"Transformative spirituality is radical truth. This collection is honest while enjoying the virtue of being hip and hopping. It offers deep and abroad appeal across generations and traditions. I commend the young Buddhas speaking out here for their joyful wisdom and inspiration. Here is a little lift we could all use after the events of September 11!"
— Lama Surya Das, author of *Awakening the Buddha Within*

"*Radical Spirit* is wonderfully engaging and down to earth. Dip in anywhere and you will find courageous seekers telling their stories with remarkable honesty, profound wisdom and refreshing humility. You'll find no pretentious 'more-spiritual-than-thou' attitudes here, nor abstract theories spun by dull thinkers. These are stories of flesh and blood humans striving in deep authenticity to create lives of spirit that make a difference on the pressing issues of our times. Bravo!"

— John Robbins,
author of *Diet For A New America* and *The Food Revolution*

"These heartfelt stories from a variety of fascinating people inspire us all to deepen our spiritual quest."
— Gerald G. Jampolsky, M.D., author of *Forgiveness*

"I have used the term 'Radical Aliveness' for years to describe the richness of coming home to ourselves. In *Radical Spirit* the passion, wisdom, and wit of a new generation of world makers storms forth. As they carry forward the true faith: deep relationship to self, other, and Earth, they touch my heart. Let them touch yours."
— Richard Moss, M.D., author of *The I That Is We, The Black Butterfly, The Second Miracle,* and *Words That Shine Both Ways*

"An Inspirational work on our transformation into the world of spirit and beyond. An exciting read."
— Lynn Andrews, author of *Medicine Woman* and *Tree of Dreams*

"Courageous, original, often funny and always meaningful. This book is a joyous expression of the divine wind blowing through a generation that may indeed save the world."
— Jim Fadiman, Ph.D., author of *Unlimit Your Life* and *Essential Sufism*

"A compelling collection of personal struggles to find the path of right living amongst the debris of the Baby Boomer, New Age, and post-modern cultures. This anthology is a veritable Indra's net of Gen Xers' inner lives. Every story is its own unique jewel, but together they radiate and reflect the same light of Spirit in a constellation sparkling with dedication and great heart. Generation X reveals its triumphant spirit in quests that are funny, touching, silly, and ultimately inspiring in their humanness."

— Jenny Wade, Ph.D., author of *Changes of Mind*

"A dream held with passion and purpose is extremely powerful. *Radical Spirit* is such a dream, a dream of a compassionate, adventurous, and engaged spiritual path. These new dreamers inspire us to stretch beyond old visions of a divine life and create something truly breathtaking."

— Marcia Wieder, speaker and author of *Making Your Dreams Come True*

"Offering profound glimpses into the hearts and souls of Generation X, *Radical Spirit* is often inspiring, sometimes disturbing, and ultimately hopeful. I can hardly wait to discuss it with my Gen X son!"

— Sue Patton Thoele, author of *The Courage to be Yourself,*
*The Woman's Book of Soul,* and *Heart Centered Marriage*

# RADICAL
# SPIRIT

SPIRITUAL WRITINGS
from the VOICES of TOMORROW

# RADICAL SPIRIT

Edited by STEPHEN DINAN

Foreword by John Robbins

NEW WORLD LIBRARY
NOVATO, CALIFORNIA

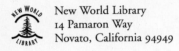 New World Library
14 Pamaron Way
Novato, California 94949

Copyright © 2002 by Stephen Dinan
Edited by Katharine Farnam Conolly
Cover and text design by Mary Ann Casler
Typography by Tona Pearce Myers

Grateful acknowledgment is given to the following publishers and copyright holders for permission to reprint the following materials in *Radical Spirit*: *Ascent* magazine and the Buddhist journal *Inquiring Mind* for permission to reprint parts of Soren Gorhamer's article, "Meditation in Juvenile Hall," which originally appeared under the titles, "Accident Prone" (Summer 2001) and "Unlocking the Dharma in Juvenile Hall" (Spring 1999) respectively; Hohm Press for permission to print excerpts of the forthcoming book, *Adventures of New Age Traveler*, as part of Mariana Caplan's piece of the same name; and Universal Music Publishing Group/Almo Music Corp. for permission to reprint the lyrics from Supertramp's "The Logical Song" in Albert Wong's article "A Fine Young Atheist." Words and Music by Richard Davis and Roger Hodgson. Copyright © 1979 Almo Music Corp. on behalf of itself and Delicate Music (ASCAP) International Copyright Secured. All Rights Reserved.

Library of Congress Cataloging-in-Publication Data
Radical spirit : spiritual writings from the voices of tomorrow / edited by Stephen Dinan ; foreword by John Robbins.
    p.    cm.
Includes bibliographical references.
ISBN 1-57731-199-fl (pbk. : alk. paper)
1. Generation X—United States. 2. Young adults—United
States—Biography. 3. Young adults—Conduct of life. 4. Youths'
writings, American. I. Dinan, Stephen, 1970–
HQ799.7 .R34 2002
305.2'0973—dc21                                      2001006367

First Printing, March 2002
ISBN 1-57731-199-X
Printed in Canada on acid-free, partially recycled paper
Distributed to the trade by Publishers Group West

10  9  8  7  6  5  4  3  2  1

*This book is dedicated to all those creative beings embodying a divine life with equal parts gusto and grace, laughter and love, service and surrender, reverence and rebellion.*

# CONTE[NTS]

# FOREWORD

## BY JOHN ROBBINS

**IN SWEDEN, THERE IS A FINE CULINARY TRADITION CALLED THE SMORGASBORD.** You stand before a long table covered with an incredible array of foods, served buffet style. You might have, at a single table, hors d'oeuvres, appetizers, soups, salads, sandwiches, fruits, vegetables, and desserts.

This book, *Radical Spirit,* is like that. You've got many voices here and a variety of paths. But they have something extraordinary in common. Each of them writes with great honesty and deep courage. Each of their stories reflects the wave of living spirit sweeping through their souls and calling them to life.

This book is full of diverse voices, each expressing the call to liberation in its unique, individual way. Reading these essays, I understand what Gandhi meant when he said that he was Hindu and Muslim and Christian and Jew, and that to reach the heart of truth was to reach the heart of all religions.

The 75 million Americans born between 1960 and 1980 have been called just about every name from the Doofus Generation to Baby Busters, and most commonly, whether you like the term or not, Generation X, popularized by Douglas Coupland in his book of the same name. They've been described as hopeless, distrustful of science, disillusioned with religion, let down by parents, manipulated by the media, and cynical about everything. They've been called the Lost Generation.

Ha!

I've had the challenge and joy of working closely with many members of this generation. I personally know many of the contributors to this volume. And I can tell you that if this generation seems lost, it's only because its members are searching for a deeper truth and a more life-affirming vision for humanity than what our society has offered them.

You may not always agree with everything you hear these authors say. For just about any rule you've got for how people should live, there will be at least one author who will exuberantly break it. They are not here merely to follow the rules of the past but to create something with their lives that attests to possibilities those of us who are older can barely imagine. They remind me of something Buckminster Fuller once said: "Our children and our grandchildren are our elders in universe time. They are born into a more complex, more evolved universe than we can experience or than we can know. It is our privilege to see that new world through their eyes."

The voices in this collection are a passionate bunch, bubbling over with life force and eager for the great adventure. Reading their essays, I have again and again been moved by their authenticity and creativity. They are committed, whatever it takes, to full awakening, to the creation of loving relationships and to the work of helping to bring about a thriving, just, and sustainable way of life for all.

I feel greatly honored to have been asked to write a foreword to this book, because I have so much respect and appreciation for these writers, and for the tasks that stand before their generation.

If I could give a gift to this generation, based on my own experience, it would not be advice. It would not be a set of commandments or guidelines designed to facilitate a fulfilled life. Speaking to this generation, I would not say, "Do this and don't do that." Instead, I would say, "I believe in you. I stand by you in faith and hope. I stand for your belief in your own capacity to respond to whatever life brings you with courage and commitment and love. If I could give you a gift, I would create a space in which you could find the ability for your souls to flourish in the world. I would show you my appreciation that you have taken birth and taken on the challenge and the responsibility and the privilege of the next step, the next link in the lineage of human spirit. I would affirm and call forth your highest nature. I would express my gratitude to you, because it is in the next generation that the next steps will be taken."

There are a lot of young people looking to their elders today, looking to my generation, and saying, "Oh shit, what are you leaving for me? Did you think about me at all?" The truth is a lot of people in my generation haven't taken on the responsibility for caring for our planet, caring for our children, caring for generations to come.

Now comes this next generation — and the exquisite voices Stephen Dinan has gathered together in *Radical Spirit.* They are here to restore our belief in ourselves, to remind us all that we can cherish each other, that we can create a joyful and just society. They are here to affirm that we can widen our hearts to include each other, and that as we embrace each other we can open to the call of the future.

This is a generation that is stepping into its power, stepping into adulthood in the midst of so much violence and destruction. I want them to know how grateful I am for their willingness to take this responsibility. I'm proud of those who are willing to be conscious, working to become aware, wanting to see what is going on and to respond to it with their full magnificence.

What, for me, are these authors whose works make up *Radical Spirit?* They are proof that there is still hope for the human race. They have their sleeves rolled up. They have their hearts open and their eyes full of vision.

Let us welcome them with celebration, and with our deepest attention and prayers.

▼▼▼

**JOHN ROBBINS** is author of the bestsellers *The Food Revolution* and *Diet for a New America.* He is the chair of Youth for Environmental Sanity (YES!) and founder of Earth-Save International. He can be reached through the Web site www.foodrevolution.org.

# ACKNOWLEDGMENTS

**MY DEEPEST BOW GOES TO THE BRAVE SOULS IN THIS BOOK** who have dared to live their lives radically committed to the divine wisdom that often leads beyond the paradigms we inherit. Their courageous example of true pioneering inspires me daily. I am especially grateful that in the circuitous journey to publication, they worked on spec, trusted that the book would find a home, and continued to offer suggestions, encouragement, and cheers.

A most gracious thanks to John Robbins for so generously stepping forward to write the foreword, showing in word and deed what it means to live aligned with Spirit. A bow to Ken Wilber for his role in launching the project. His provocative mentoring and integral vision have goaded me beyond more cramped understandings of this human adventure. A salute to sensei George Leonard, whose indefatigable gusto and mastery of the English language were essential ingredients in birthing the book. I am deeply indebted to my editor, Katie Farnam Conolly, whose strong intuition that New World Library was to be the publisher never wavered for close to a year before the book was finally accepted. She championed the book's cause on the inside. And without Michael Murphy's enthusiasm for integral transformation and his faith in me, I doubt whether I would have believed myself capable of leading this effort.

Others without whom my personal and professional journey would not have borne such fruit include, but are not limited to:

Mom and Dad, Phyllis Pay, Ammachi, Stan Grof, Tav Sparks, Haley Mitchell, Heidi Hooker, Bhagawati, Vipassana Esbjörn, Elizabeth Shaver, Stuart Davis, Marcia Wieder, Glenn Wilson, Barry Fishman, Jorge Ferrer, Mariana Caplan, Frank Poletti, Kylea Taylor, June Katzen, Valerie Vener, Lion Goodman, Ariel Giaretto, Seth Maury, Rajive Das, Jeremy Tarcher, and Keith Thompson.

# INTRODUCTION

## BY STEPHEN DINAN

**THIS BOOK GROWS FROM A DREAM I HAVE,** an image of a future in which a new brand of spirituality has fully emerged, a spirituality that takes the entire world as its starting point, that marries inner and outer work, that cultivates stillness and compassion in the midst of active, engaged lives. This spirituality is a slow dance of evolution, a tender response to the pulsing heartbeat of the universe. It builds upon — but ultimately goes beyond — traditional belief systems to create a unique path, marrying ancient wisdom, scientific and philosophic truth, and personal insight. It is a spirituality that honors periods of withdrawal, of inner contemplation, as equally as it honors the active and passionate life. It recognizes a sublime Ground, ultimately beyond all manifest form, while it also sees the realm of manifest form as the playful and ecstatic dance of that very Ground. Its God is to be found both in prayer and in lovemaking, in meditation and in mountain climbing. It sees every moment as an opportunity: for learning, for giving, for expressing a truer nature. Perhaps more than anything, it is a spirituality built upon adventure, a plunge into the unknown.

From the little I have glimpsed of this emergent spirituality, I am heartened for our future. So many ills of the modern world — excessive consumerism, rampant fear and mistrust, addiction, war, ecological meltdown, racism, gross imbalances in wealth — promise to, if not be solved, then at least be softened by this new kind of spirituality. Freed from rigid and dogmatic faiths, we can engage in a richer spiritual dialogue. Freed from the need to accumulate more material goods, we can begin to turn the tide on environmental destruction. Freed from the maintenance of falsely pleasant facades, we can begin to heal and let our creative, authentic nature express itself. Freed from the separation of rational thought and passionate soul, we can engage in further technological and social evolution far more intelligently and compassionately.

Our voyage into this new kind of spirituality has already begun. Traditions long separated by cultural and geographical divides can now cross-fertilize and produce robust new hybrids. Practices once available to only an esoteric elite are now accessible to all. The best techniques of psychology, bodywork, and healing are becoming increasingly effective tools for change. The Internet is accelerating communication, which, in turn, allows pioneers in this work to connect and go still further. Many businesses are reevaluating their relationship with the bottom line and are now trying to do good in addition to doing well. We are in an age of heightened awareness, an age in which increasing numbers of people engage in the process of evolution consciously. Our destination, though, is still barely intuited. The birthing pains are punishing. Confusion and disillusionment are rampant.

This book is a map of sorts, though not a particularly accurate one. It is more like the diagrams that proliferated in Europe in the fifteenth and sixteenth centuries as ships began to touch foreign shores. Actual peninsulas became islands. Oceans ran through land masses. America was mistaken for China. Looking at those maps, we almost always smile, both for the amusing inaccuracies penned with such confidence but also out of admiration for the boldness of the explorations. Whatever the shortcomings of their maps, those explorers risked madness, disease, and death to go still farther. Their intentions were colored by greed, but I see the spirit of pioneering in all of them. True pioneers explore, create, and adventure not just for profit or selfish gain but because the soul gropes toward a greater whole, yearns to answer the call of Mystery.

# INTRODUCTION

The contributors to this volume are pioneers in many ways, questioning the values and institutions they have inherited, seeking to find something deeper and richer, and transforming both themselves and the world around them. They are exploring new shores and reporting back so that others may follow and even inhabit the new terrain. They have responded to the call of the unknown. They have often made sacrifices and suffered to undertake the journey. What I hope you'll find is that their adventures have been worth it, that their reflections and stories are valuable for you on your path. By illuminating new truths, by stumbling into new ways of being, they help our barely imagined future come alive.

The way the book is organized mirrors the actual journey itself, which I find has three main dimensions: "Footsteps on the Path," "Landscape," and "Fruits of the Journey." In "Footsteps on the Path," we are witness to the struggle to heal, to grow, to taste wisdom, and to love more fully. We taste the sweat. We feel the tears. We laugh at the tomfoolery and irreverence. We are, I hope, inspired to go still further ourselves. These pieces highlight the mechanics of personal transformation. In the "Landscape" section, writers examine the values, traditions, and trends that shape our current world and that form the matrix from which new visions of spirituality are emerging. Several pieces explore the mechanics of transformation and the eventual fruits of practice, but their primary intent is to set the cultural context in which today's spiritual search occurs. In the third section, "Fruits of the Journey," we see the ways in which the transformative struggle rewards both the seeker and the society through heightened creativity, new lifestyles, and a desire to serve. Distinguishing these fruits from the journey itself is not wholly accurate; we are always voyagers and always students of a deeper Mystery. I do not believe the path really ends. However, in our journeys, I think a time does come to depict something of what we have seen, teach something of what we have learned, and share something of what we have felt. We can slake our own thirst at the clear spring of Spirit and bring life-giving water back for others.

In compiling this volume, I knew many of the contributors

only as words on my E-mail screen. With several, I have yet to exchange a spoken word. Something is fitting in this, that I too should meet and grow to love them through their tales, through the words they struggle to mold to the visions, dreams, and practices that have sustained them. As the project took shape, I began to feel a faint but heartening pulse, as if in the E-mails and edits tumbling across the wires of this world a deeper intelligence and life were arising. Buddhists say that sangha — spiritual community — is a vital component of enlightening practice. For millennia, sangha has been found only within the confines of a particular tradition: in the glue of ritual, the twine of practice, and the magnet of belief. Yet, as liberating and necessary as historical sanghas have been, they have also perpetuated boundaries, polarized beliefs, and prevented true dialogue with other traditions. Now, in our increasingly interconnected and postmodern world, a new sangha is being born, a sangha that includes the entire global family, that consults the full range of saints and sages, and that looks critically but curiously at the transformative tools of all traditions. It is a World Sangha, and we are part of its vanguard.

The image that comes to me is of a massive cathedral, each tradition given its special alcove, each teacher featured on a different wall, each practice finding a voice in the temple choir. On the ceiling is a kaleidoscopic dome through which sunlight is fragmented and dispersed into a dancing montage of color, the One giving birth playfully to the Many. The choir, still unpracticed, sings tentatively. Some voices attempt to drown out the others. A bold bass belts out his truth with power and force. A shy tenor sings beautifully, but almost imperceptibly. A coquettish alto allows her voice to linger seductively on each note. Still, they are learning to harmonize, learning to let their voices blend into something that, once formed, transcends any individual voice. They unite, but in a way that does not erase the unique qualities of each.

The emergent new order, that ineffable click when the cacophony of voices finds harmony, is something magical to hear. All voices find their appropriate role, and something powerful and lovely emerges that is greater than any of the parts: a new, more integral Whole. In our postmodern and pluralistic cathedral, these moments of harmony are still few and far between. The hopeful listener must still suffer through a lot of noise and discord. But, in my opinion, the moments of harmony are coming more frequently. With each year, the Integral Choir becomes more polished and pleasing, their song more distinct.

There are those who insist that realism means focusing on the darkest side of humans, the terrors of the daily newspaper, and the desecration of our home. This is, I think, true but also partial. For without the glimpses of something better, without the promise of a luminous tomorrow, realism shades into cynicism, and the powerful transformative energies of our planet slide recklessly and wastefully into the gutter. I find it is important to listen to those whose life and path shine with radical truth and love so that our passion does not evaporate and so that our divinity does not devolve into dark despair. I am therefore proud to introduce the following collection of stories and reflections, all by members of Generation X. We are a much maligned generation that nonetheless may, in the end, carry important seedlings of the life to come. These stories, when seen as a whole, form a lovely Integral Choir, singing passionately, polemically, poetically, irreverently, and compassionately of the Spirit that animates us all. Come and listen to their song. I hope you will find, as I have, that it is divinely inspired.

# PART 1

# FOOTSTEPS ON THE PATH

**IMAGINE FOR A MOMENT** that you are lost deep in a cave system with only the vaguest idea of which direction leads to freedom. Your flashlight flickers and emits a feeble glow before finally dying. You are swallowed by a limitless void, black as an oil slick, impenetrable as steel. You grow desperate, shivering against the chill that clutches your skin with ghostly fingers. But then you discover a large box of matches buried in your backpack. Hope. One by one you strike them and, as they dance in the faint breeze from the faraway surface, you follow their lead through the darkness, a circle of light illuminating each careful step.

This is how many of us begin the spiritual path. Alone. In the dark. Disoriented. But gradually we find the matches that we can strike against the flint of experience and thereby take a few dozen footsteps in the direction of freedom. Each meditation, each prayer, each release of past wounds, each moment of lucidity — they are all matches that illuminate our journey out of the darkened catacombs into which we have so often been led. Rarely are we able to see beyond a few yards in front of us. But, with trust in our hearts, we journey on. The essays in this section are intimate accounts of spiritual practices, healings, insights, and revelations that have led the authors toward a fuller life.

# RADICAL AUTHENTICITY

## BY BOB DEARBORN

All that matters is that the miraculous become the norm.

— Henry Miller

The life I am trying to grasp is the me that is trying to grasp it.

— R. D. Laing

**SOMETIMES LIFE IS EXTRAORDINARY:** a magical night on the town, a deep conversation under the stars, a wave of creative inspiration, falling in love. It's as if windows of clarity, of sharpened perspective, of really being here open up amidst the relatively list-less routines of daily life. During these periods of clear, wakeful presence, life is just plain juicier than usual. And whether sweet or sour, packing a lasting buzz or momentary high, these juicy bits of experience are simply those times when I feel particularly full of life, especially present to whatever I'm engaged in, more *on,* more *there,* more deeply who I am.

Yet, alas, most of my life has been spent asleep to this realm of clarity and effervescent aliveness. The window of my being seems too often smudged and smeared with this and that; sometimes the shades seem tightly drawn, at times I feel boarded shut. From this place of cold, dark ignorance I yearn for what is most deceptively simple: to know who I really am and to be my most real self. What I yearn for is authenticity.

Of course, in one sense, such a project seems absurd: how can anyone be other than who they are? Even when we're clueless, somnambulistic, zombified schmucks, we're still being ourselves — who else could we be? Yet with authenticity, there's a sense of direction and developmental potential — I can imagine being even more authentic than I am now — and there's also the implication of an enlightened pinnacle, a truly radical authenticity. The more radical the authenticity, the wider the embrace of my consciousness, the deeper the sense of *me*. Nevertheless, the question that dogs me is: How to get there?

For several years now I've been searching for the key to my truest nature, a key that seems well within reach when life becomes extraordinary. During such experiences there begins to grow in me a certainty that everything makes perfect sense, that beneath the warped and ragged veneer of ordinary life lies the thundering heart of God in fullest glory. The secrets of the universe begin to reveal themselves in bold block letters, paradoxes dissolve like so much Nestlé's Quik in an ocean of milk. I know beyond a shadow of a doubt that the key to living fully is all about just one thing, *this* one thing, so simple, so obvious, so . . . easy to forget.

Back in life as usual there are still the smoldering embers of intuition, a vague sense that the seemingly fragmented dimensions of my life are of a wholeness, connected by a subtle thread of luminosity that forms the warp and woof of my being. Whether I'm talking with a friend, playing guitar, shooting hoops, sitting in meditation, or writing an essay, there are moments when this radiance begins to shine forth, when my experience transforms or shifts toward deeper levels of authenticity, aliveness, and clarity. No matter the context or content of experience, there's a reminiscent quality to the transformative process that whispers softly: "This is it, the one thing that matters." And so, pushed by the fear that I might deny myself the full promise of existence and pulled along by the hope of inspired moments, I grope about in the dark, feeling for that luminous thread, hoping to catch the faint thump of a divine heartbeat.

I'm grasping for principles, rooted in the essence of my most awakened moments, that might show how to consciously cultivate a radical authenticity. I'm just dying to figure it all out, to feel that *one thing* flailing helplessly on the end of my line, hooked like a fat bass waiting to be reeled in, skinned, and gobbled up. In spite of my best efforts, however, the most profound insights and moments of inspiration usually take me by surprise, right where I stand.

I'm reminded of a hike the other day during which I suddenly, wonderfully, literally noticed the path beneath my feet. It was as if the roots and stones and sticks were giving the bottoms of my feet a massage, nudging them, waking them up, thawing them out to my awareness. There's something about the wild earth that speaks to the feet in bright, lively melodies, unlike the paved walkways or wall-to-wall carpets I've grown accustomed to. Hallways and sidewalks are not designed to be attention grabbers; their stability and predictability lull our feet to sleep so that we can focus on other matters. Forget your feet on the hiking trail, though, and you just might fall on your ass.

Most notably, as I became increasingly sensitized to the bare edge of my immediate experiencing, starting with the flow of feeling in my feet, I began to feel more present and clear overall. Perceptions became fresher and full of crisp, clear sensations. Thoughts eventually arose, but instead of the usual muddle of reruns and worries whirling through my mind, my thinking seemed connected or engaged to a world beyond itself. These thoughts did not intrude but instead contributed to a deepening sense of clarity and conviviality with the world. In this place of clarity, thoughts made more sense, feelings took on more meaning.

Something happened on that hike that happens over and over

again in my life. I wake up to a more real world, realize that I was previously asleep, then eventually fall back to sleep again. A profound remembering takes place from a state of utter forgetfulness, and then I forget again. I begin to open up and then, before too long, I contract again, back to the land of Snoozing, Forgetfulness, and Self-Contraction, where all is status quo, a world built on habit and routine.

Shifts in the direction of wakefulness often begin the moment I start paying attention to the ongoing flow of feeling, emotion, and tension arising in my body, and then choose to express myself from that awakened depth of sensitivity. That this process of sustained, sensitive expression never fails to bring with it a heightened aura of authenticity tells me something important is going on. Interactions can go from dull and pointless to intense and spirited. In a typical interaction, I invest just enough attention to register routine cues, and then I either consciously or unconsciously restrict my range of responsiveness to some pattern of propriety, an anemic repertoire of routines. I've held myself back so many times and in so many situations that I usually don't even realize I'm doing it; I become forgetful, a sleepyhead, and the result is a sickening sense of inauthenticity.

Not that small talk and social graces don't have their place. If I felt compelled to bare my soul to the mailman each morning, I'd never get anywhere and no one would get their mail on time. It's the capacity to be authentic that's so precious, and like any other capacity, it appears to be a matter of use it or lose it. Our bones become soft when not regularly used to bear weight; muscles become weak and less responsive in the face of prolonged inactivity; brain cells not regularly involved in voluntary activities deteriorate. And if personal growth can be defined as an expanding or deepening of one's conscious awareness, coupled with an expanding or deepening of one's responsiveness, then surely we'll suffer the woes of developmental arrest if we habitually ignore and hold back.

The hiking experience reminds me that there's no better place to dig for that luminous thread of authenticity than in the dirt beneath my toes. That dirt is chock-full of creepy-crawlies — like the writing of this essay, my romantic relationship, career concerns, family, friends — the more I dig, the more heads poke through the soil.

My partner and I, for instance, have become so familiar with each other's patterns of communication that the freshness and intensity of interaction that were nearly always present while we were getting to know each other sometimes get lost in insidious routines of relating. Whenever she and I go through a prolonged period of this predictable, habituated mode of being together, our relationship becomes increasingly flat. The electricity gets snuffed out. We feel far apart even in each other's arms. We may say the words "I love you," but the felt sense of a powerful loving connection is just not there.

Our plunges back into the ocean of loving connection have happened when one or both of us simply begins to communicate more fully from the immediacy of our feelings. Usually it begins with the admission of feeling distant and cut off. I then might decide to really go into things, taking the time to sense how this aloofness is actually manifesting presently, checking in with the overall flavor of feeling, tension, and emotion arising in my body. From a sense of tightness in my chest and throat might come the realization that "I've been feeling frustrated that we don't seem to really talk lately. I'm not sure why, but I feel like I want to bite your head off. I get the sense that it has something to do with your trip to New Jersey...."

To ground self-expression in the raw, here and now experience of a situation requires vulnerability, a willingness to put one's ass on the line. The depth of authenticity that my partner and I share is possible because of the love and trust that we have built over the years. But that foundation of love and trust exists in the first place as the direct result of our willingness, from the very beginning, to be vulnerable with each other and take chances — to put our asses on the line. At the heart of this process of openness and vulnerable communication lies the mystery of love, the luster of which, to my eyes, reflects most purely that luminous thread of radical authenticity.

Self-expression that springs from a sustained sensitivity to a given situation has been the recipe — par excellence — of authenticity in my life, as well as the single biggest threat to the status quo. But, at least for me, nothing is more difficult and utterly terrifying than to buck the status quo. There's simply no way, at least that I know of, that we can be authentic, wakeful, and openhearted without becoming deeply sensitive to the ways we maintain and perpetuate our inauthenticity, our forgetfulness, and our contractedness — and this process just plain hurts. Who would numb themselves to begin with except in response to scary, painful shit? So, to really be aware involves uncorking that foul stench. But that's only part one of the story. Not only does the path of sensitive, authentic expression rustle up my unfinished business, but it often flies directly in the face of all that I cling to as a card-carrying member of society. And the fear of being ostracized, especially by those I love, is usually enough for me to reach for that giant snooze button and reconsider the benefits of forgetfulness.

As children, we're often encouraged — if not aggressively trained — to ignore or disregard our direct, authentic experience. The other day this painful truth was literally driven home before me. I was at the park reading a book in the backseat of my van, side door open wide. Distracted by a mother calling out to her son, I set the book on my lap and rested my eyes. She was getting into the car parked next to mine and attempting to coax her young boy from his reverie by the creek. Exasperated, she commenced the dreaded angry mother countdown, shouting out, "One... two... three...," and making pretty darn clear that if the little guy was not in the car by "five" she would leave without him. Clearly overmatched, the boy made a beeline for the car, but not before paying me a brief visit. As his mother rolled her eyes, the boy, about three years old, pleaded, "I have to give something to the man first." He leaned his chubby cheeks into my van and held out a closed hand to me and said, "This is for you." He then proceeded to empty into my cupped hands his wonderful gift: a pile of cigarette butts!

Bewildered at first, I quickly realized by the look in the child's eyes that his gift was most sincere, so I smiled warmly and thanked him for his kindness. I looked up at his mother to find she was mortified. As I proudly displayed my prize on the edge of the seat, the boy bounced away from the van and into the smoke of his mother's smoldering reproof: "Don't you ever pick up those things off the ground again! They're filthy!" "But I found them, Mom, a whole bunch of them, and I want to give them to people," he pleaded. Mom's words were too powerful, however: "Nobody wants them!"

Part of me wanted to cry out to the boy, to let him know that I wanted them, that I appreciated his selfless gift of love. Of course, I suppose his mother had every right to discourage his butt collecting; it's an unsanitary hobby, to be sure. But to the child, those butts were magical trinkets that he was blessed to discover. So many of these gems were revealed to him on his treasure hunt that he was moved to share his good fortune with the whole world. Now his spirit of wonder and sharing was snuffed out like a Marlboro under a cowboy boot. After the car doors were slammed, mother and child pulled away, leaving my view of the park less obscured but my heart aching.

Part and parcel of growing up, for me at least, was the following message: Express yourself only in ways sanctioned by the Handbook of How to Be, no matter what your own instincts and intuitions, or else risk punishment from authority and ridicule from peers. And it's the same old story now that I'm a big boy. Go to college, get a respectable job, get married, and I'll see you in the Promised Land — namely some retirement community in Florida. Don't worry about those pangs of doubt, that hunger for something more. Those are mere feelings, and Science tells us that such subjective leanings are unreliable. God tells us that the feeling body is the abode of sin and will lead us astray. Your eyes are getting heavy my dear, very heavy. . . .

I used to feel sadness to the brink of tears, but I held them back so many times in the name of strength and toughness that these days I can rarely muster up more than a sulk or a pout. I used to be more silly and spontaneous, more playful in general, capable of such joy that I'd laugh like a hyena. I used to climb trees and skip down the street. But then it came time to act my age, a performance held together by the rigid posture of the status quo. Upholding the status quo means to maintain the stance one took previously, and thus we embody the status quo by standing still. And as any spry ninety-year-old will insist, if you keep still for too long, you'll no longer be able to move — which is a lot like being dead.

I'm always curious how other people's understanding of awakened experience fits with my own. On a recent promenade with a friend of mine, a gifted writer, I asked her to tell me flat out, in simple language, her secret to inspired expression. To my amazement, she not only took the question seriously but spent the next two hours explaining what she believed to be the heart of the creative process and mystical experience in general. As we marched up and down Franklin Street in Chapel Hill, she encouraged me to touch trees and signposts; to notice the juxtaposition of traffic lights and church steeples; to feel the pull of gravity in my feet; to think about time, space, the xylem and phloem of plant life, the plight of hungry squirrels. Above all she spoke of the need to let things in, to notice the play of detail and nuance in the world and to let that play fuel the creative process. Over some french fries and ice cream I could only nod in assent with a half-cracked smile on my face: I understood completely. And as I tried some fries dipped in ice cream for the first time, I knew we were in the presence of that *one thing*. We were positively swimming in it. I floated home that night, pondering the fathomless depths of sensitivity and awareness.

This basic principle of sensitive expression informs most of the specific practices and strategies I employ to consciously cultivate authenticity. In the practice of Authentic Movement (based on the work of Mary Whitehouse), I begin by noticing my conditioned patterns of movement as I dance or walk about the room. As the flow of feelings and sensations becomes more refined in my awareness, some feature will usually stand out in the form of a contractedness or a particular way of holding myself that inhibits free and spontaneous movement. The more I'm able to sustain my awareness of the contractedness or the sense that I'm holding back, the more and more conscious I become of that contraction as an active gesture that I'm perpetuating at that moment. As I allow movement to spontaneously emerge from this refined sensitivity, I feel increasingly free, present, and wide awake to whatever I'm doing. This practice has made me increasingly sensitive and aware of how I move and hold myself in a wide range of situations, and I'm learning how to apply this essential practice to other forms of expression, such as singing, guitar playing, and writing.

For instance, often when I start singing, I'll find that my vocal range and quality are limited by involuntary constrictions in my throat and other areas of my body. I start off sounding like shit. Squawking and squeaking my way through a Pearl Jam song, I can appreciate how artistic excellence, in any form, springs from openness and refined awareness. As I focus attention on my constrictedness during a series of long, held-out notes, my singing becomes increasingly powerful, such that the notes sound clearer and fuller, less and less choked off. Before too long, I can tear into the song with unrestrained passion ("Ohh I, I'm still alive, yeah yeah yeah yeah yeah!!!"). It's as if my sensitivity deepens to the point where the involuntary, unconscious, habitual posture of constriction begins to be experienced as a voluntary, conscious thing that I am right now doing. With that shift in consciousness comes a spontaneous realization of freedom: if I am aware that I am the constrictor, then I can stop constricting.

Similarly, when I sit in meditation, I focus my attention on the bare immediacy of whatever comes to my awareness, and layer upon layer of ever more subtle contractions and levels of ignorance are revealed. But again, with each layer embraced by consciousness comes a deeper release into freedom. As a relatively fledgling meditator, I can only trust that as my capacity for sustained awareness deepens through practice, I might eventually learn to relax the most subtle of all contractions, the entire sense of being a separate self. Perhaps with that giant step toward authenticity, I'll be flung willy-nilly into the release of a radical freedom. We shall see.

In general, to the extent that I'm unaware of holding myself back, I am prisoner of myself, locked into a particular pattern or way of being. But to think that I have found the key to freedom with this notion of sensitive expression makes me laugh at myself, the kind of demented laugh one might hear from the foreman of a wrecking crew after he realizes he's just blown up the wrong building. Opening to a bit more playfulness feels closer to that luminous *one thing* than clinging to any special key. A more playful attitude relieves me of the burden of making this or that my God. It's hard to create when the weight of the world rides on the creative process. It's hard to open to feelings when failure to do so is thought of as the ultimate failure. Letting it all go with a more playful attitude, I can take my eyes off the prize and let my gaze fall on what's before me. This also opens up possibilities to learn from others who may or may not be cultivating self-awareness per se. Too often I've gotten on my spiritual high horse, putting people in boxes like "aware" and "unaware" and ignoring or dismissing those that fall into the latter box. From a more open stance, I recognize that each person can move me on some level of my being, if only I let them in and meet them in that place. My younger brother, Jimmy, has taught me this lesson well.

Jimmy, whose brain was made toast by an allergic reaction to the pertussis vaccine in early childhood, has always been my litmus test for grandiose visions of reality. My father affectionately refers to this youngest of his sons as "the anchor." A fully grown, perpetual infant, Jimmy has saddled my parents in their golden years with a ton of worries, responsibilities, and dirty diapers. But, at least for me, my brother is also an anchor in a different way, keeping me spiritually grounded. For any real *one thing,* if it truly be that thing that cradles all my experiences in its luminous embrace, must account for Jimmy. How can I apply my lofty spiritual principles in the face of such heartbreak and tragedy?

I've held this koan close to my heart for the past nineteen years, and just so I wouldn't forget upon leaving the homestead, I've spent the past seven working with people diagnosed with various mental and physical disabilities. There was Max, fresh out of college, as was I, who suffered severe brain damage in a bike accident. He spoke of how his friends didn't come around anymore, how he could no longer control his movements and impulses, how he wished I would roll his wheelchair in front of a fast-moving bus. And Sarah, a tattooed, pierced-tongue teenager who spent most of her time on the streets, trying to cope with the voices in her head, scarred by sexual abuse, and desperately seeking friends who could tolerate her mood swings. "I just want someone to fucking love me!" she said to me with tears streaming down her face. These tortured souls and so many more, imploring me to assuage their suffering, what can I possibly do for them?

In the end, I know that all I can do is be there with them. Not just be present in the flesh, or even be available and responsible in a professional sense. To be there in spirit — eyes, ears, arms, and heart wide open — is all I can aspire to. Sometimes I succeed. There have been many touching moments, many mutually enriching experiences. Because of these people, especially my little buddha-bear of a brother, I won't stop searching, won't stop grasping for that one precious thing until we all can bathe in its radiant splendor.

As I type these final words, I'm reminded of just how difficult it can be to walk this talk of authentic expression, to dwell in the current of a life arising until I find the courage to let go and be swept away. My heart flutters open and closed as I search for a bright red ribbon to tie around this story, a way to capture the essence of what I've been struggling to convey. Perhaps the best I can do is to close with the words that came forth unbidden from this sense of struggle. So much to say. Nothing to say. A poet with no voice, no hands to write with — they're full of throat. Like a junky who can't find a vein, I'm searching desperately between my toes. There, swimming in the depths of my heart, I feel — nothing. There, hiding in the black behind the stars, I see — nothing. Emptiness, openness, sweet surrender. Could it be this and nothing more?

**BOB DEARBORN** works with people who have been diagnosed as mentally ill and has a master's degree in East West psychology. He makes his home in Carrboro, North Carolina.

# A FINE YOUNG ATHEIST

## BY ALBERT WONG

**I WAS BORN TO BE A SCIENTIST.** My dad was a theoretical physicist and he named me Albert after Einstein. His favorite hobby as we were growing up was trying to teach us about vectors, group theory, and why we floated in the bathtub. We lived in Oak Ridge, Tennessee, a science town that had been built overnight in the early 1940s as part of the Manhattan Project.

Science in those days was my religion. The world was a thing to be quantified, measured, and reduced. One day we would all be able to understand everything as part of the elegant matrix of natural law, and the pursuit of this ambition was a person's highest calling. So, in my youth, I dedicated myself doggedly to science.

As I grew older, however, I began to discover how poorly mathematical formulae described my own felt experience of the world.

I began to contact reality from the inside as a participant in the nuanced world of life's texture rather than as a mere objective observer. My vision was cracking open and a new sensibility was arising.

I was beginning to taste the delicacy of beauty, feel the agony of love, and know the sweetness of pain. What answers could physics give me when my gaze turned inward to questions of soul? I would ask my textbooks this directly again and again, and though occasionally some insight would come, my hunger for the something more would soon return.

▼

*Jerusalem, 1987. The summer after I won more national science awards than I ever wanted. The summer after Jennifer told me she was in love with my best friend, not me.*

I was seventeen and in Jerusalem. It was sunset.

I was one of the American representatives to the Bessie F. Lawrence Summer Science Institute, and we were en route to the Weizmann Institute of Science with a Jerusalem layover. The other future young scientists of the world were back in their rooms doing what future young scientists of the world do: discussing the Einstein-Podolsky-Rosen paradox, reviewing the latest oncogene research, or planning nerd pranks to play on the girls that they liked. I should have been working on my paper on the mathematical formulation of convolution products.

But I was alone, on the back deck, watching the sunset.

I had always thought of myself as a fine young atheist. Back in my hometown of Oak Ridge, I had even taken my scientific faith to its evangelical extreme: trying to get my born-again friends to see the deluded errors of their ways.

Virgin birth. *Where did he get his Y chromosome?* Created in seven days. *Look at the data on cosmic microwave background radiation.* Water into wine. *Yeah, duh. Ethanol has carbon in it; water doesn't.*

God was the tooth fairy (with a beard). The second law of thermodynamics was much more real.

But this sunset was real.

My mind flashed to Jennifer. Ever since we had stopped talking to each other six months ago, a vague, unsettling darkness had begun gnawing at me from the inside that no scientific reduction could satisfy. There were no answers in Newton's laws. The question still buried itself in my body's quiet lament.

For reasons I could not explain — was I going crazy? — I began whistling to the sunset, slowly, plaintively, the chorus from Supertramp.

> *There are times when all the world's asleep*
> *The questions run so deep, for such a simple man.*
> *Won't you please, please tell me what we've learned.*
> *I know it sounds absurd, but please tell me who I am.*

My first scientific paper was soon to be published in the *Journal of Biological Cybernetics,* and though I could speak for hours on the pattern recognition properties of the Hopfield neural network model, I was utterly at a loss with those questions that had begun to matter to me most: *Who am I? Why am I here? And what does it all mean?*

Sometimes when we were arguing, Jennifer would say that trying to talk about God with me was useless.

*You can't pin down God. He doesn't have a name. You can't put him in a box. You can't hold water. It just is.*

I would press on. I wanted to know where the tooth fairy lived.

*He's where love is. You know, like beauty.*

Yeah, right. It had all sounded, to a scientist, like drivel.

Until now.

*Sunset. Jerusalem. I have just finished whistling. I pause. The sound hangs in the air and echoes through me for a minute, maybe ten, I do not know. I only know that the heat in my body is rising and growing sharp and pointed, like static on the radio. I listen to the pulse in my neck. At first slowly, as a trickle through my lower belly, then all of a sudden, yes, the sun is pouring in and through every part of me, as if a fire hose of light has set me aflame. A flood of rays is burning through me, and my sweat is gasoline. Across my whole front side, my body is being stretched open, urgently. My skin will burst, I know it, for I can feel my seams splitting, but still with my every breath, I want to take in more. I want to drink in this moment, this blood-red sunset that cuts across the sky and screams itself through me. I want to swallow it all whole, again, and again, and again.*

The sunset had spoken no words and yet I felt addressed. To my question "Why?" it had intoned a simple, shattering "Yes": all things settled in a world beyond science, in a language beyond understanding. *Who am I? I am that I am.* I was beginning to learn how to see.

The soul has a way of remembering and then forgetting and then remembering again. I spent my next three years mostly in forgetfulness. I did what I had always planned to do, what had always seemed my unspoken destiny. I studied theoretical physics at Princeton University just as my father had done. I used his old Sears, Zemansky, and Young book on mechanics, and like him, I won the Kusaka Memorial Prize in my junior year.

But the script ended there. I had achieved all that my father had achieved in his moments of greatest glory. My duty was complete. But now I was at a loss. For, what should I do now?

▼

*Santa Fe, New Mexico, 1990. The summer that I was in* TIME *magazine as a rising young future scientist. The summer I began to leave science.*

I was twenty and in Santa Fe. The Shuttlejack from Albuquerque had just dropped me off at the El Dorado Hotel, and I was trying to bum a ride from someone up to St. John's College to check in at the

Santa Fe Institute Complex Systems Summer School. All the complexity theory heavyweights would be there. I should have been excited.

An artist woman who had also been on the Shuttlejack ended up offering me a ride, and soon I was in the backseat of her gentleman friend's car — he had come to pick her up. He was an old white-haired guy and liked talking about jujitsu. So we did.

We stopped to pick up the woman's accumulated mail; she had, apparently, been away on vacation. On top of the pile was the *TIME* magazine article that I was in. I didn't say anything, and we drove on.

He asked me where I was from.

"Oak Ridge," I said. "It's a science town in Tennessee."

He looked at me through his rearview mirror.

"I know," he said. "I used to run the place."

He had been director of research of the Oak Ridge National Laboratory during the scientific heyday of the late fifties in the years after Sputnik. I gulped. That was the life I was supposed to have, chief scientist somewhere. Somewhere.

"What happened?" I asked.

"I left," he said. And then, he was silent.

I was expecting him to say more, but he did not.

And in his understatement lay a world of mystery that called to me. *What happened? Had he just one day decided to disappear, packed his bags and gone?*

I looked at him in disbelief. He knew I understood.

"Say hello to the folks down there for me," he said. "Tell them you met me. They'll remember."

I said that I would.

My last impulse as I stepped out of the car was primal. I wanted to grab the *TIME* magazine off the top of the pile and show him my picture. *Look. See. I'm a scientist too.*

My second impulse was to grab my bags and disappear from the world, just like him.

I never saw him again.

Sometimes spirit leaves signposts in the strangest ways.

I would oftentimes not listen to the urgings of spirit immediately, and to the extent that I was wayward the vague unsettling feeling that I had known in my younger years would begin to visit me again. I would often disregard my soul's beckoning and lose my bearings again and again, until I would find myself lost deep in a woods, shivering, uncertain which way to turn and fearful that there was no way out. Strangely, within these dark times the occasional moments of transparent illumination would flash through me, and they seemed to arrive more frequently, quickening somehow, in pace with the call of my own soul's pain.

▼

*Grindelwald, the Swiss Alps, 1992. The summer I traveled through Europe, begging the great monuments of Western culture to answer my soul's call.*

I was twenty-two and at the Terrassenweg Youth Hostel. It was 2:00 A.M. The other backpackers were in their bunk beds, asleep. I was standing on the back porch looking at the Jungfrau. I was asking the mountain for help.

I had been traveling throughout Europe for the past three weeks in a flailing effort to find answers.

Atop the Eiffel Tower, I had looked prayerfully down. *Please tell me how I should live.*

At the Trevi Fountain in Rome, I had thrown my coins and prayers into the waters, hoping that the fairy-tale ritual was true. *May I live long enough to return. May I find my way through.*

In the back rows of the Vienna Opera House, dressed in backpacker's shorts, I had supplicated to the tuxedos and the music. *Please, what should I hope for in life? Which way now?*

I did not know which way to go next, and I was being slowly destroyed by the torment of my own indecision. Science, I had found, could not help me. There was no mathematical derivation for the life best lived. So I turned to ask the world.

*Should I take up my place at Harvard Med?*

*Of course you should — what an opportunity. Listen to the sound of the word:* Harvard.

*No, are you crazy? Do you really want to be a doctor? Run off to the Australian outback and find a job as a jackaroo. That's real living. Be free.*

*Don't be silly. Farm life sucks. Take up your Hertz fellowship at Stanford. You'll be a great physicist.*

*Aaaack! No, don't do it. You'll be trapped in an office for the rest of your life. Sign on to the Bread for Bosnia relief team. You can run trucks filled with flour into the war zone and save women and children. You'll be a hero.*

*Dumb. Very dumb. You'll get killed. No, what you need is to get settled on life's questions. Go to grad school in philosophy. You'll find answers there.*

*No, go back to Oxford and get a job at George and David's ice cream café.*

*No, go to Auroville.*

*No, go to Africa.*

*Go.*


Go to the mountain.

The Jungfrau. My mind was in its characteristic sleepless frenzied pitch. And once again, I began my mantra on the back porch, in supplication to the mountain. *What should I do next? Where should I go now?* I asked the question from the depth of my torment. And then I listened, hoping for an answer, a direction. At least an inkling. The Jungfrau did not give me this. The mountain gave me something else. For a moment, it gave me peace, in a moment of awe-inspired reverie as I stood witness to the arc that its southernmost edge cut into the sky. I do not think that I had ever seen a curve etched so beautifully. My mind could not fixate in its interminable cycle of self-destruction when, standing before the mountain, I imbibed the artful lines of nature's grand sculpture. It gave me no answer. But it gave me a knowing: everything's going to be okay, Albert. *Everything will be okay. Be at peace. There is beauty in the world.*

I slept that night, for the first time in many.

Was I being guided by forces unseen, coming to stand by me, to hold me straight on my way through? Perhaps, yes. Of course, it did not seem that way at the time. In the thick of things, I was, so I felt, most utterly alone.

I was leaving science, but until now science was all that I knew. I so much wanted my father to understand my departure from this most sacred field of study and would explain myself to him again and again. We would argue. In the aftermath, I would spend the night lying awake, trying in my own imagination to state my case to him, to justify my exit from science with, ironically enough, scientific exactitude. And in me, all the while, I knew all logic was futile. No words could win. But I would keep trying all night long to find the elusive perfect rejoinder, until sweet exhaustion would give me temporary salve. Until the next night. When my mind would begin to beat itself senseless once again.

Indeed, the break with my father that my departure from science created was deep and would nearly crack me open from its pain. But still I limped along, in pursuit of this inkling that there was more in life — more marrow in life's bones — and I could not but try to know life, raw. Truly, there was no choice.

▼

A series of synchronistic jolts would lead me eventually to buy a one-way ticket out to California. I had begun to listen to my inklings, and all signs pointed to a strange institute in Big Sur called Esalen. I was supposed to be there. I could tell.

Though I had never been there before, in so many of my darkest moments a thread would connect me to the place. Our histories were meant to intersect. And finally I answered its call.

I arrived at the Esalen gate on August 20, 1995, in a half-crazed mixture of hope and desperation: hope that here I would find a place where I could give voice to my own soul; desperation, for it felt as if I was near my soul's whimpering end.

I began my great fall from the ivory tower — my *katabasis* — with kitchen work. My job was the most menial and least desired in all of Esalen, and therefore also the most noble. I was a dishwasher.

And all around me at Esalen — this Mecca of integral practice — a grand carnival of soul rolled on: from aikido to African dance, from yoga to Gestalt, from Buddhist meditation to Reichian catharsis.

Esalen, more than any other place in the world, had become the nexus point for the emerging new American spirituality. For the first time in a long time, I felt as if I were home. I became, once again, a student, not of science, this time, but of life.

▼▼▼

**ALBERT WONG** is a past Marshall scholar and has assorted degrees in physics, philosophy, politics, and economics from Princeton, Oxford, and the University of Michigan. He won numerous national awards as a budding young scientist before working for the Esalen Institute for five years. He now works with Jeremy Tarcher in Los Angeles as chief research director at a think tank start-up that studies independent thinking and pioneering individuals.

# BEING IN THE SKIN

BY SUSANA HERRERA

**AT THE END OF THE RAINY SEASON** in the desert of northern Cameroon, elephants the color of sweet ripe mangoes walk across the rising sun, playing jazz on their golden saxophones, leaving footprints behind their song. Nearby in the small bush village of Guidiguis, the call to prayer rings out, waking the Foulbe and Tapouri and bringing those who are Muslim to chant at the mosque. After morning prayers, the young men herd goats, the older Foulbe lead their cows to water holes, and the women and children begin their endless quest for water and enough food to live one more day.

When the desert people first see each other, they say, "Oh say ko." It means thank you. They say thank you for being here crossing my path, thank you for being a part of this village, thank you for being alive because your life affects mine in some small way. Thank you.

The next question is, "Jam bah doo nah?" Are you in your skin? A better translation would be, "Is your soul present and alive in your body right now?" The response is always, "Jam core doo may!" I am in my skin! It's as if the very question gathers the soul into the body with a vibration of life energy. Like a bell being struck, the soul releases its sweetest music as it rejoins its earthly form.

During my two-year Peace Corps service in the desert, "Jam core doo may" became more than an answer to a question in an African language. It became a state of mind, a practice of being present, a way to ground and center in my body, in the moment, and in the country I was serving. Answering the Foulbe question with "Jam core doo may" became my soul's journey. It was a conscious step closer toward understanding my oneness with God, being alive and present and in my skin.

Embarking on a spiritual journey, taking the first step, was the easy part. It was staying on the path that became the challenge. When a seed is planted, hope of what will sprout and blossom is buried in the soil with it. Similarly, as I planted the seed of a spiritual life with the Foulbe question, "Jam bah doo nah?" I had hopes of what would emerge. I visualized how my life would look with God walking along beside me. I could see amazing beauty, smell the perfume of my spirit's blossom, and taste the fruit of all my hard work, service, and prayer. However, when I didn't instantly get these results, I got frustrated. My life hadn't changed one bit and I was still in pain.

Gradually, though, I began to understand that after a seed is planted, the roots must go down before anything peeks out above the ground to sprout and later blossom. The gestation period is a time of darkness when we have to rely on faith. It is a time when nothing seems to be happening, when, however, everything is forming and getting ready to be born. Though there was no apparent movement happening within myself and in my everyday life, and there seemed to be an absence of light, I had to believe that the seed would grow, and I continued to nurture it. For me, this was the most difficult period, because deciding to live my life from a spiritual place meant healing everything that was getting in the way.

The silence of the desert and the isolation from all I had known brought my wounds up, one by one, for me to examine. I needed to forgive, but I didn't know where to begin or how. Letting go and giving control to God through prayer and meditation were the only choice. I surrendered to the healing with every answer of "Jam core doo may." I vowed that this time I would stay alert and deal with the pain. This time I would not numb myself with alcohol, drugs, bad relationships, and long hours on the job. This time I would remove the thorn embedded deep in the flesh. But in order to take the thorn out, I would have to open the wound and dig deep.

## TRAIL OF SHAME

When I was seven years old, my father moved my mother, brother, and me into a Zen Buddhist monastery. We practiced *zazen* during the week and went to catechism and mass at a Catholic church on the weekends. As a result of my father's religious fanaticism, I learned that life is suffering and I must desire nothing. At seven years old, I learned to fast to purify my soul, to whisper instead of speak, tiptoe instead of skip, and sit *zazen* meditation before sunrise. I learned that an insect's life was more sacred than my feelings and that I must kneel and pray and ask God to forgive my sins and make me worthy to receive Him.

Several months later, my father took my brother and me to the beach. While they fought the waves, I swam far away from their violent play. Absorbed in pretending to be a dolphin, I accidentally swam into a stranger. As I apologized, he grabbed me and held me to him. Suddenly he put his gigantic hand over my mouth and with the other, pulled down my shorts. I was seized with a sensation like a knife splitting me in two; I was completely paralyzed by the pain until the man started to run with me, carrying me away from my father and brother.

I cried out and got the attention of a lifeguard. Later, when a towel was wrapped around me and the policemen asked what had happened, I could only stare at their feet. I looked up at the impatient faces of the policemen, the lifeguard, my father, and the stranger, then back down at their feet. All I could say was that he touched me. I was too ashamed to say anything more. I was afraid they would say it was my fault. I was terrified that I would never be "worthy" to receive God because I had been tainted.

Later that night, I watched through a crack in the door as my father told my mom what had happened. She was upset that he hadn't watched me more closely. They started to argue about me, and when she got up from the couch, he grabbed her by the hair and slammed her head into the wall. My legs gave way, and I slid to the floor, crying silently, just like my mother as he slammed her head into the wall another time. After what happened to her, I couldn't tell her what had happened to me. I felt their argument was my fault because I believed I should have stayed by my father; it was my fault that she got beaten, my fault what that man had done to me. Later that night I got up from bed and put my bloodstained underwear in a brown paper bag and hid it in the garbage.

Months after the incident, I grew to hate myself for not being able "to forgive and forget." I was ashamed of what had happened to me and grew more ashamed that I was unworthy of God because I was not able "to love my enemy." My father suggested that I not press charges, that I "turn the other cheek" because he didn't want me to go against the words of God's only Son and "cast the first stone." But I couldn't just forgive that man; I didn't want to love him and offer my other cheek. At eight years old, I wanted to kill the man who hurt me. I wanted him struck down by lightning. I wanted him to suffer in prison like I was still suffering. I grew angry with God and blamed him for what had happened to me. I also grew furious with myself for not being "spiritual" enough to forgive. I grew to hate the New Testament for asking me to do what I felt I could not. In order to protect myself from ever being hurt again, I closed my heart and cut myself off from God.

Throughout the years that followed, I searched for a name for what had happened to me. Since no one asked me any further questions, I learned to pretend it hadn't happened. Many times after my mother divorced my father I thought I would tell her, but years passed and the shame and the guilt of not doing or saying anything strangled me into silent submission. I moved out of my mother's house when I was sixteen and moved in with the first man who said he loved me. Suddenly I was twenty years old with a husband who had a temper. One night, I refused to let him drive after he'd been drinking heavily. When I took the keys away from him in front of his friends, I knew I had made a mistake. Fury and humiliation flashed in his eyes as he punched me, then slammed my head into a stone wall. I begged him to forgive me for what I had done. I had come to believe that this is what I deserved.

Only a small black bruise lingered under my eyebrow by the time my mother saw me. When she asked about it, I lied to her. She knew it and said, "You come home." I tried to lie again by saying it was the first time. She asked, "Are you going to let him break your neck before you leave him?" That question pierced the bubble of illusion I was living in, thus leading to the end of a painful marriage and the opening of new possibilities. With newfound boldness, I applied to the Peace Corps and took a teaching position in West Africa.

## HEALING IS IN THE PRESENT MOMENT

In the desert of Cameroon, the memories of my childhood rolled themselves out like a rug and I walked over every single event that had happened in my life. I saw how I had never been present to each moment of shame, terror, sorrow, and pain. Instead I suppressed my feelings and never allowed my experiences to fully digest. With a lot of time on my hands and the open space of the desert, my buried feelings could finally come fully forward, although I didn't know where to actually start the healing process. An answer to my prayers came, and I began to understand that the way to heal and get the pain out of my body was by writing down the stories of my life and those of my family's history.

The healing process didn't feel good; it was stark, naked, and lonely. Like a cocooned caterpillar, I was in a dark void, longing to shed the old form in order to create wings to fly gracefully through my time in Cameroon. But in the process of becoming a butterfly, a caterpillar disintegrates. It becomes a glob of goo. Healing childhood wounds felt like my guts were being ripped apart. Everything that I had constructed myself to be was melting down. My reflection in the mirror was unrecognizable. I seemed out of place in my own skin. I was the goo, transforming into a butterfly. There was no distraction, nothing to numb the pain. There was nothing I could do to speed the process. I could only be in my skin in the present moment and wait.

Again and again, I turned to writing; I began a journal and wrote long letters home. I wrote stories that celebrated learning how to swing a machete and kill an intruding snake, how to carry a bucket of water on my head, and how to stand up to the village king. When elephants ransacked a nearby compound, killing a Foulbe family, I described the gift of another day of living. Soon, though, I noticed that I wasn't telling the whole story of what I was witnessing in Africa. Instead I censored my stories, paralyzed by the thought of writing about the everyday violence toward women.

I saw my young female students at school brutally beaten with a stick for being tardy. I witnessed a student die of malaria because she wasn't taken to the hospital; her father saw it as a waste of money to pay to save a girl's life, infinitely less important than a boy's. I was invited to mourn the death of the young girl and joined the women behind the mud walls of a family compound. I took my place among the women as they began their ritual of wailing and pounding their fists on the earth, letting out their sorrow, anger, and pain. Their wailing struck a chord in me and I let out a powerful cry, wailing with them, shedding tears, pounding my fists on the sand and releasing the hurt. Later, when I wrote about the experience in my journal, it became clear that I needed to write the whole story of what I was witnessing in the desert. By telling the stories of Foulbe women, I was also telling my own.

I began to dig underneath the skin for the pain hidden there. The more I got it on paper, the more I embraced those lost parts of myself and made them a part of who I am. I felt lighter and more present in my skin and no longer trapped by past traumas. I finally wrote to my mother about my childhood rape. This time, I didn't run away and hide. I showed up and faced the fear, letting the tears come and confronting words I had never written before.

It was in healing the flesh that I actually became aware that I am more than this physical body. Those unhealed wounds had kept me frozen in a limited identity. As they released, a greater spaciousness came. I realized that I had survived the physical traumas of my past; they hadn't killed me. There was an energy, a light inside that hadn't been extinguished. The question, "Jam bah doo nah?" reminded me several times a day that we are more than physical bodies. There is something more powerful, something stronger and more real than even my mind. My faith in God returned, but it was different this time. It wasn't the faith forced upon me by my father. My faith in God became an experience within myself. I felt God beating in my heart and breathing in the life all around me.

Strange and mystical things happen where there is silence, open sky, and solitude. I began to hear an inner voice speak to me, communicating through a lizard guide. He told me there was no one to do the healing for me. I would have to go inside and rescue the lost parts of my soul. I often wrote questions to my guide in my journal, and after awhile, he wrote back. I asked why my father had committed suicide. The voice inside said that from every situation, every person, and every hurt, there are only gifts of love. The gift from my father was an opportunity to further my understanding of myself as a Divine being in a human form. My father was not dead, the lizard wrote, he had simply chosen not to be in his skin. And I had chosen to heal in my skin, to bear witness, to give a testimony that I am still here. I am alive! I am in my skin! Jam core doo may! I had survived, and others, women and men, young and old, would find strength in hearing my story.

## RETURNING HOME IN MY SKIN

I came back to America believing that I had been "fixed," that I had gotten "it," the big aha that would change the way I thought about myself. But there was still work to be done. I got a job teaching English, entered a new love relationship, and began to write a book about Africa's lessons. The challenge was to say "Jam core doo may," to remember Spirit alive and present in my skin when I got scared, when old thoughts of being undeserving of love and success came to haunt me. I learned to take little steps, to stop and breathe, to show up with my intention and let spirit do the rest.

Through healing work with hypnotherapy, I began to change the seat of my identity from human mind and body to pure Spirit. As the sessions progressed, I began to feel myself as a radiant light full of love, clarity, and wisdom. In that soul place the traumas and pain did not exist; indeed it seemed as if they had never happened at all. In that place, I could visit the human parts of me that I most needed to heal.

After many years of working to heal childhood wounds, it was finally time to release the anger and to heal from the rape. I was guided to experience the Divine light of the man who hurt me. As I felt the holy presence within him, without any words, without any actions, I understood that he was a spiritual teacher for me. I received so much joy in the realization that what had happened to me had provided a path to this moment of understanding God within this man and God within me. I understood for the first time that there is no separation between us and no separation from God. There is only one of us here. In feeling that we are all one soul, having a Divine experience on Earth, I could at last get past the traumas because those incidents are not the last word, they are not what is finally real; there is another view. What is real is the light inside us, the Divine essence experiencing itself through us in this lifetime. Forgiveness is not about letting someone off the hook, rather it is about understanding that the only thing that is real is love. God is love and that is what we are. Forgiveness of myself and of others is done in that one realization.

## WRITING DOWN THE HEART AND BONES

The work that I did in hypnotherapy gave me the energy to write a book about my experiences of the spirit that the desert of Africa had inspired. When I completed the first draft, I was struck by the fact that I had left out all of the past that had come up for me while living in Africa. In the second draft, I got a little more daring and wrote how I felt about women not being allowed to ride a bike or have their own identification card, about the violence and oppression I witnessed. Finally, in the third draft, I wrote about my childhood and what needed to be healed.

Facing the demons of my past was a first step, writing about them was a second, and going public with them, a third. In the final editing stage, I realized that my purpose in writing the book was to be of service to others. And therefore I had to include the rape. It was still too hard to tell of it directly, so I relayed it through lines of poetry in the voice of the lizard guide. It was only a small step and not the leap of faith that I had hoped to make — or so I thought.

When the book was published, I decided to share it with one of my high school English classes and, in so doing, teach the lessons Africa had taught me. In the discussion following the reading, which included the painful poem, no one brought up the violation. I decided not to point it out if they weren't ready to see it on their own. But after class, one student stayed to speak to me privately. She asked me how I could write about being raped and publish it. She didn't understand how I could want something that was so personal and "gross" to be shared with thousands of people, especially my own class. She got angry with me for writing about it, accusing me of "being proud" of it. It came out that her anger was really a mask to hide her own shame at also having been raped as a child and having kept silent. As she cried, I told her that it was not her fault and that it wouldn't matter now if no other person ever read my book, she had broken her silence. I felt at that moment that I had written the book for her, to show her that it is possible for a person to heal from the shame, to create more room inside to be fully "in your skin." And most of all, to show that we can discover ourselves to be as powerful as we think and dream we can be.

We are greater than the sum total of all of our experiences. We are Spirit. When we remember this, we give far less weight to our past and who did what to us. When we can diminish the strength of the illusion that we are limited to our past, we can begin to identify with our spiritual essence. "Being in your skin" means identifying yourself first and foremost as a Divine being having an experience in the human skin. With this acknowledgment, we can be fully present and available for Divine energy to come through us.

There is an inner light that is constantly on, a light that demands no effort for it to shine. It is always there. We need only to be in our skin to feel that place deep within us that is at one with all things. It is our very divinity. And, in touching that place, we can answer with all the passion and power of our being, "Jam core doo may!"

▼▼▼

**SUSANA HERRERA** is a writer and teacher. Her first book, *Mango Elephants in the Sun: How Life in an African Village Let Me Be in My Skin* (Shambhala, 1999) chronicles her spiritual journey in a desert village in Cameroon, West Africa, where she was an English teacher with the Peace Corps. She now teaches literature at Santa Cruz High School in California, and is writing her second book, *Laughing Girl, Howling Woman,* which focuses on four generations of her Navajo/Spanish family history.

# BY STEPHEN DINAN

**KALI IS THE DARK GODDESS** of the Hindu pantheon, a representation of both time and death as well as the raw and wild sides of the Divine. Kali eliminates what is less than holy in us, what we use to shield ourselves from a frightening world. During a long foray through India, I lingered many times on a vision of Kali stamping out the proud postures of my ego. Kali proved to be an apt symbol for the stripping of those months, a stripping that ultimately revealed something transcendent. In this context, already more than a bit bruised, I entered my first serious meditation retreat, nervous but willing to go deeper. This is the chronicle of that inner journey.

## DAY ZERO

I rickshaw up the hill into the forested acres that comprise the Vipassana International Academy, the biggest *vipassana* center in the world, beautifully sprawled across the hilltop, yet retaining a cozy, comfortable feel. The impending retreat will undoubtedly be a shock. Noble silence for ten days. No significant eye contact. Wake up bell at 4:00 A.M. Twelve hours per day of sitting meditation. No reading or writing materials. Minimal food after noon. The journey inward is taken very seriously in *vipassana*, with no touchy-feely outlets or solace.

I immediately like the feel of the center: a pleasant peacefulness perfumes the air. Most of the participants are Indian, and many carry themselves with the elegant confidence of the moneyed class. Goenka, the head teacher in the lineage, has a positive reputation and seems free of corruption. He will drop in on the retreat from time to time.

Our first night involves orientation and rules. The rules strike me as repressive, a throwback to medieval asceticism. Even the cell I am assigned is puritanical: a half-inch mattress on a concrete slab, unplastered walls, 4 feet by 9 feet in dimension, dimly lit by a single 25-watt bulb. There will be no coddling here.

## DAY ONE

Today begins with boredom and pain. I feel like a casual jogger who has suddenly, almost whimsically, decided to run a marathon, blissfully unaware that his body is unprepared. Each meditation session begins with Goenka's tapes — a combination of instructions in Hindi and English — mixed with mournful vocals that bring the Buddha's words of wisdom into musical form. Even though I cannot comprehend the ancient Pali words, the rich tones in Goenka's voice promise a place beyond the pain, a more enlightened state, dangled like a carrot in front of our motley group of grumpy, bored, and restless meditators. His voice hypnotizes me. It is a voice that vibrates through the jowls from deep in the belly. Warbling through bass notes like a veteran smoker, it has a haunting, imperfect sort of beauty. Soulful is what it is, like the voice of a blues singer or an old black storyteller, a voice of tired but hopeful experience.

Physically Goenka is an improbable guru, which perhaps helps account for his overwhelming popularity with the educated elite in India. Born in Burma to one of the very wealthy, highly orthodox Hindu families that have been enormously successful in industry, Goenka began his adult life as a man of the world chasing fortune and status. Today, he retains a conservative, businesslike appearance with close-cut hair, a shaved face, and formal business shirts rather than the rakish garb of a sadhu.

Goenka stresses that the teacher can only show the student the path, which the student alone must walk. The teacher cannot take a single step for the student, who must work out his salvation for himself. No artifice, no drama, no promises of a quick and sure waltz to enlightenment. At the end of each brief series of instructions, he croons: "You must work ardently...patiently...diligently...and persistently. You are bound to be successful, bound to be successful."

For someone like myself who relishes the rich proliferation of gods and goddesses in Hinduism, the endless maze of philosophies, practices, and icons, entering the field of bare-bones Buddhism is painfully dreary. The rich play of Sanskrit mantras across my consciousness is now replaced by nothing but sensing the flow of breath in and out of my nose. Little tickles, heat, tingling, all at the entrance to the nostrils. In and out, in and out. As the day passes, my mind looks for any opportunity to escape, darting through a boiling stream of thoughts, criticisms, and commentaries. Tickle, heat, tingle, in and out, tickle: hopelessly dull.

In the outer world, I am pleasantly distracted by a man sitting behind me who has a quarrelsome gastrointestinal problem. Like clockwork, every minute or so, another massive, barely shielded burp wells up from his stomach. His ongoing performance of eructation is occasionally accompanied by soloists around the room passing gas in the opposite direction. Indians have none of the repressive attitude toward farting seen in the West. Indeed, some of the farts are virtuoso performances, covering a full octave of notes and vibrations, sustained for five or ten seconds. My mind tires of the slow hara-kiri of watching the breath and relishes the moments when the burping and farting blend together into a symphony of digestive gas. By the end of the day, I am closer to collapse than enlightenment. I want nothing more than to escape the tedium and the searing aches of my back. How can I sustain myself for ten days of this?

## DAY TWO

My inner restlessness is compounded by a body still aching from yesterday and a sleep deficit demanding repayment. Even the burping and farting symphony, so delightful yesterday, provides no joy as I begin to feel deeply alone and frustrated. Only the sweet crooning of Goenka sustains me, a balm for the mounting aches and inner frustrations. His voice promises relief while the practice itself offers no solace. Today we narrow our focus of attention to an even smaller triangle, encompassing only the base of the nose. In and out, in and out. No spiritual experiences, no textured mantras, no devotional chanting, nothing but the bare awareness of the subtle sensations at the base of the nostrils where breath lightly touches the skin.

My mind threatens retribution. It pontificates on why Theravadan Buddhism is a soulless, arid, and ascetic waste of time. It passes thunderous judgments on my fellow meditators. It postures and preens. It is committing a rather ungracious suicide. There is nothing to do but sink alone into its dark recesses. We are urged to remain perfectly still during meditations, yet each session brings new cramps in my back and new pains in my legs, so that I am constantly readjusting and stretching, a restless body matching my restless mind. My thoughts careen as memories of the past year, old connections, new friends, and reflections all compete for attention. Most of the time, I forget my breath entirely.

Just when my departure from the course seems the only reasonable choice, Goenka's evening discourse provides a fresh ray of hope, focusing on the three essential ingredients of this path: *sila* (moral discipline based on nonviolence), *samadhi* (control of the mind), and *pañña* (direct experiential insight, especially into impermanence). He makes the day's dullness and pain seem like a plausible step in the direction of true wisdom. Nonetheless, I am grateful to retire to my cell. The two days have already seemed a lifetime.

## DAY THREE

The outer world is now remote. My tumbling thoughts turn to Chris Peters, an acquaintance who dropped all connections and disappeared into the bowels of New York City. Friends and family assumed him lost to the world of drugs, but I suspect a different motive: a radical experiment in redefining himself and a lesson in the impermanence of relationships. His disappearance has fascinated me, which perhaps reveals the part of me eager to do the same. Why not explore new ways of being? Why not try on roles, like an actor in a play? I could become a libertine, a Don Juan, a seeker of all sorts of sensory indulgence. Or perhaps I could take the robes of an ascetic, live in an ashram, change my name, and lose my past. The possibilities here in India are endless. Nothing except choice commits me to the life I have led.

Goenka shifts the focus of our meditation to a still smaller triangle on the upper lip, and our challenge becomes to feel the dance of the subtlest sensations, anything from heat to pain to vibration. Our minds concentrate further, attuning to more refined levels of the mind and body. A cold mounts during the morning and I fight sleep. I am tired of the boot camp atmosphere. More than anything, I need sleep to cure the cold, to balance my body, and to right my mind, so I skip the last two hours of morning meditation to do just that.

After lunch, however, a *dhamma* worker presents me with a note requesting me to see the assistant teacher over the rest period. Annoyed, I go to the *dhamma* hall and wait my turn to be interrogated for skipping the morning session. The man in front of me is scolded for missing meditation. My dander is up, and I do not approach the assistant teacher with contrition. Perhaps sensing this, he practically barks at me to go back to my room for the note so that he knows where I am on the list.

I return defiant of his authority and defend my right to catch up on sleep and fight sickness. He chides me for rule breaking and "doing as I please." Rather than inquiring into my health or expressing any concern for me as a human being, he sees me only as a rule breaker, the nemesis of all bureaucrats. This man is just another cog in the machinery of dogma, another top sergeant in the service of obedience. He concludes his tirade by saying, "If you cannot follow the rules, you must go." Finally, he lectures me about wasting his time, when it is his fuss over my absence that is the sole source of the problem. By the end of the talk there is an uneasy truce, but my feelings of being trapped in this prison camp of meditation increase.

For the rest of the day, the pain mounts in my back, my mind churns with vicious thoughts, and my emotions seethe. Quiet on the outside, raging inside. I begin to hate the cookie-cutter approach to enlightenment that permeates this place, hate the naive belief that following rules leads to liberation and that discipline alone breeds success. The very qualities that were so refreshing on the first day now strike me as simplistic. It's religion's oldest formula: behave yourself and go to heaven. My fantasies vacillate between storming out and strangling the assistant teacher.

## DAY FOUR

The meditation switches from *anapana* (watching the breath) to actual *vipassana,* in which we begin with the crown of the head and slowly scan every inch of the body, impartially feeling whatever sensation is present. This change of practice is welcome in some ways, yet most of my energy and awareness are contorted by the mounting pain and rage inside. During the 10:00 sitting, an insight emerges. The intensifying agonies in my back, which I must stretch during every break, are related to the claustrophobia of being squashed through the birth canal. The emergence of the memories is fueling my rebellion against the structure of this place.

Back in my room over the lunch break, I stretch my head and neck until waves of emotion and stored pain break free. Curled up in a ball, knees on the bed next to my ears, I feel an overwhelming desire to push free and to strain against the energies pinning me down. I am breaking the rules of the place, for we are supposed to relinquish all other practices and techniques, yet this intense stretching brings archaic layers of the pain to light. Goenka stresses that *vipassana* dredges up hidden layers of *sankharas* — old wounds, attachments, and fears — the pus of the psyche. Why not accelerate the process?

Stan Grof, a transpersonal psychiatrist, invented the term COEX system to describe how similar traumas group together in the psyche, almost in a layer-cake fashion. My intense need to break free is an example of COEX. The most superficial layer, the triggering event, is composed of the rules of the retreat that I have chafed against. At a deeper level, though, I feel trapped in my marriage, trapped in a less-than-ideal family life, trapped by my own conscience and superego. Still deeper is the first imprinting of birth, a layer of agonized terror from feeling trapped by constricting uterine walls. Grof writes that healing or clearing the uppermost layers of COEX systems still leaves the fundamental or earliest layers untouched, rather like cutting the tops of weeds without digging up the roots.

These intellectual insights, though, scarcely make the process easier. I am still plagued by a seething brew of murderous thoughts toward the assistant teacher. In addition, I begin to hate the volunteer *dhamma* workers who bang little gongs to stir us from our quarters and herd us back into the hall. I savor the image of slugging the next fellow to knock on my door.

During our sitting practice, the screws are turned tighter. Goenka asks us to make the firm resolution not to move for one complete hour during each of the three daily hours of group meditation. I laugh inside. I am barely capable of twenty minutes without stretching my aching back. With each shift of position, I relish my private rebellion against the outer tyranny.

At the end of the day, I reluctantly realize that the retreat is beginning to have its desired effect: a boiling over of *sankharas* — attachments, emotions, and fears. If only I could keep even a modicum of equanimity.

## DAY FIVE

During the *adhittana*, or "strong determination not to move" period of meditation in the morning, I begin to see the deeper reason for such an apparently sadomasochistic practice. There are at least two layers. First, not moving at all in a painful situation forces a change from a pain-aversive, pleasure-seeking life strategy to a stance of equanimity. Instead of squirming away from pain and grasping for comfort, we are forced to alter our bodily and emotional habits. However, a second layer is far more interesting to me. The first muscles to start aching are those that are chronically tensed, flexed, or blocked. Such muscles are both weak and rigid. As their holding patterns break down, secret emotions, fantasies, or memories erupt into consciousness. The desire to move to a more comfortable position is thus more than just a movement away from pain. It is also the subtle evasion of old traumas tied up in muscular armor. This insight makes an immediate difference in my attitude toward the strictness here. As I begin to sit in a more disciplined way and let pain build to almost unbearable levels, I crest into breaking points when muscles release, thereby allowing feelings, memories, and images to bubble into consciousness, like carbonation in a freshly opened soda.

Our meditation instruction now points toward realizing *anicca* (impermanence) in the body and sensory field, and I am overwhelmed by the essential loneliness at the core of existence. Everyone I know and love will eventually be gone, if not before me then after. Best friends of today will fade into the past. Perhaps even my wife will become a distant memory. The trickle of sadness becomes a torrent, and I am overwhelmed by the reality of impermanence. Ultimately, we are born and die alone. After dinner, my body shakes quietly through the entire hour of meditation. Tears of existential dread drip softly off my chin, one after the other.

# DAY SIX

I sleep badly and awaken at 2:30 frightened by a dream. I am helping run a talent show with several other organizers, and I sit in a chair near the front of the auditorium auditioning new acts for the show. However, a migraine headache begins and my visual field dissolves, resulting in total blindness. I calmly assure myself that the other organizers will just have to cover for me. But as time passes, I become increasingly confused and disoriented and lose my sense of direction. I cannot even tell which way is up. I fall from my chair, clutching for something, anything at all to hold onto as my inner world twists into a mystical vortex. It is like falling into a kaleidoscope. Vaguely I sense people rushing to my side to discover the cause of my collapse, but the whirlpool of lights sucks me deeper, leading to further disorientation. I awaken clutching at the sides of my bed for stability.

In the late morning session, I cross a threshold of equanimity, remaining perfectly still for the full hour. The next two hours breeze by as I watch painful sensations with perfect aplomb. I begin to relish the pain. The throb of aching knees and cramping back becomes enlivening. With my increased discipline, a new layer of *sankharas* emerges, a smutty and sadistic montage of sexual fantasies and images of everything that has ever been taboo: gang bangs, rape, orgies, anal sex, bondage. This violently pornographic movie leaves me both embarrassed and highly aroused. For most of the afternoon, animalistic sex scenes continue to erupt into my mind as I scan the sensations of my body. By the end, I feel in need of a cold shower. As the sun retreats back into the underworld, my internal thermostat turns up still higher. The pot of my psyche has been left on a red-hot burner, insights and emotions boiling down the sides.

At the start of the day's final sit, a mysteriously beautiful image appears in my mind's eye, a sensual *dakini* figure, much like those in Tibetan artwork. She twirls in a vaguely erotic way, inviting me further within. Throughout the meditation, the inner visions multiply and intensify, such that by the time I return to my cell, I am flooded with images of golden turrets, beautiful beings, and bejeweled arches, a heavenly kaleidoscope bathed in a luminous glow. As the visions intensify, my heart is set ablaze, pouring forth love for God, love for all beings, and love for the presence opening within.

With closed eyes, I scan my energy field and watch how different colors and vibrations intermix in a swirl of motion. Gradually I sense an opening of my crown chakra, petals flowering into infinity. The rational part of my mind is baffled by this inner display. A powerful energy now shoots through every pore of my body, and I feel like a Roman candle. Never have I experienced anything this intense.

Surely the visions and energy will trail off soon, I reassure myself. But the hours pass with no relief. The visions are followed by insights and glimpses of truths previously unfathomable. The sheer force of the energies begins to frighten me, for I intuit that I am tasting only the smallest drop of honey from a vast honeycomb. This taste is nonetheless almost more than I can bear. After several hours, I feel seared and frazzled, overcooked by the inner fire blazing through my chest and shooting out my crown.

Andrew Harvey, a Western mystic, says that in entering the divine domains, one commits to being incinerated, much like placing a wet log in a hot fire. Before the log can burn cleanly, all the moss and moisture and sap and impurities must crackle, sizzle, and pop in a rather ugly process of purification. I feel like the fire has gotten too hot, that I am sizzling too quickly, popping out of control.

I fight inflationary feelings that accompany the visions and battle the sense of grandiose purpose and divine mission. I see clearly why someone who touches these realms can come away so convinced of spiritual authority before their outer self has stabilized insights into mature awareness. Spiritual grandiosity is as much a hallmark of schizophrenia as of enlightenment. The breakdown of the schizophrenic's psychic membranes allows the influx of these energies without sufficient balance, reflection, and interpretation. Merely tapping these realms means nothing. The real test is what to do with the insights. Thus, I resist my own desire to cling to the visions and insights and fight my need to feel special or unique, though I am sorely tempted.

As the night wears on, it becomes clear that I must work to heal physical blockages and psychological wounds so that these temptations toward inflation will dwindle. So I intensify the pain in my blocked legs, working to the edge of agony, at which point they finally release. Layer after layer peels away, a lifetime unraveling. By morning, the ecstatic energy still courses through me, but I manage to nap for forty-five minutes before morning meditation begins.

## DAY SEVEN

The rapturous feelings refuse to subside. My body is fatigued and energized simultaneously, like a speed addict's after days without sleep. During the first ecstatic hours last night, I prayed for the process to happen as fast as I could take it. This morning, though, I am desperate and out of control, eager for the return of a bland and predictable world. While meditating, I can see my entire subtle energy body. New areas of cloudiness and blockage float to the surface, and each release brings an ever-more uniform flow of subtle sensations. Over the course of the morning, the energy subsides only slightly. A terror begins, a terror that the process is moving far too fast. I may be going insane. Perhaps I need to leave or at least stop meditating. I decide to ask Goenka himself what to do during question time over lunch.

Goenka's quarters are as simple and Spartan as the rest of the center. The bare walls are painted a muted cream, and a solitary chair and bookcase occupy the far end of the room. As my questioner group settles in about two yards from his feet, Goenka turns a peaceful, wise gaze on each of us. I speak up first, trying to keep my desperation at bay as I plead for advice on how to slow down the process. He smiles like a beneficent grandfather and assures me, "All these impurities need to be cleaned. All must go. There is nothing to worry about. Equanimity will take you out of your misery." He turns to the next questioner with imperturbable confidence.

"Wait. I'm seriously afraid that I'm losing my mind. Energy is shooting through every pore. I can't sleep and the visions keep pouring through. Please help. I think I need to leave the retreat."

"When things go too fast, just bring your awareness to your hands and feet and say, '*Anicca, anicca, anicca.*' All is impermanent." He turns to the next questioner again.

I press further: "What about the psychological dangers of such a radical opening to the depths of the mind with no support? Can't this lead to madness or at least a breakdown if people are not strong enough?"

He replies with a laugh, "Do not worry. There are no dangers on this path. It is 100 percent safe."

No dangers on this path? If someone teetering on the brink of fragmentation is put into this environment of total outer deprivation, surely there is at least a slight danger of breakdown. Goenka expects every last one of them to come through integrated and clean? *Vipassana* is powerful enough to open the most secret recesses of the unconscious. To make a statement that such an opening is not accompanied by certain dangers strikes me as unwise.

My prayer changes. I pray for the energies to slow down, the insights to come less quickly, the burning of old habits and impurities to happen at a more reasonable pace. During the final meditation of the night, the energy again intensifies, mounting as increased tension through my legs and back. Once back in my room, I plunge deeper, my altered state allowing me to sink into the intensified pain until it finally releases. New contortions allow me to leverage my body against the narrow walls of the cell, to build old tensions to the breaking point. My feet strain and shake against the bare concrete walls as sweat pours from my torso.

By two in the morning, many layers of tension have dissolved and my legs and back move with undreamt suppleness and freedom. Eventually I become too tired to go further, yet my calves still cramp badly. They feel half done, but no matter how hard I push, the final release does not happen. I hobble around the campus to loosen up, my spasmodic calves making walking almost impossible. As the madness fades, I realize that I have tackled far too much in one night, especially alone. Now I must pay with crippling pain. The foolhardy method I have discovered is equivalent to ripping a bandage off a wound instantly rather than hair by hair. Two hours of fitful sleep are not enough for a body coping with massive changes.

## DAY NINE

The light now shines at the end of the tunnel. The long hours of meditation pass quickly and with fewer pains and inner distractions. My mind is capable of a steady focus unthinkable on the first day. Today, new students test-drive the isolation cells designated for old students for a taste of what lies in our future should we return. The cells are arranged in concentric circles around the main stupa, each higher level closer to the innermost cells where Goenka and the advanced teachers do their practice. The arrangement creates a spiritual hierarchy, each step a bit closer to the golden spire of Enlightenment. When I enter my assigned cell, seat myself, and close the door, I am enveloped in darkness. Isolation is total.

Who would imagine that the setup used by prisons as the worst punishment — the dreaded "hole" — would be used as the royal road to enlightenment? I laugh to myself, imagining a jailed *vipassana* meditator begging for solitary confinement in order to deepen his practice, each month serenely announcing that he would like still another month in the hole. The darkness and silence deepen my practice, and my solidified self dissolves again and again into an inky sea of subtle sensations.

By afternoon, I feel increasingly stable and balanced, on the path to reintegration and increasingly thankful for the whole clearing and opening experience. My fears and terrors have evaporated. Tomorrow we break Noble Silence and prepare for reentry into the world at large.

## DAY TEN

The program for this last day is quite different, although morning meditation is identical. Some emotion still trickles through in these last sessions, although its reduced strength allows me to maintain equanimity. During the last hour in the morning, however, I am surprised to find myself in a positively blissful state, a warm wave of awareness bathing every cell in my body. All my chakras feel pleasantly awake, nourished by a subtle light. We close the morning practice with *metta,* a loving-kindness meditation in which we send our love, energy, and good wishes to all the beings of the world. I feel ebullient during the practice and can practically see the harmonious vibrations ripple off in all directions. I am shocked to feel as calm, peaceful, and collected as I do, and when the Noble Silence officially ends, I begin talking to fellow participants in an easy, contented tone.

Perhaps it is inappropriate to mix traditions, to speak of Kali and the Buddha in the same breath. But for me, gods and goddesses, saints and sages, exemplars and holy fools all serve to help us envision the most sacred life possible. Each mirrors what is still latent in us. Each acts as a magnet drawing us still closer to God. For that reason, I love juxtaposing the qualities of Kali and the Buddha: wild, ruthless, bloodthirsty destruction and utter equanimity, calm, and peace. Somehow they are not opposed but complementary. The severing of our ego from everything that we attach to — self-image, emotions, pleasure, stability, sleep, even sanity — leaves us in a state of Buddha-like equanimity. For me, submitting to the relentless discipline of Goenka's course felt like facing Kali's sword. It stirred up all the feelings of a real battle as cherished parts of me were lopped off one by one. This seeming cruelty was actually a great gift, for it gave me a taste of limitless freedom, a taste forever immortalized by the Buddha's equanimous smile. And for that taste, I will be eternally grateful.

▼▼▼

**STEPHEN DINAN** is president and founder of Transformative Community Network, Inc. For two years, he directed and helped to create Esalen's Center for Theory & Research, a think tank that explores the further reaches of human potential. He is a writer and a Holotropic Breathwork facilitator and holds a master's degree in East West psychology. This article is excerpted from his memoir in development, *In Kali's Garden.*

# WHERE SOMA MEETS SOUL

## BODY STORIES FROM WITHIN

### BY ELIZABETH SHAVER

**SOME SAY THE SOUL TRANSCENDS** this mundane body, but I say the body is the transmutation of soul into dense fleshy form. Rather than profane, the body, the soma, is literally a medium of sacred transmission, the organic venue for the soul's voice. In our reaching, our holding, in our opening and closing, in each expansion and contraction within the pulse of a heartbeat or the rhythm of a breath is the physiological signature of the soul.

Our bodies are memoirs in motion, living, breathing texts, individual embodied tales. In the recess of muscle and bone, our stories mingle in fluid, organ, breath, and form. These somatic sagas, stored within our flesh, are released in cellular contractions of aqueous images, emotions, and sensations. In the grace of a gesture or the silence of a sway, our bodies tell our stories. Bodily biographies of living history whisper within our cells.

To consciously contact my body stories, I must reclaim my sensual self. I "re-member," calling into awareness forgotten fragments, inhibited pulsations, and lost sensation. I rediscover, exploring anew the textured terrain of bone, breath, and blood. Accessing the body's transformative wisdom is an embodied spiritual path, and these body stories are the journey as I venture into the virgin territory of unexplored sensation to discover what lives within.

## MY BREATH UNVEILS ME

I am on my back, naked, legs drawn up, knees apart, spread wide open in this most vulnerable of positions. The cold hard vinyl of the examination table offers no soothing softness into which I can retreat. The crackling of the white paper sheet warns me of the advance of the stiff, rubber-gloved fingers of the male doctor into the most intimate gateway of my being. I hold my breath in anticipation of his penetration. Inhaling sharply, I wince as he stretches my opening, exploring the extent of muscular contraction in my vagina. I anxiously await the declaration. I have come for a diagnosis and a cure. Imagining I have the equivalent of a vaginal "broken arm," I have made this appointment with the expectation of getting "it" fixed. To my astonishment, I am told that there is nothing "physically" wrong with me or my vagina, no physical condition or injury to explain the extreme pain I experience during sexual intercourse. To my deep dismay, modern medicine can offer no miraculous or instantaneous cure.

Instead I am diagnosed with a psychological symptom known as vaginismus — common in women who have been sexually abused — where the vagina involuntarily contracts as a way for the body to say NO to penetration. To my astonishment, it is my own habitual thoughts that are causing my vagina to close, paralyzed in muscular contraction. My unconscious mind is making my body contract, creating a piercing pain.

The doctor displays my condition by squeezing his fingers into a ball. Recommending I use an elaborate set of various-sized dildos, he demonstrates the means to my cure by pushing different size fingers through the tiny dark opening of his tightened fist. I will be fixed, he explains, when the biggest one fits in.

Perplexed, I stare at my hand, curling my fingers into a clenched fist. As I consciously will my hand to open, my fingers instantaneously respond, stretching out according to my mental command. Mind over matter, or rather conscious mind over conscious matter. Yet I am unable to consciously will my vagina to open. Dumbstruck by this apparent contradiction, I feel compelled to decipher these complex and confusing connections between my body, my mind, and my soul.

Over one year later, I find myself halfway across the country, lying on the floor in a graduate class in body-oriented psychology, asked to give attention to my breathing patterns. Breathing, I discover, is much more than simply breathing; it is a gateway into my sensations, a doorway into my depths. I notice how often I don't want to breathe, how often I don't want to feel. I wish I could simply stop breathing, stop feeling, just make all the pain go away.

Lying on my back, stiff with rigor mortis, my arms tucked to my sides and my hands folded neatly across my chest...I am struck by the familiarity of this position. I remember waking in this precise pose, startled by a recurring nightmare in which a lecherous old man pursues me. I am a corpse in a coffin. Outwardly motionless, body frozen, legs locked, face stiff, a mask revealing nothing, I am deadened to feeling and response. This is my defense mechanism, my survival strategy, a retreat into the sanctuary of dissociation, a feeble attempt to rest in peace.

Suddenly the physical memory is palpable: I am staring at the ceiling waiting for it to be over. Faced with his fury at my refusal, I make the tactical decision to give in, to sacrifice my body. He can have that, but never my mind and soul. Play dead, and maybe, oh please God, maybe he'll go away...far, far away. But I am the only one leaving, withdrawing into my inner recesses, where I cannot be penetrated. Pretend and disappear. It isn't so bad. Perhaps I can die right now, close my eyes, shut down, and simply breathe my last. But that breath! That damned breath, overriding me, gulping, gasping, keeping me alive. My eyes, mesmerized by the ceiling's cryptic cracks, read monotonous messages breaking through in rhyme: one crack, two cracks, three cracks four, I would give my life to reach the door. "Come with me," he whispers urgently as he ejaculates, interrupting my delusional rhyming. The irony of that most remote of possibilities sickens me. I have never had an orgasm in my life.

Like a homing pigeon, I keep circling back into these memories, breathing into the hidden history that resides within my corpselike pose. Not breathing, not feeling, though long my protection, prove to be my demise. For what my conscious mind has minimized, my body-mind is literally not able to forget; it is not within her physical capacity. I am instinctively invited back into reinhabiting the habitual pose I experienced as death in order to understand and unlock its grip on me. I must go back into the somatics of my death in order to live.

Gliding on the current of my breath, I migrate down into the trauma dormant within me. My mind flashes to many months after the rape. Lovemaking with my new partner, I find myself involuntarily contracting, defending the entryway, my vagina refusing to be penetrated. The vaginismus says the no I cannot verbally speak. The no I do not consciously understand. The no I do not mean to send now to the one I love. Swirling within a vortex of trauma, I am confused, disappointed, ashamed by my body's betrayal, by my lack of arousal and excitement. Not understanding, I override the pain as each thrust splinters my virginity again and again. I make sure he comes, though unable to access the orgasm within myself.

Frigid, it is called, this animal instinct to survive, this primal defense response rooted in my physiology. I am the possum playing dead, knowing that the predator is less excited by an affectless prey. I am the little bird that, after hitting the window, remains frozen, feigning death, waiting. . . . When the coast is clear, she ever so slowly opens an eye, flutters a wing, awakening from the barren tundra of numbness into the fertile warmth of feeling. I am coming out of the shock of capture, only to realize that now, with my partner, I am no longer in captivity. My intellect is angry, telling me it's safe. My soma, however, is still startled.

Back on the classroom floor, I lie still, waiting.... Could my journey back to feeling, to life, lie within this breath I have for so long withheld? Breathing in I expand, taking in the outer environment, receiving the other. Breathing out I contract, releasing what I no longer need, returning to myself. Riding the waves of each pulsing breath...of each pulsing breath...of each puls...ing breath. Time is suspended, every moment s-t-r-e-t-c-h-e-d, sensuous and s-l-o-w. Every breath whispers an invitation into the elusive mystery of my being. I tiptoe up to meet myself, all my senses alert, careful to not startle myself from opening. To be with myself here feels so delicate.

Breathing deeply again, I follow my breath all the way down to my vulva, noticing the muscular tension, the micromovements of holding. As I continue to breathe into this powerful sacred region, I gently tell myself, "It's okay, you can open now." Exploring the no reveals the hidden yes.

Closing my eyes, I languorously let go into that moist place of wanting, allowing the slow warmth of pleasure to travel through my pelvis, my belly, my legs. My angst dissipates as the tenacious need to protect myself loosens its hold. The warmth spreads, while memories of my life flood into consciousness, the pleasure and the pain pulsing through me. In my breath, I am the rage and the love, the agony and the joy, the yes and the no. My breath reveals my being: opening in awakened expansion, closing in cold contraction, gasping in piercing pain, sighing in sensual surrender. My breath unveils me.

## IN PURSUIT OF THE BIG O

Several years into the exploration of my sexual trauma, I am in hot pursuit of the Orgasm, that most mysterious and exalted of all sensations. My drive to finally have the elusive O overrides any vestige of hesitancy and shame. It's time, I decide, to consult the experts. First, I muster the courage to contact a sexologist working at a well-known institute for sexuality. The initial telephone inquiry begins with the intimate details of my sexual explorations as she fires off a round of probing questions in such a dry, detached tone that my response gets caught somewhere between a blush and a flinch. Referring to cryptic categories of sexual dysfunction from the *Diagnostic and Statistical Manual of Mental Disorders,* she recommends a series of detailed and expensive psychological tests to accurately secure her diagnosis. I decline. Without medical insurance, I cannot afford to buy myself a DSM dysfunction.

Undaunted, I go to see a sex surrogate. Her name is Lola, and she lives in a dingy apartment with little natural light. A vase of wilted flowers sits on the coffee table. With a strained and almost apologetic smile, she admits to me that she has just begun to work as a surrogate. I feel myself go blank. An abyss of silence grows between us. In her anxiety to fill the void, she stammers a confession: she has just seen her first client the night before. Oh great, I think sourly, just what I need, a beginning "expert" more nervous than me. A sinking sensation in my chest informs me this is probably not going to work. *What are you doing here?!* I scold myself.

Unsure of how to extricate myself, I feel torn between my pull to take care of her and an impulse to run out the door. I choose a less satisfying and less authentic middle ground, and agree to her suggestion to receive a therapeutic massage. Lying on my back, my body stiff and frozen, I feel myself shutting down. As the massage continues, I observe myself pulling in, cutting off all sensation, deadening myself to feeling. Meanwhile, I continue telling myself and her that everything feels fine, and end up leaving disoriented and confused. Later I sheepishly tell one of my friends about the experience and then burst out, "I was looking for some beautiful, passionate woman to show me how to become orgasmic!"

"Oh Elizabeth," my friend reflects, "sounds like you were searching for yourself."

Next, I enroll in a series of workshops on sexual healing, the more unconventional the better. In one, I find myself watching a parade of women show their vaginas and tell their vaginal stories. I never realized just how many types of petals exist on so many different flowers: pink, scarlet, brown, long lips, small lips, no lips. Through the sharing of their stories, I gain appreciation for my own. In another, I learn to masturbate by following the Clockwork of the Clitoris. I am particularly fond of one o'clock. In yet another, I learn to give and receive Taoist erotic massage and "yoni healing." Alas, though I even try a promising technique called the Fire Breath Orgasm, the big O still eludes me. I never could get the coordination between the breathing and the pelvic rocking right.

I read a series of books on orgasm and am told by these research experts to practice masturbating; some recommend up to an hour a day for several months for the really serious. I discover I'm not that serious. I go to a progressive sex store for consultation on vibrators, where an enthusiastic but pragmatic saleswoman recommends the tried and true standard model rather than the gopher, whose tongue and tail offer simultaneous stimulation for any spot within their range. I go for the gopher. Later, I attend a film celebrating the art of masturbation, and, after two hours of visual bombardment of perhaps every type of hand job known to man, I leave desensitized and disillusioned, and definitely not in the mood to go home to my gopher for an hour practice session.

Where is the mystery? I wonder. I have become trapped in a goal-oriented pursuit of a group of sensations someone defined as an orgasm and then told me I should be having. And not just once, they say: multiple times, and over an hour in length, when I get really good. In my relentless pursuit of the big O, I have lost myself.

As I wander through the labyrinth of my memory, I remember losing my virginity to a man I barely knew. Just as I was moving my body in the beginnings of pleasurable undulations, he ejaculated and said to me, "You can stop moving now. It's over." I stopped, mortified. What happened when I was told to stop making natural movements that are my own? It is here I first lost myself, abandoned myself at a deep bodily level, stifling my instinctual response to conform to his pleasure. I never had sex with him again, yet the reverberations of that repressed orgasm remain.

My orgasmic response retreated into the recesses of my unconscious only to be experienced in the privacy of my recurring dreams. "See, you can have an orgasm," my dream self would tell me in these lucid dreams, "and this is how it feels." Upon awakening, I never doubted my body had just surrendered to forbidden delight. I vow to go down there, deep within myself, and retrieve the stolen sensations of my pleasure. What would my orgasm feel like, move like, taste like? . . .

In the privacy of my own home, I move through my room simulating the measured intervals of orgasmic muscular contraction. Head, chest, arms, pelvis curling in and snapping out, curling in and snapping out. Sharp staccato contractions from the epicenter of my solar plexus. I am a clam in a shell, open, close, open, close, in an accented cadence, a determined dance, accelerating toward an ultimate release. I sense, though, a forced quality in my movement: the pushing, the pressure, the trying too hard. There is only this repetitive, predictable motion, this limited percussive pattern: open, close, open, close. My thoughts parrot this compulsive beat: be orgasmic, be orgasmic, they berate me. My movement mirrors this rigid mind-set, telling me the harsh Truth of who I am. I am either feeling or frigid, hot or cold, open or closed. Either I am orgasmic or I am less than a woman.

I stop trying, allowing myself to drop into a pregnant empty pause. . . . Is there a place past labels and fixed notions of who I am, out beyond roles, beyond right ways or wrong? Could the pursuit of this most mysterious of all sensations be a pathway toward an unfathomable me?

Bathing the room in candlelight, perfuming the air with incense, I pleasure my senses and relax, simply allowing my body to move. Voice surrenders to swaying as this wordless ritual becomes my way to speak, to touch the very secrets of my struggle and whisper my sorrow in my tears. I move . . . to free myself from myself. I move . . . to find myself within myself. Dancing the hushed dialogue of my story, I move my own unfolding in a language where words no longer exist and explanations are no longer necessary.

Following my feelings of pleasure, I gently rock my pelvis, feeling how far the movement can flow. Undulations of s motions in hips, belly, and backbone form a winding river of fluidity. I am a fish swimming in the warm liquid within my spine. Smiling, I realize I am not a "cold fish." I am reveling in my aliveness. I am the salmon making its way upstream to spawn. I am the snake writhing up from within my sacrum to dance with the beckoning flute. Hips flow in fluid circles; arms entwine and unravel in a spiral, a spinning caduceus; hands form instinctual mudras in motion. Mesmerized by my movement, I let myself go, whirling, whirling, whirling, in an intoxicating wildness.

My movement slows and the energy rises up my serpentine spine. Curling in and arching out, winding and uncoiling, I sense how my sexual energy is moving me. A quivering river of molten fire, it ebbs and flows, expands and contracts, appearing and retreating in my undulations, reverberating throughout my body like ripples in a pond.

Rolling back up to vertical, I feel a supple wave of life wash over me. Ohhh, the warm rush of fluid cascading so sweetly, reminding me I am alive.

## OF THE INTIMATE AND SUBLIME

As my journey continues to unfold, new possibilities of relating emerge. At times, lovemaking is a sacrament, a vehicle for the very Divine to radiate through my body and illuminate my life. My sexual partners, beyond simply lovers, become soul allies in healing and mutual spiritual awakening. Making love is our prayer in motion, liberating layers of previous traumas and societal agendas, conditioned expectations, and bodily fears that limit identity and narrow range of feeling and response. This initiation into realms both intimate and sublime, this recognition of Soul spinning in sexual splendor, feels as dazzling as the midday sun. Its intensity burns through the fragile layers of who I once was, to reveal who I Am.

The sexual trauma that imprinted itself upon all my sexual experiences and colonized my natural bodily response also offered me a jewel, the impetus to transform. My anguish and shame were an invitation to delve into labyrinths of bodily sensation, clearing an embodied path to God. Perhaps that is why some say the pearl beyond price lies in the jaws of the dragon. Buried beneath my deepest pain lay the treasure of sacred pleasure.

There is a story about Fabbriche di Careggine, a medieval ghost town in the foothills of the Apuan Alps of Italy. After being ravaged by World War II, Italy needed sources of energy, so the state electric company built a 350-foot dam on the Edron River. As the valley flooded, Fabbriche di Careggine was swallowed 250 feet below the surface of Lake Vagli. But every decade or so, Fabbriche reappears, surfacing when the lake is drained for maintenance work on the dam. From this watery grave emerge a well-preserved Romanesque church and bell tower, houses with doors and windows agape, and skeletal trees encrusted with cracked mud.

By delving into the depths of bodily knowing, long-forgotten memories once again appear. Like Fabbriche, they arise from the aqueous depths of our unconscious onto the dry terrain of the conscious mind. Much of who we are is submerged in our tissues, circulating in the current of our cellular fluid. At times, we may dam up the river of our vitality, drowning essential aspects of our being. Yet as we dive deeper within ourselves, the landmarks of our lives resurface. The relics of our sacredness are revealed.

Upon reinhabiting my body, I became acquainted with the intricacy of my inner realm. Within this interior landscape of fluid and flesh, I found myself. Through my soma's sensuous awakening came both a recognition of the messages encoded within my physical symptoms and a reverence for the erotic essence of my existence. At the threshold of a wound healing, soma meets soul. "Come home," is the message of the body, "drop deep into me and know that I am Divine."

▼▼▼

**ELIZABETH SHAVER** is completing her doctoral degree in integral studies, has a master's degree in body-oriented psychology, and maintains private practices as an intern psychotherapist, massage therapist, and hands-on healer. She also facilitates groups on embodied sexuality from her home base in the San Francisco Bay Area.

# PICKING
# UP THE SLACK

## AN ADDICT'S JOURNEY

### BY MICHAEL DINAN

**MY NAME IS MICHAEL AND I AM AN ADDICT.** When I first made that statement over nine years ago, it felt like a shameful straitjacket. It choked in my throat as I coughed it up in a cloud of noxious cigarette smoke at my first Narcotics Anonymous meeting. Over the course of my recovery, the edge of judgment in the word *addict* mellowed. It slowly changed tone and became instead a soulful liberation. I scrutinized the rest of humanity through this lens of addiction and found them all qualifying in some respect. Now the phrase sounds to me more like a gentle observation of a universal truth on a par with the noble truths of Buddhism. Simply substitute addiction for attachment and it translates: anyone still manifesting in a clunky 3-D body should be under suspicion of suffering from some degree of addiction and could certainly benefit from the twelve-step yoga of letting go and yoking their ego to its soul source. How many king and queen babies today have been weaned at the military-industrial teat and can't be pacified by anything short of total remote control from a cushy sofa?

In Tibet, there is a class of beings called the Hungry Ghosts that are said to haunt the lower astral planes. They have tight, tiny mouths and giant, grumbling bellies and live in a constant state of dissatisfaction because they can't ever eat enough to be full. Our human attempts to eat our way out of dissatisfaction end just as dismally. Born free, we slowly morph into Borg Teletubbies. Drug addicts and alcoholics are simply the most exaggerated and dramatic examples of this phenomenon, the personified shadow of our culture's materialistic end-of-the-millennium binge.

My fellow Gen Xers and I became teenagers in the "me decade," the greed-fueled eighties. Cocaine blew egos out of all proportion, creating corporate rapists whose toxic waste was the only thing that trickled down to the people. A whole wave of former hippies caved in to materialism and became yuppies. Even the music was shallow and mechanical, full of pyrotechnics, hair spray, and soulless synthesizers.

The spirit and meaning that were missing from my formative years became my empty belly and started me on a gut-level quest for spiritual enlightenment. Before I became conscious that this was what I was seeking, though, I followed the vampire pack's lead and developed a taste for blood. I sucked my unfair American share of resources and built myself a plush technological and pharmacological coffin. Coming out of the shadows now, I feel the need to settle my account and give back the only gold I have, the story of my soul's growth. Before recovery, I was a numb petty thief lifting energy from everyone around me with increasingly obvious sleights of hand. Now, after turning myself inside out and finding my silver lining, I am a creation of my higher self. Thanks to many years of the Divine Mother's intervention, starting with my real mother dragging me to treatment literally kicking and screaming, I am finally picking up my slack and giving back, lending a healing hand to my community.

I will start my soul's story with a couple of war stories that bookend ten years of slacking away from the trials of my life through extensive self-medication. I first started drinking at age eleven over an unrequited obsession with a girl. I had pined for her quietly for several years only to find out through the sixth grade grapevine that she thought I was "too weird." This was in line with a general consensus that had been building since I learned to speak. When I found out she had a crush on a more "normal" boy, I quickly became his best friend and understudy. He drank and smoked and fought. A good mimic, I picked up those things quickly. But my young love was not convinced by my acting trick, and my sense of freakishness deepened.

Drinking was successful, however, in helping me fit in better, and quickly changed from an act into a habit. In a loud, inebriated crowd my weirdness could easily slip under the radar. And if someone did confront my strange behavior, I finally had an excuse: "Well, I was just drunk! I wasn't myself!" The next ten years were an odd odyssey: I drank a lot, smoked a lot of pot, ate a lot of acid and mushrooms, and got a lot weirder.

Then one day my charade ended. A fellow weirdo from Duluth whose bizarre sense of humor had made him a hero to me shot his own heart out with a shotgun. At the same time I lost my first true love, the first woman who saw all of me and loved me, who embraced my strangeness and called it genius. I was such a numbed-out zombie from all the drugs I was doing that I couldn't feel the wave of grief washing over me. Without a way to get out, my emotions turned psychotic. I began fantasizing about dying accidentally. I wanted to die, but I couldn't bear the thought of being remembered with anger or pity through the stigmatized lens of suicide. I began praying for a happy fatal accident that would set me free but let me keep my vanity intact.

Then, in the depths of my depression, a strange alchemy promised to turn my leaden hopelessness to gold. A woman in my poetry class was going through a hell parallel to mine. She, however, was dealing with her tragedies completely cleanly and lucidly, and, not surprisingly, writing much better poetry about it.

Several synchronicities led me to believe that she was the light at the end of my tunnel and could save me. I began focusing all of my poems at her.

I realized I had finally lost my grip when more misinterpreted synchronicities convinced me that I was meant to go windsurfing in a thunderstorm and get struck by lightning so that I could die and be revived by one of my roommates, Phil. Phil was a big clumsy welder with five minutes of half-hearted CPR training from me, which I distantly remembered from a few drunken summers as a lifeguard. My belief was that I would win a near death experience and the love of the poetess, and everything would be rosy. The deeper reality was that I was getting more than a bit impatient waiting for a happy accident to kill me. I was starting to force God's hand.

Thankfully, the storm I thought was coming for me never arrived. I wrote a poem called "Manic Depression" that began with a manic plea for the poetess's love and ended with me alone, floating in a limp wind on a gray lake, no bolt of hope in site. The poetess liked the poem, but was not impressed with the desperate show of affection. My self-destructive bent had been dressed up and veiled in myth and mystery, but its basic energy of "I'll kill myself if you won't love me" hadn't been refined much since I was eleven. She eventually told me to stop calling. I had never reached this level of desperation and rejection before, and it was the straw that broke my slacking back and brought me to my knees, ready for treatment.

I want to stop talking about the problem now. Any more would be wallowing, because here I sit, happily writing this, due solely to a continuous string of miracles. Too often when people relapse and leave the recovery community they are written off with the proclamation that "they just haven't hit their bottom yet." I understand from my own experience the ego-stripping gift of these tragic bottomings, but I think it's just as common that the missing link in recovery is a positive spiritual experience that lends a glimpse of a higher top. So, in the interest of balancing the scales, from here on I will focus on my peak spiritual experiences. They are the lightning life that surged through me in recovery, and brought my heart back from that dead gray day at the lake, shock by shock.

First off, my drug-addled, malnourished body had a long way to go to reclaim optimal functioning. Not much spirit would be able to enter me until I did some major internal housecleaning. Over the first seven years of my recovery, every cell in my body, with the exception of those of my brain and spinal cord, was created anew. This is the physical underpinning of the seven-year itch, and why year seven of recovery is known as the "second surrender." My nervous core may still have a predilection for electric intensity, but cell by cell I've built a new temple around that center. Now my high-wired fanaticism is transmitted through tissue that wants to live and manifests as a passion for purification instead of a lust for self-destruction.

Before I got clean, I canvassed for Greenpeace, rabidly attacking the corporate status quo for their poisoning of the environment. At the same time, I created fantastic and elaborate justifications for the hazardous waste I dumped into my own body every night. I was an artist who suffered from too much genius and lucidity. I needed to do some neural pruning in order to communicate with the sheep. I believed this until I got my first D— in college and realized I'd dumbed myself down a little further than intended.

In recovery, I began to realize that any change I wanted to make in the world had to start with my own body. I have eased the toxic influx by eating more consciously, eliminating pesticide-laden meat, and buying organically. I have cut back on refined sugars and high glycemic index carbohydrates, which keep blood sugar levels on a vicious roller coaster. Research has shown that limiting them helps to quell the raw, thoughtless, physical cravings for the quick sugary fix of alcohol that can happen in those blood sugar troughs. Exercise has also helped me maintain the momentum of my physical recovery. In my first year clean, I ran a marathon, which led me to finally quit smoking. It was just too difficult to smoke with all that bouncing up and down. Also, I have returned off and on to the pools of my youth to let loose my frozen rage, thrashing steadily away from that gray lake of depression and toward a new clarity.

A year and a half into recovery, I went on my first fast. After seven days, several enemas, and some intestinal cleansers, I lost a few pounds of God knows what that never came back. That fast got some toxins out of my vision too, and my purified eyes began to see a blue-green aura around me and every other living being. Later, I learned this is the etheric body. Since then, I've tried to go on four-day fasts at every seasonal transition to give the fat cells that are still saturated with waste a chance to spit their poisons out.

As my body started to function again, I became more and more able to come out of my isolation. At my lowest point of addiction, I wanted desperately to be adored for my songs, but I was so painfully shy of performing with my guitar and harmonica that the only audience I could stomach was the pot plants growing in my closet. The only emotion I could show was anger, which drove everyone close to me away. I had truly become a Hungry Ghost, unmoored from the human race. Thankfully there were other formerly ghostly souls who reached out to me at meetings and began reeling me in with their unconditional love and compassion. They spoke knowingly of the same hell I'd just come out of, but somehow had regained the ability to laugh and smile and hug. After attending for a while, I learned the mechanics of this transformation and started putting those principles into action. Meetings brought me an instant community when I most needed it. It became the family I never had, the family who really understood me.

For the last several years, I've participated in a sweat lodge circle of recovering people led by my sponsor Robert, an Apache pipe carrier, Sun Dancer, and "windigo," something like a sacred clown. Those sweats have helped me pray and sing more openheartedly, my soul pouring out through my skin's crying pores. The first round of hot steam starts with prayers to the worst off in the world, people in constant physical pain. Slowly, through the next three increasingly scalding rounds, our prayers circle back to our community, our families and loved ones, and finally ourselves. At that point of utter exhaustion, there's no energy for frivolous prayers, only the terse truth of what we really need. This practice has given me gratitude and lessened the narcissism that is the hallmark of addiction, and the truth behind the joke, "How many addicts does it take to screw in a light bulb? One, you just hold the bulb and wait for the world to revolve around you." I have learned how to surmount this selfish tendency and be responsible to the larger world from Robert's pure-hearted example in the lodge and beyond it as a father and counselor.

One major way that I've been able to put my gratitude into practice has been to work to help others get clean. For several years I worked as a drug and alcohol case manager at Hope Haven, a six-week residential treatment center right upstairs from Colvin Manor, the halfway house where I spent my first up-all-night white-knuckled nail-biting coffee-guzzling chain-smoking dys-functional-relationship-clinging year of recovery. In the last two years I've been working for Community Housing and Services as a case manager in their PTO program. In the PTO program, I work with the same homeless addicted population but for a much longer period, up to two years. The two-year length of the program is crucial because of a phenomenon called post acute withdrawal, or PAW, that goes along with chronic use. Long after the drugs are gone from your body, your chemistry is still hobbled. You don't feel pleasure. You can't sleep right. You can't think straight. Emotions swing from extreme overreaction to a dull flat line. A lot of people give up in this limbo because they feel worse than when they were using and suspect that they may be permanently damaged. They need a lot of cheerleading and advocating to help them have faith that these things can change.

At Hope Haven and in the PTO program I've worked with the worst-case scenarios: the homeless and hopeless revolving-door cases, the angry resistant probation and parole referrals, and those with major mental health diagnoses in addition to their addictions. It often feels frustrating trying to get past their defenses. For these people to let down their guard and become fully conscious, they must come face-to-face with the worst human and institutional horrors of our twisted age: rape, incest, war, murder, racism. People in this population make slow progress and often take a long time to blossom and stay clean; many die trying. But periodically, I have gotten to watch one crack open, and there is enough hope and beauty in those scenes to satisfy me that I'm right where I should be: lending a hand to those making the leap of faith into recovery. Being able to come full circle and help others in this way has given some much needed meaning to the self-inflicted wounding that I endured.

The recovery process is similar to a long shamanic journey. In shamanic cultures, the call to shamanic healing is precipitated by a grave and mysterious illness that takes the initiate to the brink of destruction. This dismembers the ego of the initiate so they can be rebuilt as a healer, a go-between with one foot in this world and one foot in the healing world of dreams. From this stance, illness, addiction, or even a suicide can be seen as potential gifts. But it takes a lot of time and healing to redeem them and find their hidden meaning.

The deepest gifts I received in my own years of shamanic dismemberment were when I gained lucidity in dreams. With regular dreams you strain your brain and groggily recall the experience after awakening. In a lucid dream, you are right there in the moment, feeling with your whole dream body the exhilaration and ecstasy of being free from the restrictions of 3-D reality. You can fly and melt through walls. You can experience the spirits of departed loved ones. You can experience past and future lives. You can fulfill your wildest sexual fantasies, disease and guilt free. You can change or create whole scenes with a thought, painting rainbows across the sky or creating an instantly audible symphony with just a flick of intention. These were the experiences that I was seeking as I tripped through chemically induced hallucinations that mushroomed out of my control. The lucid dreams I sometimes experienced as a child came back once I stopped blotting my consciousness out with drugs and alcohol. I quickly became a dream junkie, sleeping as much as I could, seeking my next hit of vision.

When I read that regular meditation increases the frequency of these experiences, I became a fanatic meditator. For at least an hour a night for the last six years I have used special tapes that induce meditative brain waves. I dissolve into the gentle flowing water on the tapes and ride the tones of crystal Tibetan bowls into another dimension. While in that wide-open state, my subconscious is inundated with subliminally encoded affirmations recorded in my own voice and designed to wash my brain of all the sour self-defeating beliefs that I picked up along my crooked way. Through this practice I have gone from having one lucid dream every few months to several a week.

The most powerful I've had resembled a near death experience. I was lying on my face in bed and realized I was dreaming. I first got turned on sexually but I've spent a lot of lucidity satisfying earthly fantasies and I wanted something more that night, so I turned over and was promptly launched through the ceiling. I was sucked up in a giant funnel, like a waterspout leading up to a sea of twinkling starlight that was liquid to the touch and sounded like a huge choir harmonizing perfectly. As I went further, the stars glowed brighter and the choir swelled and the most overwhelming feeling of peace and beauty and my own immensity overcame me. Never had I felt my personal identity dissolve so completely. It felt like I was a galactic symphony of singing stars going supernova. Everything got blinding ultra-white and I freaked out, afraid that I was dying and would be unable to return to Earth. The fear sent me back instantly to my small, solid body, but it took me several hours to feel even remotely at home in it again.

In many lucid dreams I've developed a closer relationship with Jesus, though the Jesus I've experienced has few qualities in common with the prudish rule-making Jesus of religious zealotry. Infinitely tender, he has cradled me like a baby in a pink and blue mist. Infinitely compassionate, he has gently held my hand and whispered in my ear to calm me while I writhed in pain on a dream cross. Infinitely wise, he has come to advise me, enlightened and white haired inside the Great Pyramid at Giza. After two thousand years of bowing to wash his beautiful but singular Piscean feet, many of us are standing up and starting to get to the core of his masterful teaching. We are following his example and getting off our crosses, owning our own divinity, and meeting him resurrected as a friend and equal. As he himself said: "You will do all this and more." In this egalitarian Aquarian age, Christ consciousness is finally becoming democratized.

I felt deeply fulfilled by all of these dream experiences. But then I'd wake up alone, and that desperate empty-gutted eleven-year-old would take hold. He'd tug my sheets away and send me off again in search of a partner to share my dreams with. A partner whose love could heal my deepest wounds and make my recovery feel complete. For the first three years of recovery, I had a tempestuous relationship that cost me a fair share of serenity. After it, I spent a whole year crying followed by two years of meditative and masturbative isolation trying to figure out and heal my part in that relationship's insanity. Finally, at a recovery dance, I met Kathleen Connors. I asked her if she wanted me to "do her chart," a step up from "Hey baby, what's your sign?" and she agreed. I was shocked to discover that she had exactly the same birthday as the woman who drove me crazy in early recovery. Would I be able to get it right this time?

On our first date, we ended up naked, something she was embarrassed to admit to her ACOA (Adult Children of Alcoholics) friends. Moving that fast with a recovering addict was a red flag signaling relapse. But our merger was meant to last, and every time we lost faith and became afraid, some validating magic eased our doubts. After we were together for three months, her cat Pook died. She had adopted her from the Humane Society seven years earlier at the beginning of her own recovery journey. Pook's death was a big emotional opening and it brought us much closer. Six months later, I dreamed of giving her a Claddah ring: two hands holding an amethyst heart with a bolt of lightning carved into it. Soon thereafter, Kathleen had a dream where Pook came to her as a fox zipping up and down the steps of a Mayan temple. The day after her dream, we went to the Whole Life Expo in Chicago and kept running into people involved with Mayan teachings. The first did a Mayan astrology reading and told Kathleen that her Mayan birth sign was Cauac, or purple lightning storm for short. Then, a few minutes later, we found a perfect illustration of her sign: a painting of a giant woman-tornado in a purple dress with lightning filling the sky behind her. Another painting by the same artist was of the Mayan temple from Kathleen's dream. We bought the purple storm painting, and asked the artist about the temple. She said it was a temple in Tikal, Guatemala, and urged us to go there.

Kathleen believed, as I did, in navigating through life by these kinds of magical signs, and she did not hesitate to follow Pook's lead and get tickets to Guatemala. My stormy lightning lady had finally arrived! I had the ring of my dreams made for her just in time for our trip. While I secretly wrote and recorded a proposal song called "Hades Moon," she decided on the name Moon Song Massage for her massage business. Nine months after meeting, under the stars on top of a temple in Tikal, I asked Kathleen to marry me. Legs shaking, I gave her the ring and played her our moon song, and she said yes. We consummated our engagement as meteors blazed across the sky. Then, after we'd climbed down the temple and started back down the jungle path, a fox ran up the trail and right by us. Pook?!

As we got closer to the actual wedding, though, these magical memories began to fade and we started compiling inner lists of all of the attachments and bad habits that the other would have to sacrifice for our love to last. We are both Taureans and stubborn as bulls, which makes our relationship really easy when we agree and near impossible when we lock horns. We got more and more dug into these judgments of each other, and tensions built until, two weeks before our wedding, we saw red and raged. We yelled out everything we hated about each other. Neither of us had ever been so brutally honest with someone we were so close to. After a long, frightening pause, we experienced our second surrender together. Our souls rushed in and we gushed our love for each other. We cried and held each other for hours, both having finally found someone who could love us with all our flaws, as is. Kathleen is a true moon goddess and she has gently massaged my core wound and called my dissociated soul back into my body, tingling from head to toe.

The last key piece in my recovery was the Inner Focus School of Advanced Energy Healing, an answer to the mantra "Ma Ma Ma" that I chanted inwardly for years after my first contact with the Divine Mother through the Hindu teacher Ammachi. The healings in this group of people helped me reclaim my true being. The school is truly a Divine Mother school: the main teachers in my class were two goddesses who complement each other perfectly. Alixsandra, who founded the school, is a big, round, blonde-haired momma who sings in spirit and channels Jesus. Laurel is a smaller, darker, curly-haired Jewish Sufi who leads dynamic dancing meditations and gives inspirational readings from Rumi.

They taught by following the group's energy clairvoyantly, which means the school changed from moment to moment to accommodate the students' needs. We came with the curriculum written on our energy bodies. At first, their clairvoyance made me feel perpetually naked, but thanks to their sweet love and joyful humor, I got beyond my initial shame. I stopped trying to hide my energy-body blemishes and started bringing them into the light for healing. I began to move toward self-mastery.

With each module, I could feel healing energy anchor more deeply in my body. When it first reached my arms and hands, it was so intense and unfamiliar, I was convinced it was carpal tunnel syndrome and I would soon be disabled. Now that I've come more fully unblocked, the energy showers through my body and out my feet, so unless I've got carpal body syndrome, I think I'm going to be okay. In fact, I am beginning to understand how the yogis who experience this energy to the nth degree can be free from worldly addictions. When every pore of my body is soaking in bliss, it's hard to remember that hunger in my belly.

Some of my deepest healings involved the Goodness Process. Basically, you say the affirmation "I am the essence of pure goodness. My goodness has nothing to do with my actions or the actions of anyone else." And then you work to heal the chorus of negative voices that arise to deny this fundamental assumption. It took me straight to that lump of self-loathing that jumped up from my heart and stuck in my throat when I first choked on the word "addict." And for the first time, under the steady love of my teachers and classmates, the deepest layers of that shame and self-hatred began to melt away. It was regaining this basic faith in my own goodness that gave me the courage to make my second surrender with Kathleen.

The image of the addict I once was has been shattered by recovery. After a mystical seven-year restructuring full of bad luck, struggle, and finally love, there's now a totally new vision of me in the mirror. To honor my deepening experience of who I really am, I want to introduce myself as more than just an addict. There is no statement more creative than the "I am" statement. Anything that follows the "I am" statement in your brain is bound by universal laws to eventually trickle down to be created in your life. My first step in the direction of better "I am" statements was when I took the magical name Lightning Mike after many lucid dreams in early recovery where I was hit by high voltage strikes that fried and purified my ego. Now, I want to go one step beyond the twelve steps to a thirteenth step inspired by my Moon Goddess. So I am dropping my baggage of lies and standing to my full height. I am picking up the slack in my spine and introducing a new self: "I am Lightning Mike and I am liquid singing starlight."

▼▼▼

**MICHAEL DINAN** is a drug and alcohol counselor, a singer-songwriter, a writer, and a hands-on healer in Madison, Wisconsin. His Web site is www.gutproductions.com.

# THE STRONGER PULL

## BY SOLA WILLIAMS

### WITH TERRA WILLIAMS

Let yourself be silently drawn
By the stronger pull of what you love.

— Jalal ad-Din Rumi

**RUMI'S COMPELLING CALL** had been guiding my life for perhaps twenty years before I placed his words on the altar of my jewelry studio in Oakland, California.

I had not heard of the poet-mystic back when, in a moment during my early childhood in Jamaica, I began to sense something going on behind the scenes in life. Behind what people said and how they acted, behind what I saw with my own eyes and heard with my ears, there existed a completely different world. At the time I had no words for it, but the feeling in my body told me this hidden world was magical, delightful, and filled with a vivid sensuousness. Exploring it was my life's purpose. My heart was my guide into this realm, and its pull was stronger than any obstacles I might meet along the way.

The gene to follow the heart path instead of the beaten one is not hard to trace in my family. My brother, Randy, and I came to be island born of a Jamaican father and an American-Jewish mother after my Mom "jumped ship," as she puts it, leaving a suffocatingly ordinary middle-class life in Chicago for her tropical island dream of adventure, romance, and ultimate fulfillment. And it was her mother, "Grandma Toots," who championed unpopular social justice causes, helped pioneer the human potential movement, and participated in founding Chicago's Oasis Center for inner development. Whether by nature or nurture, the roots of walking my talk go deep.

The relative simplicity of life in rural Jamaica in the early 1970s meant little exposure to television, few store-bought toys, and few artificial entertainments. Instead, Randy and I filled our days with hours at the beach, learning to swim, or carefully placing stones to redirect a small stream that flowed into the ocean at the fishermen's beach down the road from our house. Or, we might go out to sea on one of the boats owned by our sports fisherman father, learning from him the skill that was both his first love and his work. Many days we could be found in our yard after school, where, surrounded by our cats and dogs, we sat creating our own toys from bits and pieces of found objects: old clocks, boat parts, and motor fragments that we pulled apart to see how they worked, and then reassembled in more exciting ways.

Sand, stones, water, salt air, the open fire where my father would cook his "fish tea" from the day's catch of red snapper, yellowfin tuna, and marlin: these earthy elements of my childhood became for me the taste, pull, and feel of the Real.

In the winter of 1980, in a move initiated by my mother, my parents sold their deep-sea fishing and water sports business and left Jamaica for the United States, choosing Atlanta, Georgia, for our next home. Atlanta, though, rarely felt like home to me. Not only did I long for closeness to earth and sea, for lush beauty and a simpler life, for beloved family and friends, but I felt shocked, bewildered, and isolated by the racism, classism, and other "isms" to which my brother and I were exposed for the first time in our lives. To some people in our mostly vanilla neighborhood, the appearance of our diverse family at a local restaurant was a head-turning event. Their accusing stares spoke volumes about the law, still on Georgia's books, against interracial marriage. The color barrier flew up even among supposed liberals when, as teens, my brother and I invited their daughters on dates.

Now that I have some understanding about converting pain into fuel for growth and drawing power from difficult circumstances, I look back and give thanks for the struggles — social, academic, and economic — of those Atlanta years. They helped propel me toward my first substantial "declaration of independence" years later.

I was nineteen and in my first semester at Evergreen State College in Olympia, Washington. Immediately on arrival, I had begun to feel an old familiar feeling in my body: the feeling of being an outsider, the proverbial square peg squashed to fit into a round hole. The awareness emerged from deep in my body that sitting at a desk, listening to lectures, and reading books (punctuated by scattered, largely boring trips out to the field of living experience) was not my way of learning. My way, like my father's, was the way of actual, practical, lived experience, out of my head and into my hands, feet, and heart.

While this realization grew inside of me, my mother and brother reported back excitedly about a group of people known as the Alive Tribe and their work called Domain Shift, which aimed at no less than radical life transformation. Alive to the synchronicity of my malaise and this promise of resolution, I called to enroll in the next event and left immediately for Colorado. Four days of pillow punching, primal screaming, yoga fire breathing, and free-form dancing followed, skillfully intermingled with instruction on anger release, parental deconditioning, and optimal care for one's own body and the body of Earth. In the midst of shamanic rituals and trainings in directed attention, I could almost see and hear Don Juan, the sorcerer-teacher made famous by Carlos Castaneda, a strong influence in the Domain Shift work. I was being detoxified, receiving not only a body-mind cleanse but also a long-awaited initiation into a more conscious way of living. I left the event ready to leap out of my conditioning and into the promised new domain of freedom.

My first act of freedom was to leave Evergreen College bent on creating my own way of educating myself, beginning with travel. Dropping out of school meant using funds from the trust my grandfather had generously created for my college education. My decision disappointed my brother, my father, and grandfather, all of whom thought I was being irresponsible, reckless, and immature. My mother, perhaps because of our shared heart-path gene, was the first to support my "wild" plan.

So off I went, my first stop Colorado. Exposing my most tenaciously held personal myths and most severely limiting personal habits was, I knew, the necessary first step to going beyond them. Having begun this work of radical deconditioning with "the Tribe," I felt drawn to join the small group, which by then included my brother, that had gathered around them. In the course of the next two years, the tough skin and thick outer layers of my inner onion were peeled off, chopped up, and thrown into the cosmic soup. To align myself with the village, as the informal, loosely formed community was sometimes called, I ate no meat or dairy foods, practiced daily emotional purging, and regularly gave and received point-blank, ego-burning feedback. I was also a joyful participant in the shamanic ceremonies and rituals created by Diamond, River, Crystal, Summer, and Rain, Domain Shift's creators and guides.

Then, in the winter of 1992, I admitted to myself, my brother, and my housemates that this particular version of life at the outer limits of transformation had now become stifling for me rather than freeing. I needed balance. Although I struggled with self-doubt and feelings of guilt, that familiar pull toward what I love began more and more to smell like salt air, sway like feathery green coconut palms, and taste like ackee and salt fish, Jamaica's national dish.

Revisiting my Jamaican roots a few months later, alone, as a young adult, was bittersweet. In Jamaica I could be happy, comfortable in my skin. I could relax into myself in a way that had rarely been possible in the States. Once more I tasted the delicious sweetness, not only of Jamaica's sun-ripened tropical fruits but of the Jamaicans themselves. And I could celebrate being one of them: a people formed of many races and cultures, whose music, laughter, gentleness, and generosity ran in my veins. Yet the tranquil island of my childhood had largely vanished from the north coast town of Ocho Rios, where my family had lived. Down the same roads where slow-moving cows and goats once had the right-of-way, cars and buses now sped, past incongruous imports like McDonald's and Taco Bell. Saddened by the rampant tourism and consumerism and longing to reconnect with the simpler life I remembered, I turned adventure tourist, exploring for the first time the famous Blue Mountains and less inhabited tropical rain forest areas to the east. On the flight back from Montego Bay to Miami, feeling both fed and disillusioned, I well understood, in both my body and mind, the adage that you can't go home again.

I was in fact homeless, but neither penniless nor car-less, thanks to my grandfather's largesse. A solo cross-country drive formed an important part of my self-styled educational curriculum, since I believed that a world of discovery lay between me and California. A life-changing discovery awaited me, however, not on the open road, not in a forest, not even in the desert where I camped for days, but in a bookstore, where a book stopped my world.

The book, titled *The Experiment Is Over*, was written by a teacher named Paul Lowe. In this rare, out-of-print book, in crystal clear language, were the bare bones, gut-level truths I had always felt but had never been able to speak and had rarely heard from anyone else. Even before I reached the last page, I felt a pull too urgent to be ignored to meet this teacher, certain that he would be able to answer all of my Big Questions. Within two weeks, I was on a plane for Melbourne, Australia. Within another week, I was living in the same house with Paul Lowe, his partner Grace, and his small inner circle of students.

Whatever I thought I knew about myself or about the alchemy of spiritual transformation was shattered by this first in-my-face teacher! My felt sense of something happening behind the scenes had its reference point "out there," out in the culture, in society, in the world. With fearless feedback and the force of his own presence, Paul blew my cover, exposed the layers of conditioning behind my own scenes, and revealed the multiple illusions that make up this grandest of all illusions called me. This me had long considered itself a sort of victim, oppressed by externally imposed limitations and culturally constructed rules about the right way to do life, all of which felt unnatural, even crazy. Paul revealed how these limits were self-imposed, and how again and again I was bumping into walls of my own making.

It was terrifying to be unmasked, deconstructed, stripped bare. And it was exhilarating to be confirmed in one of the few truths that remained intact, which was this: Truth, said Paul Lowe, is a feeling in your own body. The reality of who you are, where you are, and how you are emerges in the moment as a strong, silent, nonverbal physical sensation. Here I was, validated at last by a respected spiritual teacher for a truth I had lived as a small boy while playing at the beach, collecting stones, making toys out of clocks and driftwood, and later, drawing. As I look for words to talk about that always wordless experience, the ones that come to mind are: extraordinarily relaxed, integrated, vividly attuned, expanded. It was this very body wisdom that had pulled me to Colorado, back to Jamaica, then to Australia and to Paul.

Years of trying to fit in, to please, to be good enough, years of sitting in my own rigidity, had worn deep grooves in my nervous system that were probably not going to smooth out after just a few weeks (or months or years) with an awakened teacher. Besides, this particular teacher was not going to let me get away with my "I'm trying to please you and be a good student" act. I was plagued by yet another habit, fairly common among truth seekers: the habit of becoming so fascinated by my own thoughts, feelings, and perceptions, and of diving so deeply into my inner rabbit hole, that I became virtually dead to the world, dead to the feelings, thoughts, and perceptions of everyone else around me.

Sometimes extricating someone from that rabbit hole requires a certain shock. One day, Paul administered the necessary shock by asking me to leave his immediate company and move out of the house. Flooded with shame and self-recrimination, I plunged into a free fall. I had lost all: identity, money, friends, teacher, shelter. At the same time, my body-mind relaxed into the fall as it had never done before.

In a kind of floating, let-go state, I headed for the community market, posted a notice about looking for a room to rent, and, by the end of the day, had a place to live. That evening, I returned to the market, knowing there would be music and dancing, and hoping to find an interesting woman to join me for dinner. Shortly, I heard someone call my name and recognized a woman with long auburn hair, bright eyes, and a welcoming smile. It was Sambodhi. She knew Paul Lowe and had driven me up to his house when I first arrived. It was the first of countless, enchanted, challenging experiences shared with this beautiful, passionate, highly gifted and treasured friend, healer, and lover — a separate story in itself.

Sambodhi immediately tuned in to my need to create a flow of money and, linking this with what she knew of my artistic bent and my attraction to things of the natural world, introduced me to her French geologist friend, Tony, who made jewelry from natural stones. I began working with Tony in his studio several days a week learning the foundations of jewelry crafting: soldering, stonecutting and polishing, metal working, as well as the artistry of balance, shape, and composition. Soldering two wires together for the very first time felt like reuniting long split fragments of myself. Like an epiphany, my body knowing told me: this is my calling. Almost at once, the secrets, the complexities, the alchemy of this ancient art opened to me.

My growing passion for stones and metal began to extend into dreams. In one unforgettable scene, I walked in wonder around a glowing, opalescent lake, and entered a state I can only describe as bliss. For weeks afterward, I saw the world as infused with light. Tony told me that opals are actually formed from water trapped within tiny crevices of silica, and that the stone is said to symbolize one's life calling. I was clearly being called. However, following that call often pits me against parts of myself that live in terror of what I might be led to do next. When I felt pulled to leave Australia and Tony's tutelage and Sambodhi's graceful lessons in love, the struggle was no longer just an individual one. For the first time, a significant other was deeply affected. Sambodhi suffered for it. She grieved while I struggled to feel.

Nonetheless, filled with entrepreneurial enthusiasm and determined to start up my own jewelry-crafting business in the United States, I joined my mother and her friend Elizabeth in Rimrock, a tiny hamlet near Sedona, Arizona. Though low on funds, friends, and permanent housing (not to mention a studio), I surrendered to my body's wisdom and soon met Christopher, a seasoned jewelry artist who, like Tony, had his own business selling imaginative, well-crafted jewelry and who was more than willing to share his expertise with an apprentice. Next, a rental situation opened up, including a motor home to live in and a great storage space I could convert into a studio. Finally, another jeweler who was giving up her business sold me her entire set of tools on a pay-as-you-can basis. So, not long in Arizona, I found myself at my own bench in my own studio, creating a line of jewelry based on what I'd learned from Tony, while apprenticing to Christopher. With his expert guidance, I tuned up my skills in casting and metal fabrication, enjoying the hands-on techniques of hammering, engraving, cutting, filing, forging, and soldering gold, silver, bronze, brass, and copper. Once again, I had surrendered to the pull and saw my dream coming into form.

Drawing on my Jamaican/African roots, I created an entirely new line of fanciful high-end jewelry inspired by the ceremonial masks of indigenous cultures. To each pendant, earring, and brooch, I tagged the following words:

> Throughout human history masks have played an integral role in the expression of who we are and how we relate to our inner and outer worlds. Masks represent archetypes brought to life through rituals of theater, religion, rites of passage, education, celebration, mourning, and communion. They

represent, celebrate, and deepen our awareness of the sacred, that which is known and felt and not always expressible through words. Opening our awareness to the sacred is essential to our being. May my artwork inspire you on your journey.

My words were more than marketing hype. To this day, they reflect the spiritual dimension underlying all of my work.

As my works of art began to embody more spirit, my body itself needed to find its own freedom so it could more fully express that spirit. I needed to taste again the sweet embodied life I once knew in Jamaica. But this time, California called, perhaps due to two extraordinary women who were exerting a silent tug on my heart and soul. My friend Candace completed the first linkage when she invited me one evening to meet Valerie Vener, a choreographer and spiritual teacher. To my amazement, these two beautiful, ultrasophisticated women immediately fell into a form of wild and hilarious banter and play. Taking the simplest, most mundane story, they proceeded to embellish it until it became an outrageously funny scene. A lifetime of laughter bubbled through those few hours. A kind of free-spiritedness that I had been longing to find in myself flowed freely.

Valerie and I began experimenting with dance and movement together. I had a real breakthrough one day while playing my Australian didgeridoo for her. Suddenly, I took this perfectly weighted, four-and-a-half-foot tall instrument of primordial sound and began twirling it and leaning my weight against it. Valerie swiftly guided me to move with the didgeridoo in more uninhibited, complex ways that forced me to loosen up, relax, and get grounded. Following her lead, we started dancing together, our movements equal and opposite to each other. Each time Valerie instructed me to let go, our dance became more vibrant and expansive. The freer I was, the freer she became. I didn't know it at the time, but Valerie was teaching me the ancient dance of Tantra, the fundamental movement of life itself. The more time we spent together the more expanded and free I felt, both in my body and in my relationships. Valerie's availability for profound intimacy allowed for greater physical, mental, emotional, and spiritual freedom.

Before long, people interested in what we were doing began to show up, and over a couple of years, a core group of men and women began to meet regularly and to bond deeply. So it came about that on a bright Sunday afternoon in May of 1998, six people escorted me on a blind date to meet a stunning, blue-green-eyed body worker named Susan. On the palm-decked outdoor patio of a Mexican restaurant called El Rio, a live salsa band kept the beat while Susan and I fell into each other as if no one else were around. Susan beautifully embodied the lightness and ease I had just begun to rediscover in myself. Her spunky playfulness and keen intelligence immediately drew me in. Depth and great presence emerged between us from our first meeting. We marveled at the ease with which we both felt seen and heard, appreciated and attracted.

So began our Tantric love dance. So it continues as we move through our third year of marriage and celebrate the birth of our first child. Gracefully relaxed in her body, emotionally open and available, my longed-for mate is also funny, wise, forthright, a woman of brilliant gifts and beautiful as well. Susan's keen attunement to the body manifests in her work as a teacher and practitioner of the Alexander Technique (a potent form of body-mind integration). Often she will walk into my studio and find my body contorted into strained angles as I set a fragile stone or put delicate finishing touches on a pendant, brooch, or earring. With a loving, tension-melting touch, ease flows from her body into my own and I return to my task rejuvenated. In the daily play of our life together, Susan and I love standing forehead to forehead, often laughing at the way our favorite place is in each other's face! At these times, all sense of separateness fades away and my body is flooded with wonder at our union.

Separate and yet one. Both art and relationship flow from this principle. I stand awed before an invisible universe of dancing particles partnering in an infinity of unknown ways to form the astonishing wholes of this visible world. What, I wonder, is the force that binds them together? Once more, the strong, silent pull draws me to explore this greatest of mysteries and to discover a way to let the inquiry speak through my art. My mind goes back to an early fascination with insects and the hours I spent observing how their tiny parts were joined together. In a recent epiphany at, of all places, a construction site, I watched huge cranes moving with unlikely grace and precision. I marveled at the clever linkage of smaller parts that made this movement possible. On the spot, the insects and cranes resonated together in my nervous system and a vision of exquisite jewelry held together with finely joined, freely moving links flashed in my mind.

Sitting at my studio workbench, I realize it is now time to make this vision manifest. An image appears in my mind's eye, revealing a gold ring of delicately linked segments. As I focus on the image it sharpens, the details start to fill in, and I see the ring crowned by a magnificent and rare Boulder opal. This, I know, will be my own ring and the hallmark of my newly named So-Link line of jewelry. To express in words the spiritual core of my work, I create the byline: "One World, One Heart, One Mind, So-Link It!"

Feeling like an ancient medieval alchemist about to begin the Sacred Work, I take from their appointed niches my special tools of transformation. The optical visor has the power to magnify a grain of sand up to the size of a pebble. An ultrafine mechanical pencil and a digital caliper that measures down to hundredths of a millimeter help me to turn the three-dimensional images in my mind into two-dimensional sketches on paper. Here, as throughout the work, I dance like an alchemist between the realms of mind and matter, my body acutely attuned to their push and pull. My mind holds a vivid picture of the gold ring and its links while at the same time I remain sharply aware of the boundaries imposed by matter, those parameters both physical and aesthetic that seem so demanding. The finished piece must be wearable, comfortable, beautiful, playful, and have maximum range of movement. The opal must be seated elegantly yet securely. The gold must be durable enough for a lifetime of wear and also soft enough to have the desired richness and luster. And what mechanical means will join the links to each other and to the bezel? In this primordial tension between inner and outer worlds, I feel poised and relaxed. Thanks to Susan and Valerie, I have learned to dance gingerly between pushing boundaries and surrendering to them. As I do, a world of possibilities opens.

Out of this place of possibilities emerges the insight to bond the links of my ring with a tiny rivet. In another revelation, I give thanks to those early carpenters who first were inspired to join two pieces of wood in a form they called tongue and groove, mimicking the opposing yet complementary shapes of male and female. Their brilliant adaptation from nature becomes my solution, along with the rivet, for joining each segment of the ring.

And so the creative process moves me. It is a meditation. It is miraculous. It draws me into timeless time. I continue refining the drawing of the ring until a feeling in my body tells me I can begin the next exquisitely delicate process: sculpting in wax each minutely sketched and calibrated detail. My tools are again my allies, extensions of my mind and body. A set of reworked and sharpened dental tools, hundreds of differently angled and sized drill bits that fit on a high-speed flexible shaft: with these instruments I cut, carve, shave, shape, and coax the featureless block of wax into an intricate and precise three-dimensional model of my design. As in meditation, my sense of time blurs. After hours and days of deeply focused concentration, the wax model reaches its optimal form. The next work of transmutation is done by the caster through whose magic (the complex and very ancient lost wax method) the ring turns to gold.

Casting is not the last step. There are still hours of work, many exacting adjustments and refinements I must make before giving the ring its final polish. Finally, though, the auspicious moment arrives. I stand before my altar, Rumi's words in view. Feeling more wonder than pride, I slip the glowing ring on the middle finger of my right hand. A wave of ecstasy runs through my body as I experience the tremendous creative force that has been gathered and stored forever in this work of art. I hold a strong vision that this concentrated energy will benefit each person who wears my jewelry. Mine, and yet not mine. I see clearly that on this journey of beauty from image to flawless form I have not been alone. I read Rumi's words once more and silently thank the stronger pull of what I love.

▼▼▼

**SOLA WILLIAMS** is a mystic jeweler whose work is the embodied expression of his inner life. He lives in Oakland, California, and can be reached at (510) 482-7492.

# THE SWEET PERFUME OF DECAYING FLESH

BY **VIPASSANA ESBJÖRN**

## WHEN LIFE STOPPED BEING A PROBLEM

Moss-and-ruby hummingbirds flutter outside my window on a passing breeze. The pungent scent of blooming roses drifts through the house as afternoon flies get stuck between the screen and the window, buzzing for their lives. Shriveled giant cacti ferment on the porch, flooded by El Niño rains, while fluorescent magenta petals bloom on the surviving cacti. This collage of birth and death, growth and rot is a reminder of my own fragile, temporal existence in this flesh. Here is a story about that collage, a story about a young girl growing up; it is my story. It is also a tale about seemingly opposing forces — life and death, East and West, the relative and absolute — and the transformational possibilities of two worlds in collision.

Yesterday I remarked to a friend just how extraordinary it is to experience this mysterious play of life. For years, the very fact of being incarnated struck me as a problem. An aching, empty feeling colored much of my youth. Over time, this emptiness has faded, revealing a luminous ground that eternally supports me. I shared with her my puzzlement over when it happened, when life stopped being a problem. Somehow during years of torment and separation, at times painfully disconnected from the Truth, an alchemical process brewed in me. I kept my trust in that stubborn internal flame, and in turn the perception of life as a problem loosened its grip. Bit by bit, the fire of truth incinerated my delusion, seared away my belief in problems. Pleasure and pain certainly still exist — I get lustful, furious, and terrified, crave easy feelings and comfortable things — yet life has ceased to be the problem it once was.

Today, life is more like a wild garden in full blossom, a place to be explored. In this garden lives a tapestry of freshly sprouted wildflowers to tend to; velvety saffron roses to savor, mindful, of course, of their sharp thorns; a craggy yet sturdy oak tree to lean against; gnarly vines to get tangled in; thick ocher mud to squish into without getting stuck; and crispy leaves falling from a dying Japanese maple, foreshadowing my eventual return to the earth. I inevitably encounter grief and discomfort as I explore the obscure and prickly recesses of the garden of my life, yet to the degree that I resist these distasteful feelings (or seek the yummy ones), only then does life become a problem.

## STRADDLING EAST AND WEST

The Divine beckoned me at an early age, but it took many years before I turned inward to see who called. At five years old, I tugged for my mother's attention as she sat serenely, eyes closed, on a black *zafu* in her bedroom in Honolulu, Hawaii. She fruitlessly attempted to be a serious Zen student by day and a corporate wife by night. When I was six my parents gave up trying to change each other and got divorced. At seven my older sister and I trekked to Northern

California with our mother to live in a Christian monastery that housed severely abused foster children. This year was laden with a mixture of grace and darkness. We lived on one hundred acres of rolling apple orchards, had free rein to ride the horses of the house, and attended contemplative chapel services that drew on teachings from both Jesus and Lao-tzu. Yet we were regularly hit with Ping-Pong paddles, rulers, and the massive, beet red hands of a domineering man, the head of the community. This paradoxical mosaic, a crash course in freedom and fear, bewildered me.

At eight we were back in Hawaii. I was living in Kula, Maui, with my mother and sister in a funky, crimson house with a curvy metal roof the color of spinach. One afternoon I sauntered home from school after a tough day of third grade. A tawny horse grazed in its pasture down the street from our house, and the sight of its graceful swooshing tail soothed me. The brisk Kula wind felt delicious after years of humid Honolulu weather. As I approached my home, though, animal howling and piercing screams boiled from our living room. These untamed sounds rode on a background of wild tribal drumming and some bizarre synthesizer. As I approached the driveway, I saw the walls of our rickety abode actually shaking, vibrating as if a tractor were plowing the shaggy carpets of my safe haven. We lived on a main thoroughfare to Haleakala Crater, and my cheeks flushed with nervous blood as I looked around to see if anyone else was witnessing this ghastly sight. Luckily, the coast was clear, so I crept up to the front door and, crouching like a secret agent, peered through the old-fashioned keyhole. A group of naked people wearing blindfolds leapt about my humble living room — jumping, shouting, dancing, and pounding cushions on the floor. The men had long hair and scraggly beards, and the women undulated with wild abandon. I shuddered with disgust and sprinted to the backyard to wait out this fantastic affair. Huddling beneath a banana tree, I briefly considered running away from home, but instead, when the sounds subsided, I skulked back to the house. Ten years later I would revisit and embrace this scene, which I came to understand as an invocational and cathartic practice called

Dynamic Meditation. I would even experience its liberating effects on my conditioned and often constricted body, mind, and soul, but that day I was simply horrified that my mom was not "normal."

When I was nine years old, my mother announced that she was packing her bags and moving to India in search of enlightenment. When given the option, my sister and I instead chose the straight and narrow path, a life with my highly successful father that included financial security, Republican values, and Honolulu's finest elite college preparatory academy. For the next seven years I straddled those two worlds: my father a CEO of a large Hawaiian company and my mother clad in brilliant orange flowing robes, a dedicated devotee of an Indian guru. While my father made a six-figure income and became a distinguished public figure, my mother gave away her belongings and took on a new Sanskrit name. Our home hosted Hawaii's top business and political leaders, while our summer and Christmas vacations were spent at the controversial ranch in Oregon, Rajneeshpuram, a utopian oasis for my fledgling hungry soul. I was raised in a world of contrasts and paradox.

As a freshman in high school, I became accustomed to, yet increasingly sickened by, the affluent and glamorous scene that surrounded me: bronzed waifs with bulimia; sixteen-year-olds driving Porsches and BMWs; and classmates being groomed for Harvard, Yale, and Stanford. I felt insignificant and dumpy. I fought back by wearing black spray-painted high-tops with the names of perverse punk bands that I pretended to like written all over them. A shaved head, clove cigarettes, and Frankie Goes to Hollywood were my symbols of rebellion. I used a fake ID to hang out at the trendy punk club on the Waikiki strip and guzzled untold quantities of vodka and peppermint schnapps to dull the anguish and boost my fragile confidence.

By this time it had become clear that something essential was missing in my life. An aching inner hole had opened onto abysmal depths that I could no longer ignore. I endured that excruciating ache for the next four years, until one fateful night while walking Lanikai beach in a storm I shouted to an unsuspecting classmate,

"I *know* there is more to life than this, I just know it's out there! I want to discover love."

## DEATH AND REBIRTH ON HOLY SOIL

Following in my mother's footsteps, at eighteen I traveled to India to be with Osho (previously known as Bhagwan Shree Rajneesh). One month after graduating from high school, I took *sannyas,* formally becoming Osho's devotee. Maitreya, an old Indian disciple with gentle eyes and wiry silver hair, presided over the ceremony. Once a figure in the Indian government, he was said to be enlightened and was among Osho's first sannyasins. He presented a Sanskrit name to me, symbolizing rebirth into a new life of a devoted seeker. For the first time in my life the gaping hole in me was filled. The day after this momentous occasion, Maitreya "left his body," as the Indians say. His was the first dead body I ever witnessed. As his corpse lay on a bamboo and canvas stretcher, adorned with a blanket of rose petals, throngs of devotees blissfully swayed around him. Tambourines, bongo drums, guitars, bamboo flutes, and lustrous voices filled the city block, as hundreds paraded to the nearby burning ghats where this wise man would soon be transformed into a pile of ashes. I danced late into the hazy Indian dusk in a state of rapturous abandon as the sweet smell of death brought life even closer. In a moment's pause, I reflected back to only one month before when I sat among fashionably dressed teens in the center quad of my high school. I had finally come home.

It was on this ancient soil that I first experienced the fullness of life, tasting true blessedness. I would sometimes walk the pearly marble path next to the tented Buddha hall alone, at night during music group. The trees that surrounded the hall had tiny sparkling lights in them, and when it rained the path turned a twinkling, leprechaun green with their reflection. As I walked along the path late one night — shimmering emerald footsteps skipping to the beat of my favorite love song to the Beloved — I remember sensing that this was it, I was for once complete. Sitting at the feet of my master, I experienced waves of devotional ecstasy. I wept. I laughed. I fell apart and reassembled myself over and over during my three years in India. My life revolved solely around awakening.

I slept on a narrow coconut fiber mat in the living room of a modest flat. A piece of woven cloth posed as a door. At dawn I would sit on the balcony of our minty green apartment building contemplating the river and the burning ghats beneath me. Dogs and goats wandered the banks as women young and old squatted to scrub their laundry against jumbo rocks. Sometimes Indian families would stay up all night in the muggy Pune air, chanting to their deceased beloved whose body lay aflame on the funeral pyre. The freshly cleaned laundry that I hung on my balcony to dry inevitably reeked of human remains after an all-night burning. The presence of death enlivened me, though; it was a call to be ever more alive in this very moment. As my peers attended some of the most prestigious colleges in the United States — getting drunk, laid, and knowledgeable — I sat along the river in India smelling the foul scent of bodies being burned. Yet it all seemed so completely ordinary.

Eventually, however, the West beckoned me home with my growing yearning to get a formal education. I also wanted to reenter "the world," as we said in the ashram, and test out my new learnings, to see whether I could be a buddha outside the Buddha field Osho had created. The next few years brought difficult tests, for my newfound happiness proved fragile outside the liberating and protected space of the ashram. Chasing after an agonizing love affair, I traveled to Boulder, Colorado, where I quickly fell into a depressed stupor. At my lowest point, I tromped to work in the slushy Boulder snow, briefly contemplating throwing myself in front of a passing car. I desperately wanted the pain to end. As high as I had flown in India was how low I plummeted when I couldn't find the source of truth within me. The fact that I had tasted absolute fulfillment made the misery even more bitter. For several years I traveled back and forth between India and the United States, in an arduous attempt to embody what I had discovered in India, amidst the trappings, seductions, and anguish of North American culture. At twenty-one I once again entered the sober world of academia, struggling to find meaning and spiritual community on the University of California Berkeley campus.

Over the next decade I slowly learned to embrace both East and West. And now I find myself to be an amalgamation of sorts, a distinctly spiced soup flavored with the curried wisdom of Eastern spiritual traditions and the tart, clever intellect of the Western mind. The broth of this soup is textured with both teachings on enlightenment and strategies to achieve worldly goals. The vegetables in the soup are a savory mix of contrasting values and experiences: poverty and affluence, service and success, inner riches and material wealth, and being nobody as well as being somebody. The gifts from East and West are leavened, kneaded, and baked within me, and my service in the world rises out of the nourishment I have received.

In embodying these contrasting poles of existence, again and again I've contemplated death. I have been haunted by it in strange but somehow reassuring ways. Death is not just a physical process but also applies to psychological and spiritual change. It reminds me of the transience of all forms and all ways of being. Leaping from one mode of existence into another — from an ashram to a university, from single life to marriage, from one country to another — I am asked to die to the old self I so treasure. And thus, as I have journeyed forward, I attempt to embrace each new miniature death more amicably, even joyfully.

## DEATH ON MY SHOULDER

Perhaps it is brought on by the blazing mountain air that envelops our secluded dwelling miles above the Silicon Valley, or perhaps it is due to the fact that I am not in school, but summertime often feels like an extended meditation retreat. It is something akin to an accelerated independent learning course on a variety of contemplative topics. I choose the weekly lessons, or rather they choose me.

Such was the case one parched afternoon when I delved deeper into the topic of death. I was mired in personal suffering; I had just become engaged and was flooded with panic and doubt about getting married and relinquishing the promise of monastic life once and for all. My sister gave me a set of tapes by Joan Halifax called "Being with Dying." For the following week I listened to these tapes for the better part of my waking hours. The Buddhist teachings on death transformed the poison of my intense suffering into food for awakening. I lived with death on my shoulder, remembering moment to moment the impermanence of life and the inevitable reaper that awaits at any instant. An urgency brewed in me. I poured over a *Tricycle* magazine issue on death, eating it with an appetite of one facing her demise. I was awed by the photos of the charnel grounds in Nepal, the spot where Tibetans hold sky funerals in which bodies are chopped from head to toe and left for frenzied vultures to devour. The thought of my body being chopped up after death and fed to these wild birds struck a deep chord that illuminated my attachment to this vessel of my body.

The following week my fiancé and I drove to Berkeley one Friday afternoon to sit in *satsang* (a gathering in the name of truth) with the Advaita Vedanta teacher Isaac Shapiro. During the two-hour sojourn, we were fighting about something trivial that seemed quite important at the time. At one point I said to him, "You know we could die any moment." Ten minutes later as we rolled into Berkeley on the Warren Freeway, traffic began to slow. And then like a surreal scene out of a movie, two teenage boys with blood-strewn faces came staggering into traffic. They were dressed in hip baggy clothes and looked to be about seventeen. Their arms flailed while they moaned and shrieked as if to both God and those of us in traffic, "Somebody HELP!"

My heart rate quickened as we pulled off the road and saw an overturned car with a limp young boy lying in a pool of blood on the pavement beside it. He looked about the same age as his bewildered friends. Crouched over the body, a fourth young man begged his unconscious friend, "Hold on! Don't give up, Cousin!" A group of onlookers wandered about the scene aimlessly, asking those awkward but somehow reassuring questions that give a sense of purpose in such moments: "Have you called 911? Do you know if he's breathing? Should we try CPR? No, he's bleeding too much.

Did somebody take his pulse?" The scene felt choreographed, as if I would peer behind the eucalyptus tree and see a camera crew and makeup team. "Cut!" But this was the real thing.

We approached the young man lying on the pavement and knelt on either side of him. I lamely lay my black knit sweater over his back as if to protect him from the chaotic energies that encircled him. I cradled his left hand, which twitched ever so slightly. I did not know if he would make it, so I silently supported whichever direction he needed to move — toward life or toward death. Whatever spiritual practice I had done up to this point was all I had to draw on: I prayed, I meditated, I opened my heart and bathed him in love as best I knew how. My mind hovered in the delicate quiet between life and death. I was humbly receiving a teaching on death by this kid whom I only knew as Cousin. I gazed up from the commotion at the hills above the freeway where my grandfather lives. He is ninety-one years old and bursting with aliveness. An old man running toward life, a young boy hurtling toward death. Strange. The hand I was holding stopped moving.

Sirens announced the arrival of officials upon the scene. We were told to move away if we were not witnesses. Before leaving I approached each of the three young men who were wandering about the freeway. Perhaps on another occasion I would be intimidated by their burly youthful presence, but that day all I wanted was to hug them, to hold each weeping stranger as they spun with shock. I cradled each young man, and we both held on to each other tightly as the universality of grief became palpable. As we walked back toward our car, I paused and looked again at Cousin on the pavement. Now he was covered with a large turquoise tarp. I silently said good-bye and wished him a most peaceful journey. Later that night while sitting in *satsang,* I peered down at my hands. They were crusted with dried blood.

Death flirts with me each morning as I say farewell to my husband. I savor the moment, for I know this could be our last meeting in the flesh. It hovers near as I traverse the steep mountain roads surrounding our house in the blackness of night. The impermanence of life shatters my self-image when I gaze into the mirror and see the rotting corpse that my body will one day become. As I cling to my position during an argument, wrangling to hold on to my opinion, a microdeath occurs when I instantaneously let go. In that moment I fall into the void, landing splat in the stark here and now. The presence of death presses in on me, shaking loose and revealing my terror of the ultimate unknown. At the same time, death is a constant reminder of the flowing fullness of being in a body, alive in this moment.

Embracing the miniature deaths of each moment has subtly transformed my spiritual journey. Once a frenzied quest, it is now more of a gentle unwrapping. The tangles of constriction around my soul are gradually loosening, so that Being shines through with greater ease and delight. I would now describe my search for God as an inward dwelling, a sweet and constant deepening into who I actually am. The truth of me arises in the dynamic space between form and formlessness, body and spirit, life and death.

▼▼▼

**VIPASSANA ESBJÖRN** holds a master's degree in counseling psychology and is pursuing her Ph.D. in transpersonal psychology at the Institute of Transpersonal Psychology, where she researches the body-self relationship in contemporary female mystics, teaches a course on women's spirituality, and works as a psychological intern.

# PART 2

# LANDSCAPE

**THE SPIRITUAL SEEKER IS NOT A SOLO ACT.** Surrounding her is an array of traditions, assumptions, and cultures. For better or for worse, we are on the life stage with a rather large ensemble cast. Most of us grow up taking the show for granted: its premises and its plots, its characters and its props. They become the setting for our strivings, the backdrop to our goals. As long as we do not stray from the script, we do not realize the extent to which our actions, behaviors, and dreams are chosen for us. But the commitment to walk a spiritual path is a commitment to radical truth about ourselves and our society. It almost inevitably creates friction, the friction of evolution at work. The spiritual seeker gradually becomes a voice for something more, and in those moments the creativity of the universe is unleashed.

In this next section, then, we pay special attention to the collision between paradigms long kept geographically and culturally separate. There is mess and mayhem as well as humor and heart in this process. As we unravel our assumptions about patriarchal Gods and information age mysticism and the strange hubris of the New Age, we begin to feel what is most real and valuable rather than what is merely a vestige of the past or a distracting detour. In exploring these issues with a fresh, playful, and occasionally ruthless wisdom, the following articles help situate the spiritual seeker on the emerging postmodern stage as well as articulate a more enlightened script to live by.

# LOOSE 'ROOS
## ON THE ROAD TO ELEUSIS

BY **ASHLEY WAIN**

Right from the first moment when one begins to explore the possibilities of man, whether one likes it or not, whether one is afraid of what this represents or not, one must face up squarely to the fact that this search is a spiritual search.

— Peter Brook in *Art As a Vehicle* by Jerry Grotowski

**IN THE FILM *MURIEL'S WEDDING,*** there is a scene in which Bill Hunter, an actor who has built a distinguished career playing "ordinary" Australians, stands on his balcony watching his no-hoper son Perry playing footy alone under the Hills Hoist. Perry is commentating on his own performance and indulging a fantasy of scoring a miraculous try (or "touchdown"). Bill's character, a corrupt and adulterous local councilor, watches him for a while. You can see in his eyes what a disappointment Perry is, how he can't quite believe this complete bloody idiot in the backyard is his son. After a few moments he loses patience and barks out: "Perry! Wake up to yourself!"

It's a classic piece of Australiana and, for those immersed in transpersonal psychology or a spiritual quest, it probably sounds like good advice. But in Australia *waking up to yourself* isn't *Waking*

*Up to Your Self.* It means snap out of it and get in line. It's a phrase to pull out whenever someone breaches the unwritten code of the culture, when the values that contain our identity are undermined. That subculture the Anglo-Saxon section of the population claimed as distinctively "ours," born in the bush poetry of the 1890s and sealed in legend at Gallipoli, debated at length ever since and self-consciously exported to the world in films like *Muriel's Wedding* and *Crocodile Dundee* — this was, roughly, the milieu I grew up in.

One level of my explorations into the realms of the unconscious has been an encounter between two cultures, between two clusters of values, those of my Australian roots and those of the weird, weird melting pot of the emerging American spiritual flowering, with all the nonsense and hubris, all the astounding insight and profound wisdom inherent in that rollicking jalopy. Of course the emerging synthesis of the world's wisdom traditions is a global phenomenon, but we encounter it as an American phenomenon, first in the stereotype of the Californian New Ager turbocharging their path to fame and fortune with past-life regression and colonic irrigation and then, if we are lucky, we encounter the depth behind the dross: those brave, sane people shaping monumental changes in the way we understand ourselves through meticulous and searching inquiry. Entering this odd cultural milieu challenged my sense of Australianness. My identity was secured by levees that the Americans seemed to have flowed over long ago.

My parents valued honesty and hard work. They believed in *a fair day's work for a fair day's pay.* In our world, nobody *should get too big for his boots.* A real man didn't make a fuss; that was a woman's job. The best approach to reality was to look it square in the face and get on with it. If you couldn't do that, then you were probably *playing with yourself* or you were *getting too deep.* The most laudable attitude was laconicism. Spirituality was a kind of taboo subject, something people did in private and rarely talked about, which they had their own reasons for. The universal mantra of comfort and consolation was *She'll be right, mate.*

I never really fit this picture too well. I would get worked up about ideas or ideals, was too serious and *too deep*. I shrank from criticism and the judgments of others, and was compulsively moral. I couldn't, like my larrikin friends, do a nude run through a hotel corridor or egg the ferry as it passed my friend's riverfront property. But I never rejected the values of "Australianness" and remained strongly identified with the ideal, if not as a picture of who I was, then as a picture of what I *should* be like and, when all my problems were fixed, what I *would* be like.

After high school I studied philosophy and politics and auditioned for acting schools. I hoped for wisdom and knowledge at university, but academic life was, at that time, in the grip of an essentially nihilistic relativism. Truth was a dirty word and wisdom was a joke. My attitudes to spirituality at this time drew upon popular stereotypes. The American "therapy culture" and the New Age were objects of ridicule by everyone, from intellectuals to my best friend Damian to television comedies. One featured a character called Candida, who squirmed on a sun bed and rambled about crystals, charts, and just really being there, you know?

One incontrovertible requirement for being regarded as a serious and intelligent human being was a scoffing disdain for all things spiritual. A second requirement was to adopt a patronizing attitude toward the United States. I remember a TV skit in which a hapless ambassador apologized to the world on behalf of the American people for, among their other crimes, "electing an illiterate B-grade movie actor as president — twice." Spirituality might well have been an American invention for all the associations that came with it, from everyone in Hollywood asking, "What's your sign?" to Rajneesh's fleet of gold-plated Rolls Royces, to Nancy Reagan's astrologer. Involvement in American spirituality meant membership in the New Age, and that meant you had 'roos loose in the top paddock for sure.

This put me in an awkward position because I was always, as long as I can remember, interested in what lay beneath the surface of things, in the depths of people, in secret knowledge. I also had a weakness for fantasy, which suffered a mortal blow from a teenage reading of Lobsang Rampa's *Third Eye,* which contained

descriptions of levitating monks and journeys beyond death. I
planned a trip to Tibet, only to discover that Lobsang Rampa was
not a lama but "the son of a plumber from Dorset." Betrayed and
humiliated, I cultivated a greater skepticism, although the urge to
explore the depths remained. The only way to do this respectably
was to study philosophy or, taking a more embodied approach, to
become an actor.

My first encounter with "American spirituality" happened in
1994, my first year out of drama school. In three years of actor
training in Melbourne, I had discovered my body and a few of the
interesting things it could do. I'd started to come alive emotionally
and was standing up straight for the first time since adolescence. In
our Neutral Mask classes, taught by a remarkable man called David
Latham, who knows what it means to be an individual and nurture
the individuality of his students, a whole new dimension of life
revealed itself, a realm of archetypes, of elemental energies and
numinous experience. I was bitten: this was the doorway to the
depths I sought, and I continued to work with the Mask after graduating. But I also struggled to get work, to initiate projects, and
even to believe in the worth of a career in the arts industry. I had
hoped to enter an art form, but the kind of theatre I had wanted
to be a part of didn't seem to exist. Everybody referred to "the
Industry." Left with too much time on my hands, I found myself
reading voraciously, especially Joseph Campbell, who had influenced David's approach to the Mask. Toward the end of the year, I
came across Tarnas's *The Passion of the Western Mind*. In the epi-
logue Tarnas presents a cogent philosophical summary of the psy-
chiatric research of Stanislav Grof that hit me with the force of
revelation. The next morning I set out to buy one of his books.

I inquired first at Dymocks, a major bookstore. The guy there
suggested I try the Theosophical Society Bookshop because "they
are probably the only ones who carry that kind of thing." I imagined Damian staring at me suspiciously as I admitted visiting
the world of the flaky ones. I decided not to confess to it, found the
place, and, with a look each way up the street, ducked inside.
Sweating with embarrassment, I stood looking at the little Grof

section on the shelves. Behind loomed a much larger section called "Crystals." To the left was a mind-boggling array of dream catchers, incense sticks, and self-hypnosis tapes. And bugger me if his books didn't have awful cringe-inducing titles like *The Adventure of Self-Discovery* and *The Stormy Search for the Self*. I browsed, but the word belies my demeanor: close to the shelves, shoulders hunched in, hoping I wouldn't be spotted by anybody I knew. Ridiculous really, like meeting an acquaintance at a nude beach: you're both there, so who cares? But this was a private affair; I didn't want to be caught with my spirituality hanging out. *Beyond the Brain* struck me as the most reasonable title, but there I was with *The Adventure of Self-Discovery* in my hands, like a one-way ticket to Palookaville. I adopted an appropriately offhand attitude at the cashier, as if I were buying it for a friend.

My day was free, so I retreated to the safety of my room and read almost the whole book in one sitting. That was a remarkable day. Here was someone writing about things that I had long ago dismissed as fantasy as if they were daily occurrences. Here was a lucid account of a vast range of spiritual experiences, from past-life recollections, encounters with deities, ego death and spiritual rebirth to identity with the Void. And Grof wrote about these things in clear, grounded language free from speculation and unnecessary theorizing. It was Karl Popper on acid. And the method for accessing these states, for undertaking this transformation, was breathing, faster and deeper, to music. It had to be a hoax. It was Lobsang Rampa again. Except that this time a simple experiment could verify Grof's claims. We couldn't be that close to a whole universe of transcendental experience, could we? Faster breathing? It couldn't be that simple.

In true Popperian style, I decided to refute the hypothesis by replicating the experiment (while hoping to God it was all true, which is not so Popperian). A few months later, in Perth, a generous facilitator offered me the chance. Those early sessions were not as astounding as many of those recounted in Grof's books — they involved mostly strong physical sensations, often associated with birth, many powerful emotions, some strange visions and stranger odors — but I felt significant changes. These were most evident during rehearsals for my first play since leaving drama school. The work came much more intuitively, more spontaneously, and with a greater sense of embodiment. The intellectual junkyard had apparently been swept clean, or at least tidied up. I was excited enough by the possibilities of the process to enroll to train with Grof to become a facilitator.

Nevertheless, I approached the training with some apprehension. No matter how sound and grounded the work was, no matter how many hours I was prepared to regurgitate the history of psychology and the philosophy of science, most people would regard the whole thing with suspicion, and some would think me mad. The process was called Holotropic Breathwork after all. In Perth "gone troppo" means gone nuts. And "holo" certainly sounded New Agey. It didn't seem important that holotropic, which means moving toward wholeness, describes exactly what the breathwork was about; it was a question of style and stereotype. It was a question because I was weak when faced with the judgment of others, of being grouped with loonies, of being dismissed as a flaky failed actor, as a cross between Candida and the guy who wrote that Mars and Venus book. It was one thing to undertake the process — it's kind of thrilling to become a demon or a wild animal or a baby in the birth canal — but it was another thing altogether to be open about it, to become a facilitator, to actually tell people that I was a — a what? A *Holotropic Breathwork facilitator* (a.k.a. A New Age Lunatic Who Wants Your Cash). I arrived at the first week of training excited and defensive.

On the first morning we had introductions. I expected these to be short, sweet, and polite. Instead they were long, emotional, and intensely personal. I struggled. As the mike circled, I thought of *Absolutely Fabulous,* the episode where Edina joins a New Age group and finally asks in frustration where she can buy her own talking stick. What were these people doing? We weren't in California. We weren't Californians who referred to our "process" as if we were carrying either a precious child or an affliction, who tearfully shared our painful personal histories. Inside me friends were saying, "Get over it"; Mum was saying, "Don't wallow"; Dad was telling me, "When you fall off your horse you get right back on." How to describe this to my friends? How to give due respect to these people here and still keep a safe distance? When the mike arrived, I was brief, polite, and stated the facts, showing everyone how it should be done, how a serious person behaved. It never occurred to me that I might be the one with the problem, even as I half-consciously tried to impress with my "objectivity."

But Stan, as everybody called him, didn't seem any more impressed with me than anyone else, and neither did his assistant, Tav Sparks, who was to run most of our training modules. To watch these two guys work was a revelation. Here were two men who lived outside time. They gave whomever they were working with their entire attention, and would stay with a breather for seven hours or more, serving not as a negation of themselves but as an expression of themselves. Simple things really, but I had never seen anyone act quite like that before, ever. We so often have somewhere else to be or our own barrow to push.

Witnessing things like this would silence the inner critic, but other aspects of the training had me clambering for ways to maintain a familiar self-image. There was the stigma attached to therapy, the implication that something was wrong with me, that I couldn't deal with life. I assured people that I wasn't doing it to fix problems, but out of curiosity and because it related to aspects of my theatre craft. I cringed inwardly when Tav referred to the Goddess, rather than God. And phrases like "I really feel for you," and "I'd really trust yourself there" veered too close to a Candida skit. When people talked this way the phrases were usually platitudes, but here they expressed genuine empathy and reflected a deep understanding of what constituted a therapeutic environment. Sometimes, to close a session, we held hands in a group. I didn't tell any of my friends about this part. It was difficult to accept that there could be a truth within the stereotype.

These concerns were only a small part of the story and never arose in the sessions themselves, which evoked many powerful and some incredibly beautiful experiences: murderous rage, numinous energies, experiences of being born and slowly dying, and, of course, an encounter with the nurturing energy of the divine feminine, probably to prove to me that what I thought would be embarrassing was in fact beautiful, and humbling.

*Humbling* became an important word for me. One tiny sixty-year-old woman showed the strength of a bull and the courage of a soldier in many terrifying sessions; I often gave up in exhaustion and fear, knowing the process was incomplete. These people I had half-consciously denigrated were the same ones who held me for hours when I regressed to a state of utter abandonment. I began to feel such gratitude for the acceptance they had all shown me, and for the humility I had gained as a result. When I completed the training last year, it felt like the one endeavor that, without reference to any outside opinion or benefit, had been completely worthwhile.

I stayed with Damian in Sydney for a few days following the final week of the training. Although skeptical, he asked about it. I told him it was great. Then he asked, "How were the fruitcakes?" I balked at the word, probably for the first time, realizing how I had let this image persist, and had even helped create it. In the photo of the training group I showed him, there were teachers and nuns, psychologists, artists, counselors, and academics. It wasn't a mob of fruitcakes. They were a warm, honest, vibrant, and skilled group of people. By hiding my true feelings for the group to avoid being seen as a loon, I'd done everybody a disservice.

Later that night my girlfriend ended our relationship, which spanned the same two-and-a-half years as the training, and which had been as important to me, as wondrous, confusing, and tempestuous. A time of devastation and emotional upheaval followed. My process took on a life of its own. The following three months of extreme turmoil and confusion compelled me to reassess my commitment to breathwork and intensive self-exploration. Why was I doing this? Did it actually help me, or anyone? Was I trying to escape reality? Wasn't it dragging me further from the friends, values, and security of my cultural heritage? I finally sat down to get to know the madding crowd, the ravenous horde of inner critics, to see if they had anything worthwhile to say.

What had pushed me to pursue this unconventional path? Admittedly, if I had found excellent roles and satisfying work straight out of drama school, I would probably not have come across this field at all, so this journey emerged partly from the failure of my worldly ambitions, ambitions that were already faltering, caught between a yearning for true nourishment and the demands of our industry. Secondly, having seen Grof's map of the landscape, it seemed obvious that to ignore this rich and profound realm of experience meant choosing a relatively impoverished life. Aurobindo wrote that the song of awakening should be a lullaby for those who still wish to sleep. Fair enough, but if someone's taken you to the window and pointed to a world of vastness, depth, and beauty, *can you sleep?* Also, I wanted to be a good man. I wanted to help others, but moodiness and self-doubt often hamstrung my capacity to actually make a difference. This motivation transformed as my experiences deepened because, of course, it is not *goodotropic* breathwork, it's *Holotropic* breathwork; it's not about becoming good but becoming whole, which means owning the downright evil as well as the divine within us. Now I find that the helping happens anyway, but not through trying to be good.

Was all this a way to avoid facing reality, to escape from ourselves? Thinking back over hundreds of sessions answered this question clearly: nobody escapes the reality of themselves in breathwork for long. They face it again and again, often in pain or fear, and sometimes in rapture. In comparison, the reality I seemed to be avoiding comprised watching television and movies, talking about these over coffee, acquiring objects of "value" without considering what was truly valuable, pursuing personal ambitions only to compensate for a sense of deficiency, and self-sedation by nicotine, booze, Prozac, or gossip. Not to demean these things in themselves: I love movies, drink booze, occasionally smoke cigarettes, and have been a dreadful gossip, but partaking of these things doesn't qualify for me as facing reality. They are often an escape or, at best, only a fragment of the story.

Looking reality square in the face means acknowledging what we value and what we can be responsible for. In more than one breathwork workshop parents have wept for the pain and falsehood they have passed on to their children. Someone in the training once asked what was the hope for our children when, in every workshop, we saw evidence of the abuse, neglect, and suffering we were carrying. Tav said, "Yeah I know, I think about that with my son, but you know what? For me it stops here." He was pointing to himself. He wasn't saying that he could completely control what he passed on, or that he was perfect, but he was taking responsibility for himself, for his intention not to harm. Most people who come to breathwork intend to discover the truth about themselves or to heal the past. There's nothing flaky about that.

As for the cultural conflict, under a steady gaze it looks as earth-shatteringly important as last week's Hollywood gossip. It's true that holding hands in a circle doesn't fit the ideals I learned to aspire to. It's true that talking about personal problems with a microphone in my hand meant looking like people I had learned to see as fools. But if this process allows us to know ourselves, to open up to others and heal the collected crud preventing us from living full lives, then should superficial self-images stop us? Grof's books are called *The Adventure of Self-Discovery* and *The Stormy Search for the Self* because that's what they are about. People use words like Cosmic Consciousness and Great Mother Goddess because they need these words to describe an experience that has leapt unexpectedly from the depths of their being. If our culture cringes at these words, it reflects the paucity of our experience and our obsession with style at the expense of substance. Digging beneath the surface of my culture's heritage, its substantial values — facing things squarely, keeping your feet on the earth, not obsessing about yourself, a sense of humor — all appeared as indispensable elements of any true quest. And honesty, the value my parents impressed upon me most strongly, is, if it is heartfelt, the basis and the means, the rudder and the wind of the journey.

Since I started breathwork there have been many blessings: my first deep and wondrous love affair; the privilege of supporting people as they expressed rage, rapture, or tenderness for the first time in their adult lives; feeling at home in my own culture instead of confined by it. I launched all this evidence back at my doubt and judgment, and I guess you could say that it added weight to my side of the seesaw. Sitting opposite the inner critic and being the heavier kid was so satisfying that for some time I failed to realize I was still on the playground.

One morning, four months after the strong phase of my process started, just past the worst of it, I was lying on the floor after a session of Tibetan yoga. I became aware of the voices in my head telling me I should get up and be more practical, I should go outside and chop wood or something, I should get a real job, and so on and so on. Allowing the thoughts to be there without reacting revealed a feeling of pressure and then, at the boundaries of my body, a sensation like a thick black goo. I watched with curiosity, exploring the details. Suddenly, the boundaries dissolved, as if my skeleton and flesh had opened like a doorway and let me out. There was no sense of separation at all. Imagine *being a room:* you are the walls and the ceiling, all the objects in it and the space in between. And somehow in this state you can look at the body and the person you thought you were and see how all your problems, judgments, and fears are founded on separation; how the boundaries are an illusion you've bought into, a concept you learned, a fold in the fabric, a bright and wondrous joke.

Here was a glimpse of life out of the playground. Seeing through the *you should be*s revealed a sense of *I am* that does not engage in the conflict. This experience made it clear to me that truth doesn't fall on either side of the debate; it was present as an unfiltered reality, requiring no explanation or interpretation, from which the vagaries of judgment and defensiveness, theory and speculation, culture and psychology seemed like the rules of a children's board game, something to distract us or amuse us, the parameters of an adventure that is not in any way final.

A complete truth can admit no boundaries. My interest in breathwork is another form of the impulse to study philosophy, to authentically embody a human story on the stage, and to avoid lying to others. My spiritual search is simply an orientation toward truth, knowledge, and wholeness. And although my loves, friendships, work, reputation, and sanity have all seemed lost at times in this game, there is no choice about whether to play it. The deep questions are just there, unbidden. To be able to ask them with an autonomous heart is such a blessing, and the answers that have started to come to me are rich and real, wondrous, worldly, and satisfying in a way I could never have imagined and cannot hope to convey.

▼▼▼

**ASHLEY WAIN** has worked in the theatre as an actor, director, and teacher, as a guest lecturer at high schools, introducing students to current thinking in psychology, philosophy, and the spiritual traditions, and as a facilitator of Holotropic Breathwork. He holds a degree in philosophy and is a student of Jean Berwick, a teacher in the Ridhwan School. He has conducted innovative research intensives for actors and is currently conducting research on Mask, nonordinary states of consciousness, and Ritual Theatre at Monash University in Melbourne.

# IN THE ARMS OF THE GODDESS

BY ABIGAIL SUTKUS

**AFTER EIGHTEEN YEARS OF STRICT CATHOLICISM,**
hearing the words "God as Female" in my theology class freshman year
of college was life altering. For me, God was synonymous with He, and
the possibility of God as She opened the door to a whole new world.
At first, it was a struggle to even hold the possibility of a female God in
my mind, God as He was so deeply ingrained. Yet, I searched for images
of Her, information about Her, and gradually She was revealed.

Reading about the ancient and current cultures that worship
the Goddess helped Her come alive. I imagined Her...breasts,
hips, vulva, womb...and the ability to birth. Over time, I was able
to see myself in Her; I became proud of my own body, of myself.
Despite this beauty I perceived in Her, I had no experience of the
Goddess; She was a distant being existing only in my head.

Where could I go to find Her? There were no churches, no

temples. How could I learn to know Her? I was not raised to recognize Her presence. Where were the others who worshiped Her? The community I came from revered only Him. After substantial searching, I discovered a graduate program in women's spirituality and a women's circle. My ritual experiences within the circle have provided me the vehicle I needed most to connect, initially with other women, and ultimately with the Goddess Herself.

*We turn to the East*
*A woman speaks...*


*Spirits of the East, of Air*
*Dawn*
*New beginnings*
*Wind that blows through our hair*
*Breezes that caress our bodies*
*Breath that sustains our existence*
*Creatures that fly*
*Be with us*
*Guide us as we begin new journeys*
*Give us clarity in thought and vision*
*Inspire us*
*Teach us your softness*
*And, as we take a breath*
*And breathe you in,*
*May we be reminded of our own Spirit*
*That dwells within us, always*
*Welcome East*


*We turn to the South*
*A woman speaks...*


*Spirits of the South, of Fire*
*Of passion and creativity*
*Of sexuality and sensuality*
*Blood that runs through our veins*

# IN THE ARMS OF THE GODDESS

*Energy that permeates the universe*
*Come, join our circle*
*Bless us with your vibrancy*
*Warm us*
*Sweep us into your realm of desire*
*Burn away our insecurities*
*Ignite our fires*
*That they may rise up*
*And shine forth with your brilliance*
*We welcome you*
*Spirits of Fire*


*We turn to the West*
*A woman speaks...*


*Spirits of the West, of Water*
*Of the deep oceans and the rushing rivers*
*Of waterfalls, rain, and tears*
*Waters of the womb*
*The womb of our mother the Earth*
*And the wombs of the mothers who gave us life*
*Be present with us tonight*
*Stream through our hearts*
*Cleanse us and purify us*
*Activate our intuition*
*Remind us of your life-giving capacity*
*Your healing power*
*Your fluidity*
*Teach us to ride our own waves*
*Welcome West*


*We turn to the North*
*A woman speaks...*


*Spirits of the North, of Earth*
*Of the crone and the ancestors*

*Mountains and the trees*
*Food that we eat, and creatures*
*That share this sacred planet with us*
*Join us*
*Ground us, nourish us, and sustain us*
*Remind us of our rich depths*
*And of the powers that lie in the darkness*
*Activate our healing capacities*
*And our memories*
*Of the ancient lineage of women healers*
*Help us to honor our bodies*
*To celebrate them, and revel in them*
*As we gather here*
*Held in your loving embrace*
*Welcome North.*

The circle is cast. An energetic container has been created. I stand with the other women around the altar of candles and flowers carefully arranged atop a grass mat, sacred craft of the women of Hawaii. The room is dark, lit only by the candles spread throughout the room, and music whispers in the background. Tonight is dedicated to Laka, Hawaiian goddess of the dance. The dancing will soon begin, but not before the check-in. As always, the ritual begins with each woman having the opportunity to share her feelings and experiences since the last circle.

I am weighed down by the issues I carry with me to this, my first circle. I have recently returned from a trip to Sedona, in retreat with my spiritual teacher, confronting a deep mother wound, a deception around the circumstances of my birth. As a newborn baby, I was separated from my mother for the first month of my life. Torn with indecision and with little support, my young mother placed me in foster care.

Initially, the enormity of being given away and the magnitude of my mother's lies were too much for me to bear. My journey to Sedona was an attempt to finally face this pain. In the circle, I share my discovery from this retreat: the wound with my mother has created a fundamental mistrust of women, coupled with an ingrained pattern of relying on men to fulfill my emotional needs. I express my desire to heal and deepen my relationships with women.

After each woman speaks, sharing her own experience, the altar is lifted aside and we spread throughout the room. A rhythmic melody fills the air and we begin moving with its reverberations. Flowing with the sweet sounds, we sink deeply into our own internal rhythms. Like trees swaying with the wind, our bodies move, each woman's authentic self revealed in her dance. The room is alive with beauty.

Mesmerized in movement, I savor my sensations. Opening my eyes, I see several women drift toward each other. Belly to belly, hips flowing in fluid circles, their bodies move in unison. On the couch, two women rest, hands linked, limbs intertwined. These women are tender and affectionate; their interactions are foreign to me.

Before long, a woman lies down in the middle of the floor. Several others surround her, one at her head, one at her feet, and one at her belly. The women move their hands over her body, using gentle and firm touch as their intuition guides. Voices tone, chant, and sing, tuning into the energy, creating subtle shifts. Other women continue to dance, raising energy and sustaining the sacred circle. Gradually, a different woman lies in the center, and others, in turn, dance, chant, and heal.

I feel the urge to lie down in the center but hold myself back. The atmosphere is welcoming, yet I am hesitant. I am new to this circle, to connecting with women in this way. Instead, I dance around the woman on the floor, gradually participating in the healing. Though awkward at first, I begin to feel the energy vibrating in my hands. It is exciting, intoxicating.

I have never seen women in this way: generating energy, exchanging energy, holding energy, expressing themselves so fully, and giving to one another on such a deep level. The power in the circle is palpable. I feel like I am in another world, witnessing and yet also somehow participating. We weave an intricate, yet strong energetic web; it connects us to each other and to something beyond.

After several hours, the energy dissipates. We gather the gifts that we have brought from home and reform a circle. The priestess explains the Native American belief that whoever sits across from you in the circle has a teaching for you. Exchanging gifts with the person directly across from us, we share what we brought, what it once meant, and why it was chosen.

The exchange is a divinatory process, with the gift holding meaning for both giver and receiver. The woman across from me is going through a divorce, and her gift is her wedding bell. Upon seeing it, I blurt out, "What am I supposed to do with this, break it?" These words erupt from the knowledge that her relationship is over. I do not see its significance for me. The other women laugh and say maybe she's "passing the torch," that it's my turn to get married, but that doesn't resonate with me. We finish the exchange and close the circle. I leave confused.

The women in the circle were connected to themselves and to each other in a way I had not yet experienced but yearned for, so I made a commitment to attend the circles regularly. The rituals provided me a forum to work toward healing my relationships with women, and forming bonds with the women in the circle gave me the courage to reach out to women in other realms of my life. Gradually, new friendships blossomed.

Throughout this time of growth and transformation, I pulled back from my connections with men, creating sacred, solitary time for myself, as well as room for my burgeoning relationships with women. Within this space, I came to recognize how I had equated my happiness with a romantic relationship. Remembering the bell, I understood that I did indeed need to break it, not as a symbol of the previous owner's marriage, but as a symbol of my own pattern of depending on men for safety, security, and happiness.

▼

Walking in the candlelit room is familiar; I have been here many times in the past six months. Yet, as I look around more closely, tonight is different. Over the fireplace is a Happy Birthday banner and balloons. One of the women approaches. Handing me a piece of her artwork, she kisses me and whispers, "Happy Birthday." I am stunned. The ritual only coincidentally falls on my birthday; I am not expecting a party.

I cannot contain my smile as we call in the directions, east, south, west, and north. We sit, and the priestess selects a candle from the altar. She passes it around, asking each woman to make a wish for me. My sisters bless me with peace, joy, pleasure, inner knowing, abundance, strength, and an understanding of my power. When the candle reaches me, I hold it for a moment and thank the circle, placing it on the hearth to absorb the energy of the evening.

Several bowls filled with water sit on the altar. Flowers float in the sacred water, collected from lakes, rivers, and oceans, blessed and scented with essential oils. Breaking into groups of three, we ritually purify each other. As I anoint one woman's forehead, face, hands, and feet, I look up at the other women receiving cleansing. It feels ancient, witnessing women nurturing and healing each other in this sacred way.

Closing my eyes, I take a deep breath, preparing myself for my turn to receive. One woman places my hands in the bowl of water as another runs her hands through my hair and over my face. Again I breathe deeply. One pair of hands gently washes and massages my hands while the other pair soothingly glides over my back, arms, and legs. My body tingles in sensual delight as the hands touch me and the water evaporates from my skin. Sinking further into my sensations, I surrender, the cool, scented water dissolving all negativity.

With the purification complete, it's time to dance, and as the music begins, my movement flows easily. We have not danced since my first ritual, and I laugh and sing in excitement. Several songs later, I feel a tap on my shoulder. The priestess urges me to lie down on the floor. Other women encircle me, one at my head, one at my feet, and several at my sides. As their hands touch me, I feel immersed in their energy.

Quickly, however, I find myself resisting. Critical, mistrusting voices begin to whisper: "You should get up. That's enough. These women don't want to do this for you. They're only doing it because they have to." Despite these voices, I refocus my attention on the hands massaging and gently touching my body and remind myself whose hands these are: they are my friends, my sisters, these women sending me profound energy and love. I concentrate on staying open, allowing myself to receive their love, letting it fill me and then overflow, back to them and to me once more.

After much energy has been exchanged, my friend escorts me to the couch. I lay my head in her lap, feeling her soothing fingers run through my hair. I close my eyes, savoring the moment. After a short rest, I return to the floor with the rest of the women to participate in the hands-on work. We continue dancing and healing until well into the morning.

As I reflected on that night, I realized how significantly my relationships with women had shifted, both inside and outside the circle. The affection and closeness between the women, which had felt so foreign during my first ritual, were now natural to me. I was participating fully in the circle, and I had formed several important friendships in my master's program. With this new support network of women, I felt happier and more secure than I had in years.

However, a few months later, during another visit with my spiritual teacher from Sedona, I uncovered a new layer of my mother wound, an extreme sense of abandonment. Later that night, there was a ritual that included the telling of painful stories. . . .

As I sit in the candlelit circle, my heart is heavy; the deep sadness that surfaced during the session with my teacher remains. Still, I listen intently as each woman tells her story. To share in these women's wounding is deeply intimate, and I can feel another level of connection being formed.

When it is my turn to speak, I relay the experience of spending the first month of my life in foster care. As I finish my story, the circle is silent. For a moment, the women just sit there, holding me in my pain. Slowly, they begin to mirror back my story in mantra-like form, repeating my exact words and phrases.

*I just called to ask a couple questions... shocked... like it was normal... like I should have known... I had to hang up... you can vacuum under her crib and she doesn't even wake up... so many lies... they didn't want me enough to keep me... didn't know what to do with me... she wasn't my mom... taken care of by a stranger... alone... afraid... everything I knew... gone... Where is my mom?... WHERE IS MY MOM?!*

As I listen to their voices, tears stream down my face. I can feel myself again as that desperate baby, so lost and confused. To hear my story echoed in the circle touches me deeply, meeting a profound longing to feel held and supported by women. Afterward, a woman escorts me to the couch and wraps me in a blanket. I close my eyes. She places one hand on my forehead and the other around my shoulders. As soon as she touches me, I feel surrounded by intense love; it is as if she is holding me when I was a baby. Her love penetrates me to the core, and for the moment the pain is gone. I feel as if I rest in the arms of the Goddess.

*Turning to the directions*
*A woman speaks...*


*By the Earth that is Her body*
*By the Waters of Her living womb*
*By the Fire of Her bright spirit*
*And the Air that is Her breath*
*The circle is open*
*But unbroken . . .*


*The women all cheer . . .*


*And the Goddess,*
*Blesses Her women!*

▼▼▼

**ABIGAIL SUTKUS** holds a master's degree in women's spirituality from the New College of California in San Francisco. While studying there, she became involved with a women's circle in Lafayette, California, called Daughters of the Goddess, which inspired her chapter in this book. She is currently living, teaching, and circling in Chicago.

# SEEKERS WANTED, APPLY WITHIN

## FINDING A LIVELIHOOD FOR THE MODERN SPIRITUAL LIFE

BY GEORG BUEHLER

**IN COLLEGE, I BECAME PASSIONATELY INVOLVED** in spiritual matters. I devoured books, I visited teachers, I meditated. I chartered a student organization called the Self Knowledge Symposium (SKS) and hung out with other people equally enthralled by the possibility that we could find Answers for ourselves. And then, as we neared graduation, we started to ask the same real-life, profound yet mundane question that dogs every college student: what am I going to do now? Which is really a euphemistic way of asking what your parents are asking: "When are you going to get a *job?*"

The Job is, after all, the central point of American identity. We are profoundly identified with our livelihoods. The answer to "Who are you?" is usually answered with a vocation: I'm a carpenter.

I'm a lawyer. I'm a C++ programmer. Yet, after aspiring to follow in the footsteps of Jesus or Buddha, to go after the Divine with all I've got, it seemed ludicrous to just go out and "get a job" like everyone else. If the spiritual quest is what I really care about, surely there is a way I can be doing it all the time — isn't there? In a typical Generation X fashion, I was ready to do some radical tinkering with the traditional lifestyle, if that's what it took.

## PUTTING CAREER ON THE TABLE

Most people never really factor their livelihoods into their sense of spiritual life. Lots of people ask for work that is "meaningful," "significant," "fulfilling"... but I didn't hear too many people saying, "I wonder how my job will affect my spiritual life?" Career was a given, an unquestioned necessity, something everyone did. Even those people I saw in meditation halls and retreats were, by and large, never really questioning their jobs. The prevailing attitude went something like this: "Well, this meditation stuff is all well and good, and it adds meaning and perspective to my life. But I'm not going to pick up and go to a *monastery* or anything. I still want to have a *life* and all."

There were others who resonated with my desire for full-time spirituality, but for whom it still seemed like too much of a sacrifice: "Yeah, I know what you're talking about, I would love to quit my job and just work on this spiritual stuff... but my wife would *kill* me."

And then there were those who were right there with me, who knew that they wanted to put the spiritual quest at the center of their lives, and yet had no idea how. "What can we do? As far as I know, there are no monasteries for open-minded spiritual seekers of no particular tradition. Looks like we're just going to have to muddle along, find some way to stay alive and make a living, and keep looking for a better situation."

I could relate to all these positions. I myself have not found any monastery to retreat to; I seem fated to live out my spiritual aspirations in a secular context. But to unquestioningly give eight or more of my best hours, every day, to something that is not directly relevant to the spiritual life seems awful. It runs the risk of trivializing the spiritual; it makes God an extracurricular activity, something to do in one's "spare time," something not worthy of full-time attention. Or, as J. D. Salinger's character Zooey Glass sarcastically puts it: "God is my hobby."

So, the question hit me hard upon graduation: how does my job fit into my spiritual search? At best, I imagined a job or career that had a direct bearing on my quest. At the very least, I had to make sure it didn't get in the way.

## EVERYDAY ZEN VERSUS EVERYWAY ZEN

Of course, I can't go too far in this line of thinking without some well-meaning self-appointed sage touching me lightly on the arm and saying with a beatific smile, "But spirituality is not limited to any particular activity! Everything you do can be spiritual if you are alive in the moment. So all this talk of 'right livelihood' is irrelevant. Just *be!*"

This line of reasoning always strikes me as either (a) the highest state of wisdom or (b) complete and utter bullshit, depending on who is saying it and why.

On the one hand, I have no doubt that, from an enlightened perspective, that assertion is absolutely true. If you are Awake, if you have obtained a level of witness consciousness that is constant and unwavering, then you could do pretty much anything in your daily routine and still be spiritual. From the eternal perspective, everything is perfect and nothing need be done.

On the other hand, the exhortation to "just be" is an extremely potent rationalization for never changing a damn thing about your life. I am always suspicious of spiritual prescriptions that don't involve any work. Especially with the newer, less dogmatic spiritual perspectives emerging on the scene, laziness has a way of masquerading as wisdom.

I *do* believe that, for a spiritual person, everything they do can be a spiritual practice. But that is *only* because the spiritual seeker has consciously and deliberately constructed a life for himself that affirms his spiritual direction. The genuine seeker engages himself in practices and habits that benefit his quest: the books, the meditations, the friends, the teachers, the students, and all the other things that keep him on track. Likewise, the seeker gets rid of those things that get in the way of the search: the bad diet, the distracting TV shows, the obsessive attachments. Spirituality is no accident.

There is a difference between everyday Zen — looking for spiritual lessons in the here and now — and what I call every*way* Zen, the conscious commitment to shape every aspect of one's life around a spiritual aspiration. They are by no means mutually exclusive. The whole goal of everyway Zen is to maximize the possibility of here-and-now revelations, the visions of God immanent. But paradoxically, even if God is everywhere, it might be easier to find him in some places than in others. We must at least accept the *possibility* that we will have to radically alter our way of life in order to find God. And it's no help to say, "But I don't know what I'm supposed to do! What are all these spiritual practices I'm supposed to be embracing, anyway?" If you don't know what to do, then the first step of the quest is to find out, and that in itself can be a full-time job.

When my Zen teacher, Richard Rose, was asked about prayer, he replied, "Your *whole life* should be a prayer. And if your whole life *were* a prayer, it would be instantly answered."

So, we're still on the hook. We have to make sure that our livelihoods are conducive to the spiritual path we are undertaking. Maybe that will mean finding ways to inject spirituality into common, ordinary roles, and then again, maybe that will mean throwing everything out and starting fresh.

## OPT OUT

So, faced with the employment issue, the obvious question arises: "How much money do I really need to make?" If I'm hoarding my energy for spiritual purposes, then perhaps the best strategy is to sell as little of my time as possible. This line of reasoning spawned the most stereotypical of Generation X strategies: slackerdom.

I don't hear the slacker label too often nowadays. In the early nineties, when young people faced a tight job market and cynicism was still cool, "slacker" struck just the right tone of willfulness and nonactivity. Today the cynicism is drying up, but the urge to forgo full-scale careers is still alive and well, recast in the more descriptive phrase "voluntary simplicity."

The thinking behind the simplicity movement goes something like this: "Everybody is stressed out and unhappy because they work at jobs they don't like to buy things they don't need. So we're just going to opt out — not buy all the frills of modern Western culture, and just live on the bare necessities. We might lose a certain level of convenience, but we will gain our freedom."

There is a compelling cleanness in this kind of thinking. Think of it as budget cutting with a vengeance. The simplicity movement is no different from any household's struggle to balance the budget. The only difference is that *everything* is on the table. Who needs a house in a suburban neighborhood? Who needs a car? Who needs health insurance? At the crux of this movement is a very obvious (and therefore very overlooked) principle: standard of living (how much you consume) does not have a firm correlation to quality of life (how happy you are).

I bought into it. Or, more accurately, I cashed out. I quit my job as a molecular biologist and moved to West Virginia to live on an isolated farm in the mountains. The land was owned by my Zen teacher, Richard Rose, who had converted his family farm into a rustic retreat center for spiritual seekers. He was more than glad to rent out the tiny log cabins in the woods to people who wanted to live a life of spiritual austerity. It *was* Spartan but beautiful in the summertime and blissfully free of expense. Rent was fifty bucks a month. We heated with wood, cut for free from the hundreds of acres around us. There was no electricity in the cabins, but a vegetarian diet was manageable with dry goods and lots of peanut butter. I figured I could live on less than $1,000 a year. With a "burn rate" so low, worries about income seemed almost trivial; indeed, a little more than a month of minimum wage labor could fulfill my needs for a whole year.

I spent about eight months in my "Walden" phase, reading and writing and meditating and going for long walks in the woods. I had almost nothing at all, and yet I had everything I needed. It was one of the most beautiful periods of my life, precisely because it was so free of desire. Such simplicity made me realize firsthand how little one really needs to be happy.

And, moreover, it blasted away the number one rationalization that always stood in my way, namely that total simplicity was no longer possible in the postmodern world. If I wanted to follow in the footsteps of the Buddha, it was still possible. So many of us are stuck with a Bible school notion of historical revelation, that God was easier to find when we were all herding sheep and living in villages, but now that we have airplanes and science and cell phones, it is impossible to "go into the wilderness." But, as it happens, it is just as possible, and just as difficult, as it ever was. I'm sure most of Jesus' friends and family thought *he* was nuts to hang out in the desert for forty days.

Of course, I knew it couldn't last. Rose had warned me, in his West Virginian drawl: "Don't stay out there too long, or you'll get simple. Monk simple. You'll go to sleep. You need other people to keep you on the move." And I could tell that it was true. I was very happy, but I wasn't enlightened. My meditation was not yielding any insights, and I had a sneaking suspicion that my time alone would only bring diminishing returns. There is no magic in the woods, other than the magic we bring with us.

## THE COST OF SOCIETY

In the woods, I had been so free of needs that I was having a hard time understanding why anybody needed to make much money. Coming back into society, I learned why: to buy the company of others.

Living on the farm was cheap largely because I wasn't doing anything that put me in touch with other human beings. I was living in the middle of nowhere, three miles down a narrow bumpy dirt road, twenty miles away from the nearest grocery store. I wasn't going to movies or classes or cafés. Rough work boots and stained T-shirts were good enough clothes for me, and there was no one around to demand any higher standard of dress. My cabin was dark, dingy, soot stained, and hardly a comfortable place to host a guest — but I didn't have any visitors. Had I lived at this level of poverty in Raleigh, I would have been considered backwards or weird; but there were no neighbors to worry about up in the hills of West Virginia.

In short, I realized that human contact was my most expensive luxury, the only real luxury there is. An apartment near the university, clean clothes, a couch worth sitting on, food worth sharing, an Internet account and the computer to run it — what I considered the basics of my lifestyle were all geared toward maintaining contact with good, well-educated, ordinary people.

In other words (loud rumbling noise as I swallow my spiritual pride) I just wanted to fit in.

*Now* I was starting to understand the real price of simplicity. It is possible to break away from the mean level of consumerism in our society, but it will cost nothing less than society. Living out of synch with others means social isolation. Some of my peers thought it was a good deal: they all opted for an impoverished and somewhat isolated existence, in exchange for free time. I couldn't make that deal. The devil of materialism got me where I least expected it — in my desire to be around others.

## THE JOE JOB

So, if complete retreat from the world wasn't going to do the trick, I looked at the next best thing: working a low-maintenance, undemanding job. We called it "the Joe Job," the show-up-for-work-but-don't-strain-yourself kind of work. This was typical slacker employment: coffee shops, bookstores, carpentry, jobs that used the body but left the mind free for other pursuits.

Of course, being an overachiever in all things, I went for the lowest and Joe-est of Joe Jobs: security guard.

Now, being a night watchman is the closest thing in the world to getting paid to merely breathe. If you have a short haircut and a pulse, you probably qualify for the job. I got a position on the graveyard shift at the Blue Cross Blue Shield building in Chapel Hill, and got paid to sit around in the lobby and read and write to my heart's content. Working at night was a pain, but it let me take writing classes at the university during the day. And it was nice to walk around the building at night, lost in thought as I paced through the vast quietness of darkened empty cubicles. I felt almost like a ghost there. The vast proliferation of Dilbert cartoons, the snarling office humor plastering this human warehouse made me think of all the unhappy people enslaved to their monitors, while I floated through it all, untouched. I was free to listen to the near silence of morning, to hear the birds fluttering in the corporate campus trees, and to see dawn reflected off the glassy ponds and gleaming skyscraper windows.

Unfortunately, this meditative quiet was usually broken by the other security guards. Security, because of its undemanding nature, has a tendency to attract the dregs of humanity. Some were good people, stand-up working-class men and women; but many were not. The bad ones had only one way to pass the time: complain incessantly about everything and everybody. They bitched about the supervisors, bitched about the other guards, bitched about the regular employees who treated them like dirt, bitched about the schedule, bitched about the pay... it was like standing under a waterfall of negativity, an unending cascade of petty nastiness. Sartre was right: hell *is* other people. It was my first reminder of what I now consider to be the most important factor in finding a spiritually friendly workplace: work with good people, the best people you can find. No amount of freedom or money can compensate you for the psychic damage of having to hang around complete assholes.

## FAMILY TIES

Around this time I made the most momentous decision of my life, the most profound and most mundane decision: I got married. I resisted the urge to get married for as long as I could stand it. Not because I thought sex or relationships or marriage were bad, or evil or anything; far from it. But I fully recognized that they come at a high price. I could see a trend in our society: relationship leads to marriage, marriage leads to children, children lead to houses, houses lead to mortgages, mortgages lead to inescapable careers...and careers, children, houses, and spouses all put together eat up every single solitary bit of time and energy, miring us in mundane concerns and suffocating spiritual ambition.

My Zen teacher always advised his students to temporarily pursue a celibate life, not because he thought marriage was avoidable but because he thought it inevitable: "Someday, nature will expect you to fulfill your genetic destiny. Damn few people escape the urge to make more of themselves. Having children will be a wonderful, profound, selfless experience...and you won't get much else done in the meantime. So put it off for a while, if you can...."

So, when I finally did fall in love with a wonderfully spiritual woman, and couldn't resist the nesting urge any longer, my thoughts on livelihood became much more sober. Love is the most potent and binding of obligations. Your love for your children (even your unborn, future children) will drive you to all sorts of achievements you would not undertake for yourself; security becomes more important, and the burdens of "real jobs" more unavoidable. Now integrating work and spirit was not merely one potential option among many, it was the only option if I wanted to keep my spiritual sense alive and well.

## HAVE LAPTOP, WILL TRAVEL

I started looking for another path to freedom, the high road to freedom: entrepreneurship. If I worked for myself, I would have the maximum amount of control over my schedule and workplace. I could do what I wanted, whenever I wanted, so long as I could drum up the business. The only question was: what business?

As if on cue, technology came to my rescue. The rise of the Internet and its surrounding software industry had given birth to a wide class of wandering *ronin* (literally masterless samurai) techno-warriors, intelligent freelancers whose skills in Web design, programming, graphics, or networking were in high demand. Lured by the smell of money and prodded by my own latent geek genes, I became a technical jack-of-all-trades consultant, a smelting of writer/designer/ programmer/whatever-the-hell-you-need-tomorrow — a go-to guy. The only requirement was to communicate well and to learn as quickly as possible. Better yet, it brought the right combination of job security and job *in*security: I never had to worry about finding another job, but that didn't mean I could afford to get soft, either. And the skill set was blessedly applicable to spiritual ventures: I was setting up the selfknowledge.org Web site, starting E-mail list servers for spiritual groups, and desktop publishing the posters and print ads that enlarged my own circle of spiritual-minded friends.

## THE POSTMODERN MONASTERY

The biggest downside to being an independent contractor is, well, being independent. That is, still alone. It was very painful for me, the "ragged individualist," to finally admit that I was most effective when I worked in a structured context with other people. We are gregarious critters, we humans, and we tend to do our individual best in all endeavors when we join with others. The advantages of peer support, peer pressure, opportunities to share information, to teach and be taught are abundantly obvious in nearly all lines of human activity. Athletes have their teams, scholars have their universities, artists have their schools, and ... of course, monks (even modern day mendicants like me) have their monasteries. My work with the Self Knowledge Symposium at North Carolina universities had taught me that working with other people is the single greatest aid on the path, perhaps even more important than having teachers or traditions to follow. With the right group of people, collective effort *finds* the teachers, or even *creates* them from within the ranks.

So, with the obvious benefits of having fellow seekers, it was only natural to wonder: wouldn't it be cool if a bunch of us seeker types could work together in a common business?

I got my wish when I joined Raleigh Group International (RGI), a software publishing company that was founded and staffed mostly by SKS people. With about thirty employees, RGI looks a lot like any other fast-growing software company. The office has an open floor plan, with more computers than people, and Nerf footballs flying past overhead. The salesmen dial and laugh and throw darts and practice their golf putts across the wide carpet floor. The system administrators and developers work late into the night. While the dress is business casual, neither slovenly nor uptight, the atmosphere is 110 percent Business. There is not a single business plan or employee manual that even mentions spirituality.

And yet, the place is pervaded with spirituality, strictly because many (though not all) of the people there are into esoteric matters. The CEO, August Turak, sets the tone; his many years as a full-time Zen student did not prevent him from eventually establishing a stellar executive career with the likes of MTV and Adelphia, and later with his own company. Like the Trappist monks he still studies under at Mepkin Abbey, Augie has a life of *ora et labora,* an even mix of work and prayer. On his desk a well-thumbed copy of *Moby Dick* might sit next to *The Spectrum of Consciousness* or *The Ego and the Dynamic Ground* — which are probably burying the quarterly sales report. A conversation in his office can change from a business meeting to a Zen dialogue in a heartbeat. When his mind inevitably drifts into spiritual topics, his musings can make the physical world seem ethereal and unreal, while making the Divine palpably present.

The values that Augie demonstrates attract seekers and non-seekers alike to the company. The seekers are happy to have a place where they don't have to hide their meditation pillows, where they can get time off to go to a meditation retreat, where they can turn around in their chairs to find a good conversation on Jungian psychology, and where their boss is also a profoundly wise man. And the nonseekers, good people with no particular interest in spirituality, still find the place welcoming, mostly because politics are almost completely absent and there is a strong sense of trust. RGI has the usual small-business strains, the frantic pace, the "competitive stress disorder"; even when we're doing well, it's hardly cushy. But, as the multibillionaire Warren Buffett points out, the only point in having money at all is so you only have to work with people you like.

## THE REALLY-HAVE-IT-ALL GENERATION

Generation X is the *really*-have-it-all generation: we keep attempting to find the right titration of work, family, and spirituality that will somehow add up to a meaningful life. We don't seem to have much more perspective than the previous generation, who also tried to have it all, but with slightly less pretense. Adding spirituality to the mix has not cured us of the mistaken boomer notion that we can plan out our path to happiness. Such attempts to find a perfect life are doomed; once we get everything scripted out, God has a habit of missing his cues. But until life shakes me out of my hubris, I will keep hanging on to the hope that I've found a suitable path. My work is supporting the good of my friends, my family, and my community. My coworkers share in my greatest spiritual aspiration, and remind me and encourage me in that aspiration every day. I find myself forgetting, in the middle of the day, that "work" and "spirituality" were once separate entities — what better livelihood could I ask for?

▼▼▼

**GEORG BUEHLER** balances his time between a software company, his writing, and his spiritual life. He lives in Chapel Hill, North Carolina, with his wife and his son.

# BY RABBI DANIEL KOHN

## THE SEARCH FOR DAVID CAIN

As a fairly typical Midwestern male, I was always attracted to the "macho" side of life; guns and war filled my childhood imagination. Growing up watching the TV show *Kung Fu,* I had admired the central character David Cain's prowess in martial arts combined with his profound commitment to peace and harmony. Although I dabbled in karate and Ninjitsu, I never found a real-life version of David Cain or his martial and spiritual discipline. Nonetheless, I had faith that somewhere there must exist a discipline combining the best of enlightened Eastern philosophy with the discipline and grace of martial arts.

I first heard about aikido in a slender volume entitled *Zen in the Martial Arts,* by Joe Hyams (Bantam Books, 1982). One chapter explained its essential principles as a defensive, nonviolent expression of Japanese religious philosophy. Although it was to be years before I actually found an aikido *dojo* (studio) and saw aikido in action, I was hooked. I now knew that such a martial art, as I had only hoped and dreamed that I would find, did in fact exist in reality.

## THE WORLD OF KABBALAH

*Kabbalah* is a Hebrew word that means tradition (literally that which is received) and refers to the mystical, esoteric theologies and practices of Judaism that have developed over thousands of years of Jewish history. I, however, am not a kabbalist, that is, a Jewish mystic. Yet, I was drawn to enter a six-year course of rabbinical studies that ultimately led to my ordination as a rabbi in the Conservative Movement of America. Though I still sometimes wonder why I chose to become a rabbi, I'm sure it reflected my search for a larger, grander reason and purpose for my life. In the course of my rabbinical studies, that same search led me to kabbalah.

From my humble perspective, kabbalah developed because at various times in Jewish history, the Jewish people felt spiritually cut off and separated from God. Kabbalah was — and still is — an attempt to reconnect individuals with the Divine and reestablish a sense of more intimate communion and communication with God. Its popularity these days may reflect our widespread thirst for more direct and intimate spiritual connection.

On the one hand, God is infinite, omnipotent, omniscient, and unknowable. God is so vast, boundless, ethereal, and immeasurable, that God is completely beyond human comprehension and contact. Yet, on the other hand, the Bible and all subsequent Jewish holy texts maintain that God is also palpable and present in the daily world of humanity. God cares about human beings, God knows our thoughts and desires, and God loves and cares about each one of us. Therefore, it is also possible to come to know God and enter into a close relationship with the Divine. Kabbalah developed in order to accommodate these diametrically opposed aspects of God and merge them into a single, unified system through the theological construct known as the Ten Sefirot.

The word *sefirah* (plural, *sefirot*) is related to the Hebrew word for "to count" (and also to, perhaps, "sapphire" and "sphere"); the Ten Sefirot refer to ten different vessels of God's essential nature. The *sefirot* are basically facets of God's "personality." We all have many "faces" that we display to the world, some of them quite different from the others. This applies to the *sefirot* of kabbalah, in that each of the Ten Sefirot represents one distinct quality of God. The Ten Sefirot are links in an interconnected chain that connects the infinite, unknowable qualities of God with the knowable, experiential aspects of God.

## FINDING AIKIDO

Perhaps it was fate that, during the last years of my rabbinical studies in New York City, my roommate turned out to be a long-time student of aikido. He took me with him to practice one evening. From the outside, I would have never suspected the *dojo* was a major, national center of aikido. On a fairly dilapidated street in lower Manhattan, the *dojo* looked more like a garage than anything else. The door was beat up and the whole facade gave the impression of neglect. Inside was a small sitting area with a bench and desk. The rest of the room consisted of a long, canvas-covered mat. The walls were white, the ceiling was white, the mat was white; it was the kind of white that, if I looked at it long enough, my eyes would swim and I would lose my sense of depth and perspective. It was a mind-numbing, but also mind-emptying, kind of whiteness.

People slowly came on the mat, each student dressed in a white *gi* (traditional martial arts uniform) and white belt. An elite few wore long, flowing, black trouserlike skirts called *hakama*. In this style of aikido, only black belts and higher wore these dramatic and elegant skirts. People slowly warmed up and then began sitting down on their knees in rows facing the front. At the front of the studio was a shrine. Recessed into the far wall was a picture of a very elderly Japanese man with a long white beard. I later learned that this was O Sensei (literally great teacher), the honorific title of Morihei Ueshiba, the founder of aikido. Everyone sat very quietly in a kneeling position for a few moments, and then the senior Japanese instructor came on the mat. He strode confidently in front of the ranks of people sitting respectfully before him. He kneeled down directly in front of the picture of O Sensei, and everyone bowed together. Then the instructor turned and bowed to the class as they bowed toward him.

After a short series of stretching exercises, the teacher demonstrated a technique with a volunteer, and then everyone began practicing that movement. This continued throughout the entire class, with the movements growing ever more vigorous, complicated, and energetic. Toward the end of the class, the instructor demonstrated powerful throws, sending his demonstration partner flying many feet through the air, only to end up rolling out of the throw at the last minute.

What struck me during this time was the silence of the class. Despite the necessary thumps, thuds, and occasional grunts of the students, no one seemed to talk. Or if they did, it was in a whisper. Even the instructor didn't talk much. Occasional comments in his heavily Japanese accented English were lost to my ears. People were expected to learn through visual absorption and direct physical movement. There was no overintellectualizing of a movement; rather, simple physical practice was the dominant mode of learning. And despite the vigor, the power, and speed of the movements, no one seemed to be getting hurt. Everyone rolled out from throws gracefully. People slapped the mat to signal the threshold of their ability to withstand a pin or a stretch, but everyone seemed to be enjoying themselves.

It was magic. Thus began my introduction to the world of aikido. I began at the bottom, at the lowest level of the educational ladder, but filled with excitement.

## THE KABBALAH OF AIKIDO

As I have continued to practice aikido and pursue my religious studies as a rabbi, I have discovered an amazing number of similarities and parallels between kabbalah and aikido. First, they each seek to perfect and improve the world. In some schools of kabbalah, the world is understood as being "broken" and in need of fixing. Indeed, who can look at the world and declare that everything is perfect about it? Millions of people in the world go hungry every day for lack of food and have no place to sleep at night except on the streets. Ethnic groups and nations still war with each other and harbor hatreds based on superficial differences. Is this the way God intended for the world to be?

In one school of kabbalah, God originally planned to create a universe filled with God's presence. Justice would prevail throughout, as would peace and harmony. However, in the process of imbuing the universe with God's presence, the spiritual structure intended to convey God's presence throughout the universe broke down. As God began to create the *sefirot* and fill them with the divine illumination, something happened. The *sefirot* proved unable to contain the intensity and brilliance of the primordial light and shattered in an event called Shevirat ha-Kelim, the "shattering of the vessels." In the midst of this cosmic catastrophe, the divine light became fused with the material, physical aspect of the shards of the *sefirot,* and all of these pieces fell into God's creation below, the world of humanity and everyday reality. Our physical world was created from the remnants and shards of these shattered vessels, and thus the world we live in is not perfect, despite God's plans and intentions to create a perfect world. This cosmic catastrophe led to the creation of the world as we see it now. Homelessness, hunger, hatred, violence, and war are the results of a broken world. The goal of kabbalah is to begin repairing and healing this world.

This goal of perfecting and healing the world is also at the very heart of aikido. The founder of aikido, O Sensei, often said that aikido is the way of harmony for the world. In one lecture, O Sensei stated that the goal of aikido is to "bring humanity back into balance with all things" and that we must all be "part of the infinite growth toward perfection. To bring about the end of malice and suffering is the vital mission entrusted to us."[1] In fact, O Sensei even

---

1 Mitsugi Saotome, *Aikido and the Harmony of Nature* (Boston: Shambhala, 1993), p. 31.

stated among his five principles of aikido that "aikido is the path of strength and compassion that leads to the infinite perfection and ever-increasing glory of God."[2] This is the core of aikido. It is not esoteric knowledge reserved only for advanced students and masters. Everyone who practices aikido, from the beginner to the highest black belt, is engaged in improving the world on some level.

Even the name of this new martial art that O Sensei created contains its message about repairing and healing the world, for aikido can be translated as the "way of harmonious energy." This peaceful goal of aikido was recognized and acknowledged early on in its development. In the immediate aftermath of World War II, when the U.S. Occupation forces prohibited the Japanese people from learning martial arts, aikido was the very first art permitted to be practiced again. O Sensei's fame grew and his disciples traveled to other countries to spread aikido's message of peace through martial arts training. Aikido has become an international movement to bring about harmony, peace, and universal love.

Another significant parallel between kabbalah and aikido is that both understand that healing the world must involve a system of small, concrete steps to train people to be more loving, ethical, and peaceful in their own lives. Judaism is a religion that emphasizes the importance of concrete acts of charity and loving-kindness as a means to improve the world. According to kabbalah, singular acts of charity, prayer, meditation, and moral behavior can have a profound effect upon the spiritual fabric of the universe. Even the most seemingly insignificant ritual and ethical acts can help to heal the cosmos and reconnect God's infinite essence to the mundane, material world of our reality. Individual actions have a power and influence that far exceed their limited scope within the realm of the personal and individual.

So, too, in aikido, the goal of promoting and working to establish universal peace and harmony is predicated on not merely training in the techniques of the martial art but in applying them to daily life on an individual scale. Of course, the first step in

---

2 Ibid., 17.

working to establish peace and harmony via aikido is to train in the martial art itself. This is because the very techniques themselves and the philosophy that suffuses their every movement is based on diffusing conflict and violence.

A famous story is told about O Sensei during a time in his life when he taught an early form of aikido to Japanese naval officers. One officer who had heard of O Sensei's great martial prowess was sure that he could defeat O Sensei and demanded a sword match with him using wooden practice swords. O Sensei did not even bother to take up his own weapon; instead, every time the officer would strike at him, O Sensei moved out of the way with lightning speed so that he seemed to disappear, avoiding every blow. The officer, growing infuriated with this tactic, attacked all the harder and with greater speed and fury. However, O Sensei deftly stepped aside, avoiding every single strike, until the officer had expended all of his energy. Thoroughly winded and exhausted, the officer laid down his sword and humbly requested that O Sensei accept him as a student.

The principle of avoiding an attack can also be applied to the realm of social interactions. When confronting angry family members, friends, or coworkers, we need not be drawn into the spiral of hostility. Sometimes, simply controlling our reactions, smiling, nodding our heads, and humbly agreeing with the criticism is all it takes to diffuse someone's anger. "You're right, I'm sorry" are perhaps the last words that someone would expect us to say in a confrontation; however, they can often be the most effective in resolving differences and neutralizing the vehemence in tense social confrontations. Avoiding an attack, whether physical or verbal, is a small but important first step in trying to bring about more peaceful, harmonious relations between people in the world.

Kabbalah and aikido are cross-pollinating each other in my life. My personal, spiritual practices have been powerfully enhanced by my aikido training. And my practice of aikido has been influenced by my religious background. O Sensei once said, "Aikido is truth and truth knows no religious or cultural boundaries."[3] The longer

---

3   Ibid., 19.

that I practice aikido and study Jewish mysticism, the more parallels and interconnections I discover. Over time, I have noticed that the convergence and synergy of my aikido training and Jewish observance have improved the quality of my life overall. I have found a discipline that has enabled me these past ten years to improve both my emotional and spiritual health together.

## LEARNING TO JUST BE

Randori (freestyle) is an advanced form of aikido practice that is the closest to real conflict that is ever practiced in the *dojo*. In Randori, a defender is attacked by multiple assailants, attacking however they choose and as fast as they choose. This is the hardest and most demanding training situation in aikido. I would love to claim that I am comfortable with and skilled in facing these kinds of multiple attacks; but the truth is that I am not. Freestyle attack is the single most difficult training experience for me to this day and represents my greatest, ongoing challenge in aikido.

Freestyle training sessions are difficult not because of the many physical obstacles involved but, rather, due to the mental and psychological challenges. The key to learning to successfully confront multiple attackers is to sink into a state of deep calm so that one's thoughts flow freely and easily. One should not even have to consciously decide which technique to execute, for it should just happen naturally. In such a state, a defender is able to perceive the movements and the dynamic energy of the attackers and simply avoid and then redirect strikes. While in this state of flow, a defender is always attuned and prepared for the next attack.

It is not easy to achieve this state of mind because it is far more natural for people (myself included) to temporarily freeze up in panic and feel the muscles stiffen due to the sudden, massive introduction of adrenaline into the bloodstream. Rather than relaxing and opening up our spirits, we tend to stiffen and develop tunnel vision, focusing on only the most immediate threat to our safety. In a situation of multiple attackers, such a reaction actually tends to reduce our ability to deal with the situation effectively. Even the most graceful of aikidoists, when beginning to learn Randori, suddenly lose their elegance and look like Frankenstein ineptly wrestling with a pack of nimble wolves. This is why Randori requires years of practice, so that our minds, bodies, and spirits are functioning at their peak capacity when they are truly needed. Such practice helps develop confidence and a sense of calmness in the face of multiple attackers.

On occasion I have been able to perform outstandingly well in these situations of multiple attackers. When this happens, it feels like being the calm eye at the center of a storm. Nevertheless, as much as I had trained for the Randori part of my black belt examination — a simultaneous attack by four attackers — I never felt comfortable with my level of proficiency. My training sessions never seemed to achieve a state of flow, and I felt as if I was rushing the timing and exerting too much energy. I knew how it should feel, but I just couldn't make it happen, at least not on a consistent basis.

When the time came for my freestyle demonstration during my black belt test, I kneeled at the far end of the mat trying to slow my breathing. I didn't even look at my attackers arrayed on the other side. I was vaguely aware of my fear and exhaustion, but at that moment they seemed far away. I knew I couldn't wait forever, though, so I bowed, giving my attackers the signal for the attack. They came rushing in, far faster than I could have imagined, and almost without thinking, I dropped to my knees directly in front of my first attacker and this destabilized him enough to completely throw off his balance and nullify his attack. When I rose to my feet again, I knew my attackers were moving very fast and rushing in toward me, but somehow my perception of how much time I had was greater than in past sessions. I had the time to take a step or two, the leisure to feint a strike, and the opportunity to lead an attacker into a fall.

It felt magical to be so present in that moment. At one point, two attackers seized me at the same time and began to hold on to me. In training sessions when this happened, I would begin to panic and start exerting muscle power and energy to fight my way free. At that moment, however, I knew this strategy would fail because my attackers were far stronger than me and were working together. I felt clearly that I would never dislodge them with my strength alone. So I didn't even try to fight them; I gave up — and whirled in a circle to the outside. I could have said, "Abracadabra," and the effect wouldn't have been any less amazing; they flew off me as though we were magnets and our polarities had suddenly been reversed. Seconds later, it was all over. My teacher clapped, signaling the end of my test, and suddenly everyone in the room was clapping as well. It was quite a moment. It has also been a moment that I have rarely been able to duplicate.

Aikido is all about *ki* training. *Ki* is the Japanese word used to describe the unique energy that all people are capable of projecting and directing. *Ki* is the energy of our bodies, the heat we exude, the smells that surround us, and the palpable yet invisible essence of who we are and how we are feeling. Randori is designed to force people away from relying solely on the physical input of their five senses and to rely on their ability to perceive and direct other people's *ki*. During a freestyle attack, the five senses are secondary to a defender's ability to spiritually expand their circle of perception and work within this powerful, almost scintillating energy field.

Normally, I am unable to do this and it is truly frustrating. But even more frustrating is knowing that my frustration itself constitutes a barrier to my success. For a crucial component of being able to turn one's self into a giant, organic *ki* field is the capacity to be calm, confident, and humble. It strikes me as deep truth that the moment I give up trying to conquer Randori will be the moment I will be able to master it. I know this intellectually but have so far been unable to let go sufficiently to experience it regularly.

## SENSING A LARGER WORLD

When I first began training in aikido, everyone talked about *ki*. It was the power that is supposed to flow through all aikido techniques. People of higher ranks used to chide me when I worked with them, saying, "Use your *ki*!" But no matter how hard I tried, I ended up using my muscles. I was convinced that this mystical, elusive *ki* was beyond my grasp, a power too rarefied and hidden for me to be able to comprehend, much less utilize. It was only when I began to despair and stop trying so hard that I began to catch glimpses of this mysterious, powerful energy. First in other people's techniques and then, slowly, even in my own. When I began to relax and let my mind go blank, I gradually began to experience a sense of connectedness that I had never noticed before. I felt joined not only to my training partners but also to myself and the world around me. Every time that I am able to experience this, I feel as if I am participating in something holy and profound.

In the kabbalistic creation story, immediately after Shevirat ha-Kelim, God began to repair the damage and rebuild the *sefirot*, linking God's presence to the world. According to one school of kabbalah, God has restored nearly 99 percent of the structure of the *sefirot*; however, God intentionally left that 1 percent unfinished so that human beings might become partners with God and help to complete the work of God's creation.

The task of human beings is to search out and find these shards of fused broken vessel and divine light (called *klippot,* shards) and engage in spiritual and religious acts that will help release the divine sparks of light trapped inside these pieces of broken vessels. The sparks will then return to their divine source, further strengthening the connection between the world of humanity with God's unknowable and infinite essence. This process of uplifting the sparks is called Tikkun Olam, restoring and repairing the world.

The behavior that releases these divine sparks is acts of loving-kindness, charity, and love. To these I would add the practice of aikido, and the ability to create a bond of *ki* and love between people. For in that creation, I believe we release the divine sparks and repair the shattered *sefirot.* When performed with proper concentration and devotion, all of these actions can help to release the divine sparks and bring the brilliance of God ever closer to our mundane world. Both kabbalah and aikido have already helped to bring more divine light into my own life.

▼▼▼

**DANIEL KOHN** is a rabbi and spiritual leader at Congregation Kol Shofar in Tiburon, California. He has practiced the Japanese defensive martial art of aikido for over ten years and currently holds the rank of Nidan (second degree black belt). Daniel is the author of *Practical Pedagogy for the Jewish Classroom: Classroom Management, Instruction, and Curriculum Development* (Greenwood Publishing Group, 1999) as well as *Sex, Drugs, and Violence in the Jewish Tradition* (Jason Aronson Publishers, 2002). Daniel also volunteers for the Ask a Rabbi service on America Online (www.jewish.com). His contribution is partially excerpted from a manuscript in progress entitled *Kinesthetic Kabbalah*.

# THE HEART OF THE MATTER

BY HALEY MITCHELL

**THE LIGHTS ARE DIM** and the staccato beat of the music begins to penetrate me to my core. Electricity is coursing through my veins, and I am on fire with desire for God. My separate will dissolves and a new energy dances through me with wild abandon. I am a fiery rocket streaking across the room at lightning speed. A feeling of exuberant freedom overtakes my body and sets my skin on fire. My deeply lustful woman within steps forth, gyrating and moaning on the floor in fits of orgasmic rapture. I roll and I rock, groping for other intoxicated beings with whom to share the ecstatic flood. My soul merges with the meditative music. Dancing and frolicking across the room, I toss off layer after layer of clothing. And when I finally collapse, I feel myself held in God's sweet embrace.

▼

That first experience of deep connection to God came while I was in college. After immersing myself in fraternity culture during my freshman year — playing beer pong to gain the attention of pubescent boys clad in Greek letters — I began asking myself if there wasn't something *more*. I wanted to taste a God-infused brew that wasn't on tap at the bar. A childhood friend who shared my disillusioned feelings and my longing for divine connection suggested a nine-day intensive with a spiritual group called the Miracle of Love. Desperate for the nectar that I smelled on his breath, I signed up for the course.

I had no idea what was in store. The nine days were a systematic dismantling of my ego, where I was forced time and again to face the deepest pains and the darkest parts of my psyche. I visualized the face of my childhood playmate who lost her life in an innocent game of hide-and-seek. I despaired that her life had ended so prematurely, and my stomach ached in feeling her loss. I relived the trauma around my parents' divorce, brought on when my father's supposed friend seduced my mother into an affair. I allowed myself to fully face the nagging dread from those years that my mother would commit suicide to end her suffering, as her mother had done.

To my surprise, the deeper within I dove, the more relief and freedom I found. As I surrendered into the center of my heartache and felt its most searing core, my numbed feelings began to revitalize. Since grade school, I had heard my father's mantra that "you've got to be tough!" In my youth, I believed he was right. In the face of my mother's breakdown, I had turned off the faucet of my emotions in order to be a strong support for her, so much so that I didn't cry for seven years. During the intensive, though, I finally allowed myself to fall apart and cry the tears that had never been shed in my youth. And in embracing my deepest pain, I rediscovered my humanness.

In the open space that emerged by the end of the intensive,

participants shared in ritual release. This final day, described at the start of this article, we celebrated our emerging Selves. For the first time, I actually *allowed* all the facets of my being to integrate in one scintillating whole. So long repressed, my divinity demanded to finally stand in the limelight.

The ecstatic experiences continued after I left the intensive and returned to school. For many months, I would awake in the middle of the night, afraid of an energy that seemed determined to enter my body. The sensations were the same each time: while asleep, I'd be bathed in a bright light with a Christlike essence. This foreign presence seemed to want to merge with my soul. Each time I would wake in a panic, demanding this energy leave me alone; I was afraid that I would either die or become possessed if I allowed it to enter. However, I did notice that it had a positive, benevolent vibration. I trained myself to remain calm and eventually invited the energy in. When I did so, I felt a short-lived but radiant bliss. The nighttime visits then suddenly ceased. At first perplexed, I began to realize that the energy no longer needed to penetrate from outside; it lived within me, and I began the slow process of integrating it into my being.

I continued my exploration with the Miracle of Love for several years, deepening my newfound connection with the Divine. But I was eventually beckoned by the Brazilian Amazon. I had studied ecological anthropology in college, and I was determined to do something about the constant destruction of rain forest. So when the opportunity arose to research economic alternatives to logging, I packed my bags and headed south.

In the field, I shared a mud hut with the chief of the Tembé tribe and eighteen of her closest relatives. Challenges of daily life included sinking canoes, malaria-stricken children, lumber poachers, and egg-laying insects burrowing into my feet. Mere survival was a battle, but the Tembé managed to survive the inevitable setbacks by sharing resources. Living in this completely foreign world, disconnected from my own tribe, I nonetheless had an experience of deep community. I came to value, and now actively seek, a Tembé-style community where people's lives are intimately interconnected.

▼

Bringa rests in a tattered hammock, its colored threads frayed and faded from years of use. He is from the Tembé village of Canindé, which also serves as a government outpost in these tribal lands. Three scrawny brown chickens cluck below him, scavenging for lost morsels on the hut's dusty floor. In the corner two naked children play with their newest toy, a stained piece of string fastened to a tin can, which they drag behind them while mimicking the loud rumble of a diesel engine. Bringa is known among the villages for his skilled navigation of the tribe's clumsy boat through the perilous rapids downstream. Whenever called upon, he willingly brings goods and people in and out of the village, earning him the respect of the community.

I sit while he quietly whittles a wooden stick with his mammoth machete and rocks himself back and forth. He explains that he is bedridden with a swollen foot that is infected for no apparent cause. Unable to join the other men to hunt, build canoes, or tend the fields, he cannot provide for his family.

The focus shifts when Brasilisei, who lives across the village, comes to visit carrying her newborn grandson on one hip. In her strong arms she carries a half dozen freshly gutted fish. She silently passes the heap of fish to Bringa's wife and arranges herself in a nearby hammock. Little is made of the gift, just a silent exchange between friends. A trail of visitors follows, each encouraging Bringa in his healing process and bringing foodstuffs — fresh eggs, cashew fruit, papaya, corn — to ensure his family's survival while he is sick. With each gift Bringa nods in appreciation, but this display of communal generosity is nothing out of the ordinary.

A week later, Bringa shows no improvement. His foot remains swollen and the herbal remedies do not seem to be working. I offer some antibiotic cream, but he is uninterested. As night falls, I worry that his condition will deteriorate. I awake in the middle of the night, surrounded by the thin gauze of my mosquito net and the black solitude of the Amazon sky. Distant rhythmic drumming reverberates through my bones, sending shivering waves up and down my spine. The faint drone of tribal chanting summons me from my hammock. Through the dark, I stumble toward the sound, which appears to be coming from Bringa's hut.

Once there, I perch outside the open doorway, trying to discern the shapes within. The shrill vibrations of the chanting raise my hair on end. Male and female voices echo through the hut, inviting in the tribal spirits. Still half-asleep, I shift into a trance-like state, allowing the energy to wash over me like waves in a swollen sea. The darkness of the hut is punctuated only with the glowing red tip of ritual cigars. The village shaman, known as the *pajé*, once told me that a few puffs of this pure, organic tobacco allows the smokers to journey into a nonordinary realm, communing with the ancestors and bringing their healing energy to the patient.

As my eyes adjust, I watch the participants evoke protective totem animals and embody the movements and the sounds of each. One tribal elder hops with a quick, froglike motion. A full-figured woman flaps her arms with the grace and elegance of a regal bird, while yet another slithers snakelike across the hut.

Sensing I am privy to a very sacred ceremony, I crouch outside, careful not to move a muscle or make a single noise. My supposed invisibility is belied when a woman turns in my direction and remarks that I look quite uncomfortable squatting in the shadows. She inquires why I remain outside where I cannot fully participate in the ritual. The *pajé*, master of ceremonies, turns to speak to me. I tremble. The darkness, he complains, makes it difficult to see his patient — would I supply a flashlight to illuminate the ritual? I laugh full-bellied as I walk back to my hut.

▼

The Tembé's seamless integration of the sacred and the profane stood in stark contrast to the separation of worlds in my own culture. For them, the spiritual realm is not a faraway domain entered only by priests clad in holy robes. Instead, the gods are woven into the tapestry of daily life. When I would stand aside during their shamanic practices, assuming a foreigner would not be welcome in their sacred rites, I was always encouraged to participate. The Tembé shared their homes, knowledge, and friendship; I was even invited to partake in their pious communion, considered no different from sharing a common meal of rice and monkey meat.

Just as the Tembé interweave the spiritual and material realms, their community members are also interdependent. When people "fail" or need help, neighbors lend their support to set them back on their feet. If one man's hunt bears no meat, he can count on his neighbors to feed him. When a family needs to build a new house, the entire village pitches in to collect the materials and build the foundation. I remember one village meeting where I scratched a mark in the sand for every mention of *communidade*. In a two-hour period, I made twenty-six marks.

My year with the Tembé awakened my hunger for a deeper level of connection to the people around me, a desire I had long suppressed as a part of my strongly individualistic North American culture. Since most of us North Americans do not depend on each other for survival, we have created a culture fixated on independence. But each wall that we construct to separate ourselves from each other also serves to keep us from God. We learn to repress our natural desire for interdependence, though our souls yearn to be part of a strong community. Relating intimately with others allows us to touch and feel our essential commonality with other beings. Fundamentally, we are all one in God. Community is thus central to spiritual life.

Several months after returning from the Amazon, I embarked on an adventure of a very different kind: Corporate America. My days of manual labor and survival skills were replaced with luxurious dinners, first-class flights, and rigorous analytical training. And although my life was glamorous on the surface, underneath I longed for the team spirit that I saw among the Tembé. Instead of feeling connected with my peers, I felt isolated and alone. More than ever before, I needed to rely on God to pull me through. Eventually, though, it all unraveled, which in itself turned out to be an act of grace.

▼

My throat tightens and my face begins to flush. I cannot avert a looming sense of doom. My eyes begin to water. "Don't cry. Whatever you do, don't cry." I clench my jaw, attempting to suppress the mounting anxiety.

Outside the glass walls, other consultants at the firm linger as they pass, like drivers rubbernecking at a roadside accident. The members of my review committee sit in silence while I fidget, alone, in a chair on the opposite side of the room. I smile half-heartedly, hoping for an encouraging nod in return. Instead, their faces remain blank, causing my stomach to tighten into a clenched knot. None of my "team" meets my eyes for more than a second. Finally, the leader speaks:

> As you know, Haley, our firm must maintain rigorous standards. Our clients expect platinum performance, day in, day out. People at the firm really appreciate your enthusiasm. You're a real team player. But, we regret to inform you that you are not meeting our expectations as a consultant. Honestly, we don't feel that consulting is really the best "fit" for you.

The rest of his words fade into a babbling stream of syllables as I stare at the faces of my colleagues. Unresponsive. They analyze my performance with the same rational reasoning that they've been trained to use on all business problems. My composure crumbles, and tears begin pelting down on my freshly pressed suit, leaving wet ringlets. Nausea overtakes me as my achievement-oriented ego shrinks smaller and smaller in my chair. I tune back in to the leader's commentary for a moment.

"We systematically evaluated your last client case, and your performance was not satisfactory."

Outside the glass wall, familiar figures linger longer than usual. My cheeks are undoubtedly crimson, my mascara smeared. I slump, no longer caring about proper posture. I imagine the gossip is already circulating: "Her review is not going well. Not well at all." At least I won't have to deal with the further humiliation of announcing the verdict.

They hand me my review summary, a detailed document with scores attached to each aspect of my personality. as I thumb through the pages, I am surprised by the results. The reviews are sprinkled with comments about being a great team player, my willingness to stay past midnight to help my colleagues, my respect for others, and my commitment to learning.

I turn back to the review board. "My performance was good in four of six areas. Why are you saying that I am not meeting expectations?"

"We have those six areas for review, but the only ones that are really important are the two in which your performance was substandard: problem solving and practicality/effectiveness."

I am devastated. I have worked harder at this job than I have ever worked in my life, trying to teach myself the business skills that I didn't learn as an anthropology major in college. However, my interview polish proved inadequate in the trenches of the daily grind. I feel worthless. Not good enough. Not smart enough. Not "effective" enough. Just plain "not enough," and it hurts. How can I face the world? How can I face my father? I feel utterly and completely alone.

▼

At the time, it didn't register that the core qualities I was developing in my spiritual practice were undervalued by "the system." The community values I brought back from Brazil proved peripheral. The loving-kindness I was cultivating through *metta* practice was "appreciated" but not central. In my meditations, I dissolved my barriers with other beings, learning to treat everyone equally. Again, this trait was not critical to a successful consulting career. Instead of recognizing the mismatch of values, I wallowed in the shame of failure and assuaged my dismissal with a steady diet of chocolate.

After a few months, I began to realize that the termination was perhaps a great gift. After all, I had been miserable making presentations on the future of semiconductors or linking cells in Excel spreadsheets at two in the morning. The real work I valued involved more than the hard numbers of business. It was evoked by the spirit of the Tembé, and perhaps even more so by the spiritual practices I had been exploring since my teens.

I now realize that the intensive, the Amazon, and the corporation were more than just separate adventures. Each symbolizes a central aspect of my being. I thrive on the intelligence, speed, and innovation of the business world. I crave the nurturance, support, and deep connection a strong community provides. And my spiritual practice sets me free by putting me in touch with God. When I stand exclusively in any one camp and ignore the others, my deepest Self is not satisfied. Business without heart is mere prostration at the individualist shrine. Heart without business is just fluff. Either without community is lonely. My soul hungers to bring *all* its aspects forward and to bathe in the creative energy that emerges from the union. This combination of forces greatly accelerates the process of spiritual awakening.

But how to combine them? I tried to merge business and community by settling down in Silicon Valley, but I found a place where the social fabric was unraveling as fast as the stock market was climbing. Heart was mocked as touchy-feely. And when I returned to my spiritual seeker hangouts, I found that my heart was satiated but my intellect stagnated. I also wasn't ready to abandon the business world altogether. If any place needed heart, it was Corporate America, the great engine pumping the lifeblood of our country. To bring a greater sense of compassion and community into our society, I would, I reasoned, have to begin with the people — the CEOs and politicians — making decisions that affect everyone else's lives.

A door to integration began to open. I was invited to run a start-up venture philanthropy group called the Full Circle Fund, founded in the fall of 2000 right as the Nasdaq took its first major plunge. It was not an especially good time to begin a nonprofit, especially one involving young Silicon Valley business leaders. But, assuming that the heart's impulse to heal suffering is more steady than stock valuations, we moved forward. We began examining community problems, talking to experts, and applying money, skills, and networks to tackle key social issues.

Yet one central ingredient was still missing from our approach. In drawing together this group of aggressive business executives, I initially assumed that matters of the heart were taboo. But as we moved forward, it became apparent that spiritual work was actually central to our mission. Humanitarian efforts require us to bring all aspects of our being to the table. We certainly need entrepreneurial ideas and business-minded savvy, but we also need loving presence, an abundance of compassion, and deep tolerance to heal profound societal wounds.

To really solve our communities' problems, we must be open enough to our natural caring to unleash its power to create change. But this openness can bring with it immense pain. In my case, when I was exposed to images of war, famine, and death during the Miracle of Love intensive, I initially numbed myself; it was too much to bear. But as the meditations continued, my heart cracked open, finding at first only a bottomless pit of despair: holocaust corpses, stacked like logs; children, faces gaunt with hunger, being eaten alive by flies; elderly patients, abandoned in the virtual coffin of convalescent homes to face death alone. Surrendering and feeling that ocean of pain was brutal. Yet, doing so allowed me to tap a new wellspring of desire to help others. While numb and dead inside, I could ignore the calamities around me. Once open, I began to let my natural compassion shine.

To invoke that same compassion in Silicon Valley professionals, I am developing a Philanthropic Leadership program at Full Circle Fund. At its root, philanthropy means "lover of humanity." This program is designed to open young business leaders to their innate loving hearts and explore methods that elicit their fullest potential as human beings. Putting job titles and income figures aside, members will reach into each other's souls. We'll share our dreams, disappointments, and visions for a vital society. We'll join in the evolution of spirit to reinvent ourselves and the world around us. Together we will explore ways to clear barriers to creativity, find the care in our hearts, remove limiting beliefs, and live out our true callings. When we marry deep internal change with deep external change, our work will create much greater impact than it could if it depended on either type alone. As a result, we will be more present and heartfelt in our hands-on work with local nonprofits. In addition, we will have the tools necessary to transform the companies we run.

It remains to be seen whether the Philanthropic Leadership program will take hold in this dot-com crowd. It may integrate the realms of business, spirituality, and community, which have been relatively separate in my life. On the other hand, it may not take root. Whatever happens, I will treat it as a perfect gift, another rung on the ladder of my journey. The failures of one moment often become fertilizer for the next big success, which in turn may lead to another failure. Life stretches us beyond the familiar until we stand on the precipice of the unknown. At that point, threads of seemingly irreconcilable experiences may suddenly weave themselves into a comprehensible whole. When we embrace whatever comes as a gift, our true heart begins to blossom, leaving us more open and more capable of living each moment compassionately and joyfully. We begin to see, in retrospect, the uncanny perfection of life's unfolding.

As I continue to weave together the various threads of my life, I see how my time at the firm gave me the skills I now need to run a burgeoning nonprofit. Because I was once "one of them," our corporate members honor my opinion and accept my guidance. The Tembé showed me a society where communal values are central. Their emphasis on and respect for teamwork showed me how to create community and value it in my new endeavors. Finally, my Miracle of Love memories continue to remind me of the sweet nectar of the Sacred. As I touch the core of my being through meditation, I find myself opening deeper and deeper layers of my heart.

When I compartmentalized my tribal, spiritual, and corporate worlds, I found myself feeling incomplete in each. But as I interweave these threads, I become more empowered, stronger, and confident that I am living in alignment with Divine Will. As I learn to simultaneously open body, mind, and heart and embrace them as part of a coherent and balanced whole, I can better play my part as cocreator of Heaven on Earth.

▼▼▼

**HALEY MITCHELL** directs the Full Circle Fund, a philanthropic venture group based in San Francisco. As a Fulbright scholar, she spent several years exploring economic alternatives for indigenous groups in the Brazilian Amazon. Haley earned both her B.A. in anthropology and her M.A. in international development policy at Stanford University.

# FEBRUARY VIOLETS

BY RACHEL MEDLOCK

**I AM DRIVING NORTH** on Interstate 85 toward Washington, D.C., to see a Van Gogh exhibit with Kristin, who is sleeping in the passenger's seat beside me. It is already December 20, but the sun shining through the car windows is so warm that I've turned on the fan. We've just crossed the state line into Virginia, and it's about time to fill the tank. I wait for an exit with a cheap gas station and turn off. The slowing momentum of the car wakes Kristin, who sits up and blinks in the bright sun. She tells me she's getting hungry, so we look around the main strip to find a suitable place to eat. Nothing but fast food. We resolve to wait for a better place, but as I'm leaving the gas station, Kristin spots a small sign for Bagels, Inc., peeking out from behind a much larger Wal-Mart sign. I pull into the lot, and we head inside.

The place is new and immaculately clean, filled with home-made signs and the smell of fresh coffee. A woman in her mid-fifties leaning against the counter smiles at us as we come in and asks — in a rich New Jersey accent — what we'll have. Something about her demeanor (is it in her eyes? her friendly voice?) immediately sets me at ease, and I'm glad we decided not to delay lunch for the next town. We both order a bagel and a cup of coffee and go outside to sit on the curb in the sun.

"Isn't this odd?" I comment to Kristin as we sit down. "Southern, Podunk, small town Virginia, and we're eating at a bagel shop owned by a Jerseyite."

Kristin smiles from around the edges of her Styrofoam coffee cup. "Yup . . . and that lady . . . there's something about her. . . . "

"You noticed it too? Something in her eyes — I can't explain it. She just. . . . "

"She knows," Kristin finishes.

"Yeah. Exactly. There's a wisdom about her."

We sit on the curb for more than an hour, sipping our coffee, talking about road trips, spirituality, bagel shops, and Carl Jung. Kristin tells me about the other waiters and waitresses she works with at the diner, about the way they are all on a journey of their own, untangling their own riddles, solving their own koans.

"You know," Kristin says, "everybody's searching, each in his own way. Everybody's dealing with the same stuff; they always have been, too. Year after year, era after era. Always."

I raise my face to the sun. People come and go from the shop with bags of bagels and white Styrofoam cups. Gaggles of teenagers in pickup trucks and cowboy boots. Long-haired young women with babies on their hips. Old men wearing ringlets of gray hair and wide smiles.

Everybody. Always.

The day is waning, and we need to reach D.C. before rush hour. We go inside to throw away our cups. On our way out the door, the woman behind the counter waves and calls, "Thanks!"

"Thank you!" I reply reflexively, without turning around. "See you later."

Kristin and I stand outside the National Art Gallery in Washington, D.C. Neither of us is wearing a heavy coat. Her fingers turn numb white for the privilege of holding another cigarette, while I shove my hands in my pockets and stamp my feet on the sidewalk trying to keep the slow blood circulating. In the nearly four hours that we wait in line to see the Van Gogh exhibit, our noses turn bright red and our ears lose feeling as they try to protect our temples from the winter wind.

But we don't spend time complaining of the cold. Lost somewhere in the middle of a line of four hundred plus museum goers, we are laughing, joking, telling each other stories as we inch closer to the entrance and to the promise of the warm blast of air that will greet us at the door. The four hours pass as quickly as they can outside in the middle of December without a winter coat, and Kristin and I are finally admitted into the exhibit.

It's packed with people pressing up against each other, not speaking, not making eye contact, but subtly elbowing and shoving their way closer to the paintings while still trying to pay attention to their audio tours. Kristin and I worm our way among them toward the paintings, spending almost as much effort fighting the crowd as studying Van Gogh's work.

Getting through the exhibit takes only a quarter of the time we spent waiting in line. In an hour, I have reached the last painting, which hangs between the two exits and has a quote from a letter Van Gogh wrote to his brother, Theo, a short time before his suicide: "They are vast fields of wheat under troubled skies, and I did not need to go out of my way to try to express the sadness and extreme loneliness." I don't remember the painting's name. I remember its crows, its golden yellow wheat fields, its deep blue hues reminiscent of a spring sky before a thunderstorm. I stand in front of this last painting for at least a full five minutes while other patrons divide and file out of the exhibit on either side of me, spending no more time on this last, capstone piece than they spent on any of the others. I am witnessing a man's last attempt at expressing the inner recesses of his Soul; they are witnessing the culmination of some sort of "cultural experience." I wonder how it is that they remain so seemingly unmoved.

Kristin comes up from behind and stands next to me. For several minutes we stand silently in the sea of moving people. Finally she turns to look at me. Smiles. She understands that there is no need to go out of her way to try to express the Meaning expressed by the painting.

"Let's go," she says. I nod, and we leave the exhibit.

It is 3:00 A.M. on January 4 at Mepkin Abbey, a Catholic monastery in South Carolina. I am walking from my cottage to the morning services at the chapel in the dark. Yesterday morning I brought my flashlight, but this morning there is no need because the moon is so bright. It casts a milky, silver glow to the grounds: surreal and alien, yet beautiful all the same. The morning is bitterly, hungrily cold. I try to pull up the hood of my sweatshirt and hunch my shoulders against the wind that is sprawling into the gravel road between the pine trees, but I can't do it: I keep looking up, craning my neck to get a glimpse of that clear, white moon. My hood falls off and my ears freeze to the side of my head, but I still can't take my eyes away from that moon. I think of all the travelers of ancient days, of how many night journeys they spent walking just as I am now, guided only by the moon, a rough road, and an overwhelming desire to know, to understand the Mystery of wheat fields under troubled skies, of perfect moons, of chapels at 3:00 A.M.

Once inside the chapel, I do my best to keep up with the monks as we sing the morning's Psalms. As the only female in the choir, I have no one to measure my voice against, and I stumble along from verse to verse. To my great relief, we finally sit down for a few minutes of silent prayer. I close my eyes and try to observe the raucous internal dialogue jabbering in my head, when I am suddenly struck by a memory of something Father Christian had said: "The totality of God is beyond our ken." *Ken,* such an archaic word that so perfectly encapsulates the impossibility of ever truly understanding the Mystery of frigid January mornings like this one. I stop my mental fidgeting for a moment and say a silent prayer:

*Lord, I am but a flit of a butterfly wing,*
*One half-stroke in a world of monsoons,*
*One brief spurt of breath — and my time will be gone,*
*Lost amongst a sea of nameless faces,*
*And other fragile, frantic wings.*
*I will disappear as the single drop in the ocean does,*
*Or one star in the heavens.*
*And, Lord, though I understand none of it,*
*I rejoice, and would have it no other way.*

A sunny, beautiful day for February, I think to myself as I look out at the quad from the third floor window. I am in Duke's Counseling and Psychological Services office, filling out the paperwork for my first visit. Among the papers is a questionnaire asking me to self-evaluate myself in different categories. Do you have trouble concentrating? I mark always. Are you easily irritated by friends and associates? I mark frequently. Have you experienced a loss of appetite and/or changes in sleep patterns? Somewhat. Do you have thoughts of death? Occasionally. I turn the paperwork back in and pretend to look at an out-of-date magazine while I wait my turn. A tall, skinny lady in her mid-thirties calls me back to her office. I take a seat on the couch across from her desk.

"So . . ." (she glances at the paperwork) "Rachel. What brings you here?" For an hour I try to explain my inability to focus, my loss of interest in school, my need to be anywhere but here at Duke, but I want to explain the people at the Van Gogh exhibit who didn't see a thing. I want to tell her what it feels like to be a seeker surrounded by people who aren't seeking for anything, other than a comfortable future. I want to tell her how, for the past three years of my life, I have watched my peers clinging blindly to the assumptions they were raised with, unwilling to find their own Path, unwilling to open their eyes to a universe that does not revolve around our little selves. I wanted to tell her how badly it hurts to sit through class after class filled with talented young people clamoring toward their futures. These peers of mine — ambitious, headstrong, and scared to death — hurtle toward their destinies. Law school. Business school. Medical school. They are destinies of wealth, prestige, and power; just as often, they are destinies of divorces and broken families, nervous breakdowns and alcoholism, midlife crises and the loss of Meaning.

But I can't explain any of this to the counselor before me, or my need to escape it before it becomes my destiny as well. Instead, I mumble on about not being able to concentrate, work, sleep. She nods and "mmm-hmms" encouragingly whenever I get stuck. She diagnoses me as depressed and recommends that I look into counseling and antidepressant drugs. I nod numbly, make an appointment for the next week, and stumble out into the February afternoon sun.

Tuesday afternoon. I'm walking through the parking lot behind my dorm with Laurie; I already skipped my morning class, and I'm trying to decide if I want to skip the next two as well. The weather is warm again today — even for North Carolina it has been an extremely mild winter — and I am loath to spend my afternoon inside a windowless classroom, listening to a professor drone on about nothing I particularly care about. I catch a glimpse of my car out of the corner of my eye. I halt.

"Laurie."

Laurie stops, too, looks at me quizzically. "What?"

"Where can I drive to on I-85?"

"I don't know. South Carolina?"

"I don't want to go south."

"You could take 70 East and drive to the beach."

"Too far. Have to make it back by seven — I have a Pub Board meeting."

Laurie's brow knits in thought. "Virginia...?" she says tentatively.

"Virginia." I check my watch. "How far is Virginia?"

She shrugs. "Two and a half, three hours."

"Virginia...."

"Rachel? Why do you want to drive to Virginia?"

This time I shrug. "Why does anyone ever want to go anywhere?"

I change my direction and walk to my car instead of my dorm. Laurie is still standing in the same spot, looking confused. I wave to her as I pull out of the parking lot.

It is a perfect driving day. It is slightly cloudy, so the glare isn't bad, but it's so warm out that I can't resist the urge to roll down all the windows and turn up the volume on the radio. After an hour and a half, I begin to see the green and white marker signs announcing the approach of Virginia: 55 miles. 42. 31. 11. 6. Why did I want to drive to Virginia? I ask myself. What about classes, homework, grades? Aren't I one of the "good" students? The kind who doesn't randomly skip classes to drive to other states? Why this restlessness? This wanderlust? This need to seek something out? And what makes me think I'll find it in Virginia?

I turn the radio up. I start singing along. I look into the windows of other cars. I wonder if any of them are playing hooky to drive to Virginia, too. Then I get a vision of hundreds and hundreds of people — school teachers, college students, electricians, accountants, maids — all getting into their cars, pulling onto the interstate, heading north without really knowing why, watching the signs roll past one after another, thinking, "I'm driving to Virginia, I'm driving to Virginia — why am I driving to Virginia?"

I smile. We are the Pied Piper's new children. I nod to a fat mustachioed man who happens to make eye contact with me. I want to yell out the window, "It's okay! It's good to drive to Virginia on warm winter days!" But he looks away quickly, and I remember that he probably isn't driving aimlessly the way I am, but has a destination, a purpose, people waiting for him on the other end. I'm the only one driving just to drive.

I cross the state line. I have time to drive a little further before I turn around, but I've hit a stretch of road construction and traffic is slowing down. I pull off at the next exit, but I still don't feel like immediately turning around.

I take a left at the light and drive past the interstate exit. Ah, small town, Podunk, southern Virginia; it reminds me of my own home in small town Georgia. All small southern towns make me nostalgic for home.

But this one more so than others.

The main strip feels familiar. I see a cheap gas station to my left. A Wal-Mart sign behind it. And peeking out from behind the Wal-Mart sign, almost invisible from where I am, I see a small banner reading Bagels, Inc.

Could it really be...?

I hit the brakes and quickly switch lanes. Within a few moments, I am pulling into the same place Kristin and I had stopped at some months before. The bell jingles as I walk inside. Everything looks exactly as it had before. The counters are spotless, the floor is well swept, the same two flavors of coffee — hazelnut and vanilla — are sitting in self-serve canisters to the left of the register. And behind the register, leaning slightly against the counter, is the same woman. She's smiling warmly as if she'd been waiting for me all day long.

"Hi there," she says in that heavy New Jersey accent. "What'll it be?"

I order a bagel and coffee, and head outside to sit on the curb. What fairy tale have I wandered into? I think. I sip on my coffee and watch the locals come in and out. Gaggles of teenagers in pickup trucks and cowboy boots. Young women with babies on their hips. Old men wearing ringlets of gray hair and wide smiles.

Everybody. Always.

I sit, my back against the post, another nameless face in this sea of people. Another raindrop in the ocean. It is all beyond my ken.

Lord: I understand none of it; will I ever?

I go back inside to fill up my white Styrofoam cup with more coffee before I go. The woman is still behind the counter, sweeping up her bagel crumbs.

"They say it's going to reach 70 degrees today," she says.

"Is that so?" I want desperately to have a conversation about anything but the weather with this woman. I want to tell her about the way I'd been here once before, and talked to her before, and that her bagel shop seemed to rise up out of nothing, just for me. But. . . .

"Yep. It's that El Niño, I'm tellin' ya."

"Yeah, well, I ain't complainin', y'know?"

She laughs heartily. "I know, I know."

I know you know, I think, but I just smile and nod with her. I put a lid on my coffee and head for the door. "Thanks." I add silently, You've made an incomprehensible day a little easier to understand. "You have a good day."

"You too. See ya later!"

"Okay!" I call as the door jingles close.

March, supposedly the beginning of spring, draws closer. But our warm spell has worn off and Old Man Winter is back to his old ways. I am walking to work, my sweatshirt hood up, my hands in my pockets, my head down. I am lost in a cloud of thought today, wishing again that I didn't have to be at school, wondering what I'm going to tell the lady at Counseling and Psychological Services when I go in at the end of the week for my follow-up visit.

Some flash of color on the ground catches my attention. Between the gray, flagstone sidewalk and the gray, Gothic stone wall, there is a patch of violets. Violets. In the cold of February. Against the drab background, they seem like the most vibrantly purple flowers I have ever seen in my life. Violets in February: a promise of renewal. A promise that the cycle of life will continue for another year.

It is an unending process of going out and coming back, of small deaths and resurrections. It is horrible, and wonderful. And, Lord, though I understand none of it, I rejoice, and would have it no other way.

▼▼▼

**RACHEL MEDLOCK** graduated from Duke University in May 2000 with a degree in English. While pursuing her writing and the spiritual path of the "tortured agnostic," she pays the bills with her multimedia graphic design company, Athena Graphic Solutions (www.athenagraphics.com) and lives in New Haven, Connecticut. At the time her article was written, Rachel was a junior at Duke and a member of the Self Knowledge Symposium.

## COMING OF AGE IN A TIME OF DARKNESS

### BY RONAN HALLOWELL

## AT THE CUSP OF DESTRUCTION

The Earth and her peoples are in the midst of an epochal transformation, made inevitable by patriarchal and technological exploitation now causing widespread social and ecological devastation. High school mass shootings. War. Greed. Denuded rain forests. It is easy to feel apocalyptic when faced with the ills of contemporary society, its vacuous consumerism, and the machinations of transnational corporations. Capitalism has penetrated the entire globe, depleting the planet of its natural resources and turning them into an endless array of products and polluting by-products. Although the triumph of technology has some positive attributes, its tendency to control and dominate nature has created an unhealthy rift between masculine and feminine.

This rift, coupled with the "death of God" and the death of meaning, has created an unprecedented spiritual crisis in humanity. Western tradition emphasizes an extreme individuation where we seek autonomy from the unity of the primordial matrix. The resulting isolated ego has either left us "alone and afraid in a world we never made," or made us paranoid egomaniacs hell-bent on self-gratification and control.

As I have attempted to understand the root causes of our contemporary malady, I have explored various spiritual traditions that might assist in healing ourselves, our communities, and our world. When I began to study shamanic traditions, I noticed the deep parallels between my own existential crisis and what the world is facing. We are, in many ways, experiencing a shamanic initiation writ large.

In shamanic traditions initiation occurs through ordeal. The neophyte is faced with an immense crisis through a descent to the underworld, where he faces dismemberment and death. The most horrible hells and demons are encountered and overcome through surrender and communion with elemental forces. The shaman's confrontation with dark forces is often resolved through a sacred marriage of masculine and feminine energies.

We may thus be collectively challenged to rebalance masculine and feminine energies so that we may successfully emerge from our initiation and foster a new era of healing where we overcome some of our more destructive tendencies and allow our prodigious gifts to blossom. As we stumble along this path of initiation, ancient rituals such as the Native American Sun Dance provide guidance and inspiration. It is no accident that they are being revitalized and new cultural spaces such as rave culture are drawing on elements of these ancient, authentic rituals to provide individuals the opportunity for self-transformation. Our planet has no other choice.

During the past ten years, I have experienced many initiations through Sun Dances, raves, and psychedelics. For me, finding balance between masculine and feminine energies has included reclaiming my divine child. The divine child is a beautiful blend of masculine and feminine innocently playing with the world in awe and wonder. This reclaiming of the divine child needs to be coupled with the development of the sacred adult because we cannot remain children forever. The initiation process forces us to "grow up." However, if our initiation is successful, we can be grown up while retaining our divine child in our hearts. It is just this task that humanity is faced with, although the shamanic journey can only be taken one individual at a time.

## THE NIGHT'S DARK INITIATION

*In the night's dark initiation*
*All of duality's veils*
*Suddenly came crashing down*
*Seared by the acid burn*
*Of hatred's apocalypse*
*Plunged in a sea of chaos*
*Gasping for a breath of air*
*I stared back at death's lonely stare*
*To see yet another shadow of my true self*

When I arrived in San Francisco I was twenty-two years old, living in Lower Haight, trying to find work, hanging out with street kids at Buena Vista Park, and embarking on a three-year exploration deep into the mysteries of high doses of a variety of psychedelics. Alongside the psychedelic experimentation, I began to study the world's wisdom traditions and the history of consciousness at the California Institute of Integral Studies in San Francisco. Although many trips included ecstatic states of breathtaking beauty, other experiences felt like I was dying or dissolving into madness. These experiences of the dark side of existence resembled the Bardo hells of the Buddhist tradition. At one rave, I accidentally ingested a massive dose of LSD that completely overwhelmed my senses. I ended up in an alley on Halloween night vomiting uncontrollably. I seemed to hear every rape, murder, car crash, police siren, and other cry of urban suffering that night. The pain of the world seared me in a strange and excruciating way that, in spite of its fierceness or perhaps because of it, taught me about compassion. While retching in the alley I felt as if I were being assaulted, my body pulverized and my mind tortured. I was totally bereft, like one of the dirty, dejected homeless kids I knew on Haight Street. In the midst of this misery, a beautiful African-American woman walked past me and said, "God bless your soul." The mercy of her voice and eyes deeply comforted me and showed me that compassion does ease suffering. Though I still had an ordeal to face, her caring prayer gave me strength. After a number of these frightening episodes, I sought a way to channel my drive to explore shamanic states of consciousness into something more grounded.

Synchronistically, at the time that I was curtailing my psychedelic experiences, I discovered the Lakota Sun Dance tradition. The Sun Dance is a ceremony that originated among a number of tribes from the Great Plains. People who pledge to dance don't eat or drink water for four days, and many dancers endure painful piercings. At my first Sun Dance in the state of Washington, I did not know what to expect. I knew no one at camp and was fifteen hours from home. I felt somewhat intimidated but also intrigued. Despite my feelings of self-consciousness, a number of people welcomed me, and I began to feel more comfortable.

After setting up my tent and eating, I changed into my shorts and prepared to enter the sweat lodge with about twenty other people. It was a beautiful night with the moon shining bright, the coyotes howling in the distance, and the fire flickering and crackling as it heated the rocks for the evening's purification. This lodge was led by an elder from the Pima Nation, a seasoned veteran of Sun Dancing. After we all squeezed into the small domed hut, nine red-hot rocks were placed in a pit in the center and sprinkled with cedar, which produced a pleasant aroma and a solemn atmosphere. Once all of the rocks had been brought in, the door was closed and we entered total darkness. The elder began to pour water on the rocks, making them sizzle and produce clouds of hot steam.

As the temperature increased, the elder began to speak. He addressed us as his grandchildren. His voice filled with a tender compassion for each one of us. Even though he did not know us each personally, he knew that we were all vulnerable humans filled with both great joys and deep sorrows. He knew that we had come to the Sun Dance to find a lost and forgotten part of ourselves, a part crushed by the coldness of the world. The nine rocks in the center of the lodge, he informed us, represent the nine months we spent in our mother's womb, a time each of us have in common. He told us that the sweat lodge is a vehicle for returning to the womb of Mother Earth and that through the purification of the steam and prayers, we can remember our own childlike innocence.

As the elder continued to speak, his voice cracked with tears that bore witness to the intense suffering of his own life. Outside the lodge this elder had looked like a fierce warrior who spoke very few words, but in the humid darkness of the lodge he was a tender grandfather praying for each of us to have the strength and courage to take responsibility for our own healing. As the purification continued, it became hotter and hotter, and I crouched lower into the fetal position. We sang songs together and prayed from our hearts. Some of the people in the lodge were of Native American descent, and they spoke of the terrible suffering of their people. It is one thing to understand historically that Native American peoples were virtually exterminated by Europeans, but witnessing the human toll of such abuse brought up great sadness. Feeling the anguish of the other people was overwhelming. In the midst of this, many people were wailing, and I began to cry. I cried such a deep cry that night, my armor stripped away to leave only a vulnerable child. Being in that womblike state allowed me to touch a place inside myself that I rarely expose. Through letting myself become vulnerable, I began to reclaim the divine child inside me while also accepting my role as an adult.

For me, accepting my role as a sacred adult means participating in life and helping others. During the rest of the Sun Dance, I learned how to be a fire tender for the sweat lodges, which entailed building and stoking the fire, carrying rocks, and helping with whatever else needed to be done. Fire tending put me in intimate contact with the ceremony by being close to the arbor (the tree-lined ceremonial circle) and by helping Sun Dancers who were sick from heat and exhaustion. It was extremely intense watching the dancers sacrifice themselves so dramatically, and it was powerful helping them through their suffering. The Sun Dance is an interactive experience, not simply a ceremony to watch. It emphasizes the spiritual participation of everyone present. Helping out as a fire tender allowed me to contribute to the ceremony in addition to receiving the many lessons the dance had to offer.

I was so moved by the first ceremony I attended that I decided to write my master's thesis on the Sun Dance and intercultural dialogue. What followed was a two-year whirlwind of intense fieldwork and study where I attended seven Sun Dances over three summers while participating in a Lakota circle led by an elder medicine helper and undertaking my own vision quest with the guidance of two Native American Sun Dance leaders. One of the primary values of Native American cultures is respect for the young and old and the consideration of how one's behavior will affect future generations. In our world today youth are in crisis, struggling to find meaning in a labyrinth of chaos. Most of us were wounded in some way during our childhood and youth. By healing our own past, we can help young people today find their way and contribute to a better future for generations to come.

## THE VOICE OF YOUTH: HOPE FOR A WOUNDED WORLD

To embrace the earthy and ebullient spirituality that can help us evolve out of this dark time, I think we must reclaim our youthful passion. We must listen to the voice of youth, not only so we can clearly see the horrible situation we face but also to be encouraged by the vigor and hope that youth inspires. This hope comes through most clearly in the image of the divine child. The divine child is the epitome of awe. She is enraptured with the present, dependent and naive in a world that demands love and protection. But for many children today this innocence is shattered earlier and earlier due to the breakdown of society, the crisis of values, and an antispiritual climate that turns a deaf ear to the cries of the oppressed. Our children's divinity is poisoned by violence, fragmentation, and evil.

Despite this, we all still possess a remembrance of our own childlike innocence, and it is that capacity for awe and wonder that we need to rekindle in our world today. For although we face an end to one cycle in the Earth's story, we are called to be the forerunners of a life renewed and to help launch a new era of possibility.

In *Return of the Mother,* scholar and mystic Andrew Harvey speaks to the importance of the divine child when he says,

> This state of consciously reclaimed childhood, in which all the passion, pure sensuality, and lyricism of the lost or hidden child is consciously reintegrated into a purified and organized adult awareness is the end of yoga and the attainment of the kingdom of heaven itself. To be a child in this glorious sense is to be in heaven here, to be one with the Tao, to possess the Grail, to be in union with the Mother.

The divine child grows into the seeking youth, the ambiguous adolescent who faces the difficulty of channeling chaotic energy into a coherent adult identity. The youth stands at the midpoint between the divine child and the corrupted or sacred adult. The corrupted adult has lost touch with her inner divinity through socialization into a sick society, whereas the sacred adult has been initiated into the mysteries of self-knowledge and compassion.

The voice of youth is raw but it is real. Youth internalize and express the neuroses of the prevailing adult world, yet at the same time the divine child of youth cries out to be remembered and cherished. So we must listen to youth, must hear its shocking pronouncement that nothing's shocking, that our culture has forsaken basic human values and repackaged them as fragmented chimeras. The breakdown of the family and social fabric has created a lost generation wandering in a labyrinth of confusion and hype.

Although the voice of youth can be a primal scream, spewing out the perversity of our dysfunctions, it can also serve as a prophetic song of the divine child, restoring in us the solace of belonging, the yearning for love, and the possibility of manifesting our most lofty and beautiful visions of divine life. For youth are struggling between the optimism of childhood and the reality of adulthood. Our society would do well to provide youth with new models of adulthood that allow them to realize their sacred self. To enact these new models of adulthood, I believe we must each recapture our own divine child and be willing to accept our roles as sacred adults, adults who seek solidarity with kindred spirits and who hope to make a more compassionate and loving world.

## RHYTHM OF WHOLENESS: PEACE THROUGH MUSIC

Music is prophecy...the herald of the future.

— Jacques Attal

Throughout my coming-of-age process I have found that it is not enough to criticize the problems in the world; we must share positive visions that can enliven us with the courage to cocreate a new world. We need to tap the joy of life to overcome the incapacitating effects of despair. During my journey, music and dance have been the two activities that have kept me sane and have given me hope.

While a college DJ in Boston, I was introduced to the rave culture. At my first rave in 1992, I had an incredible mystical experience while trance dancing. I was in New York for the New Music Seminar, a major music industry event that showcases new talent. This was the first year that featured techno-rave/dance music as a main event. The event took place in an old cathedral at a New York club called the Limelight.

The DJs for the evening were Derrick May, Juan Atkins, and Kevin Saunderson, three of the originators of techno-house music. The music they played built upon an intense pounding beat stimulating a primal response that was excited by my intake of a psychedelic cocktail. With my inhibitions loosened, my body became supercharged and my mind lucid. When I closed my eyes, vast fractal oceans receded into supernovas of light. This powerful array of effects paralleled an opening of my heart. Through a process of surrender and praise, embodied in my wild ecstatic dance, I experienced the wisdom of wholeness. This joy and insight, such as I had never experienced, arose from my connection to the primordial beat. My heart burst open in awe at the wonder of the world. I danced in a circle with people of all colors, and I felt a true kinship with others for the first time. This gift of rejoicing and praise lit a fire of hope inside me. I felt deep down that, if as individuals and as a human civilization, we can access our true divine gifts, we can make the world a better place.

Shortly after this rave I had the privilege of hearing the master Nigerian drummer Babatunde Olatunji perform. He and his troupe of drummers and dancers communicated deep spiritual wisdom through celebration and sound. Babatunde spoke wisely between songs on the healing power of music. He told us to "feel the love in the music and use that love to help heal this world." His performance struck a primal chord in me and demonstrated the power of music and dance in conveying wisdom and joy. After these initial experiences, I became more involved with raves through DJ-ing and producing underground events with a positive vision. Though much of rave culture has succumbed to consumerism and addiction, its best aspects can be incorporated into new hybrids that can help foster a culture of celebration.

Music and dance are for me the best metaphors for the true nature of existence: we enter into the rhythm of wholeness through them. They express the most creative aspects of the human endeavor. Music can serve as a mind-numbing commodity or it can contribute to the raising of consciousness. Those of us who have been called to explore our spiritual nature, both young and old, can use music and dance to actualize our most beautiful potentials.

Although I have found great insight through my own ecstatic dancing at raves, my Sun Dance experiences, where people dance in suffering and sacrifice for renewal, taught me that the ecstasy of the dance is not just one of hedonistic pleasure but also one of sacrifice and giving. In our culture of greed and individualism, we are not encouraged to think of the well-being of others. If we are to contribute to a sustainable world, we must live, not for ourselves alone, but for others as well, especially for the young and for those yet to come.

My psychedelic, Sun Dance, and rave experiences have opened

me to the numinous dimensions of life and have shown me that my access to these dimensions depends upon my intimate participation. I must be fully present to understand the wisdom available through spiritual practice. This presence also requires the cultivation of ethical discernment and the ability to see myself in relation to all that is. If we can begin to understand ourselves in the larger scheme of things, we can begin to find balance in the midst of upheaval and chaos.

Our world today is a battlefield of legacies, egos, and despair, but the spiritual life holds the promise of renewal. I believe we must stop living in denial and stand up against the injustices and abuses that threaten our world by first turning inward to know ourselves deeply, so that we may in turn know others and find a space to live with each other in peace. If we can remember the awe and wonder of the divine child in each of us, while still accepting our roles as sacred adults, we can manifest the resources needed to mend our broken hoop. As the writer James Baldwin said so eloquently,

> An old world is dying, and a new one, kicking in the belly of its mother, time, announces that it is ready to be born. This birth will not be easy, and many of us are doomed to discover that we are exceedingly clumsy midwives. No matter, so long as we accept that our responsibility is to the newborn: the acceptance of responsibility contains the key to the necessarily evolving skill.

If we accept this responsibility, not as a burdensome obligation but as a divine challenge, we can harvest the fruits of celebration and contribute to a life-loving renaissance.

▼▼▼

**RONAN HALLOWELL** is a DJ, writer, and student of the world's wisdom traditions. He holds an M.A. in philosophy and religion and has taught at Naropa University and the Whidbey Institute and now resides on the island of Kauai. He can be reached at kualapa@yahoo.com.

# MEDITATING IN SENSURROUND

## BY ERIK DAVIS

**IT WOULD BE NICE TO BEGIN THE JOURNEY** with
who we are. But who we are is a house of mirrors, a tangled knot,
a great and terrible Oz that, in the final analysis, may consist of
nothing more than, well, nothing. The self, I am afraid, may be
more of an onion than a fruit, and who we are is the skin we shed.

So instead we start, as the Yankee Tibetan Pema Chödrön suggests, from *where* we are, which is another way of saying where we've
been. It is no accident that the freshest spiritual writing these days is
largely autobiographical and confessional. When it comes to spirituality, that amorphous and easily misheard inner call, we have come
to trust experience, however mundane and confused, more than
belief systems or philosophical reflection. Practice, along with the
mutations in subjectivity that practice brings, is our primary tool.
But this tool warps the hand that holds it, and that warp is our story.

For my generation, the turn toward practice and personal experience in matters of the spirit is part of our heritage, not just as Americans, who have always fetishized know-how and the explorer within, but as kids who surf the spiritual wake of the baby boomers. In their desire to crack open the nut of spirit and eat the meat within, the sixties generation raided the world storehouse of mystical techniques. They *experimented* with spirit, along with drugs, sex, food, and unconventional social structures, and their protocols and inconclusive results still dominate the spiritual scene. We came of age as they gradually turned away from the heady dreams of Enlightenment, chemically induced or otherwise, and moved toward everyday responsibility, sobriety, and the practices that support a mindful but ordinary life. Our own turn toward autobiography reflects this legacy as well, but it also expresses, I hope, a tiny bit of spiritual wisdom often lost in the absurdities and revolutionary excesses of the counterculture: that we are not just children of the moment, but of history, and especially of the biological and social forces that shape and constrain our bodies, our perceptions, and the still infinite potential that lies shrouded within the hooded self.

But again, we start with where we are, or rather where we have been, which in this particular case means a tent in the mountains of Southern California. The portable alarm clock chirped to life at 3:30 A.M., finding me in an all-too-familiar state: disoriented and in the dark. Tugging on loose black pants and yanking a long-sleeve pullover over an Aphex Twin T-shirt, I staggered out of my tent into a night filled with stars and satellites. It took a moment before I recalled my exact coordinates: east of Los Angeles, in the San Bernardino Mountains, on the grounds of the Zen Mountain Monastery. It was deep summer, in the middle of 1995, and I had just driven down from San Francisco for *sesshin,* a weeklong silent retreat consisting largely of interminable hours of *zazen.* Barely half an hour after rising, with a blast of coffee in my gut, I was at it again: sitting with my legs scissored in the half-lotus position, eyes hazily gazing at a blank wall, my mind gradually settling into the breath that filled and fled my belly like the air in a bellows.

A week later I would hurtle down the mountain into the heart of Los Angeles to attend SIGGRAPH, a huge industry convention devoted to the latest advances in computer graphics: video games, animation, Web technologies, virtual reality. But I wasn't thinking about any of that at the mountain center; in fact, I was trying not to think about much at all. The monastery's strict regimen gave me a rare opportunity to tune out the details, distractions, and seductive chimeras of our yammering information age, the glut of signals and noise that I, like so many folks today, navigate for bread and butter — and sometimes, it must be admitted, for a sense of self as well.

For people habituated to media, its abrupt and total absence can be both refreshing and alarming. Cult deprogrammers (notice the technological metaphor) warn that authoritarian religious groups severely restrict or eliminate access to information from the outside world in order to inculcate their worldview in new recruits. While a number of sects have certainly abused such tactics, the deeper implication of these warnings is that today's barrage of media is healthy and normal, and that the stream of images, ads, and information that saturate our world is not *already* infested with vivid and manipulative seductions, with cargo cults of consumerism, greed, and celebrity worship.

In any case, I felt a brief media fast would do no harm. In fact, I hoped it would allow me to do some deprogramming of my own. Our ordinary stream of consciousness flows from deeply ingrained habits: cultural, biological, karmic. Practice partly consists of creating the space for these tics and knots to gently deconstruct themselves, until the whole constricted sense of "I" begins to loosen like an old sweater.

But sitting there hour after hour, watching my body settle into a relaxed immobility and my brain trance out on its own babble, all I encountered was a tumultuous buzz of restless chatter, what sages have dubbed the monkey mind, but which I rapidly came to think of as TV mind. I was amazed how much media clogged the pipes: Led Zeppelin songs, *The Simpsons* episodes, Wallace Stevens poems I read in college, the most recent reports from the latest distant war. Though I occasionally channel surfed into moments of pregnant stillness, I spent far more time realizing what anyone who feels lonely or anxious and instinctively flips on the television knows: media is much easier to process than a moment of unvarnished experience.

A number of channels were showing *The Erik Davis Story,* though most of the episodes appeared to be reruns. I weathered collegiate video porn and scratchy 8 mm films of embarrassing childhood flubs, high-production fantasies of future triumphs and tests of the Emergency Anxiety System. But as the tatters of autobiography flapped by, they also begged for an answer to the inevitable question: well, how did I get here?

As a kid growing up in Del Mar, the suburban Southern California beach town name-dropped by the Beach Boys in "Surfin' U.S.A.," I was exposed to about as much traditional spirituality as you can string on a pine tree. I was a child of *Gilligan's Island, Bugs Bunny, The Hobbit,* and the sandy arroyos and red-rock cliffs of my hometown, wild places where my friends and I created fantastic playgrounds of elves and superheroes on the way home from school.

When I hit teendom in 1980, my fondness for such reveries bloomed into a fondness for drugs, especially LSD, pot, and psilocybin mushrooms. My friends and I stoked the dying embers of the California counterculture. We read Carlos Castaneda and *Be Here Now,* traveled to Dead shows, took psychedelics seriously, and meditated at the local Siddha yogi joint. I was a huge reader, and became particularly fascinated by religion and the occult. Like the Lovecraftian dungeon novels and science fiction classics I also devoured, the metaphysics section of the mall bookstores offered up coherent but astoundingly imaginative worlds that somehow mirrored, mocked, and resolved the tensions of the rather disappointing one I greeted every day. Because I was basically raised a heathen (I learned the Gospel from a scratchy copy of *Jesus Christ Superstar*), I had no sour taste of dogma in my mouth; I found atheism boring and accepted the appealing if somewhat fuzzy notion that all paths led to God. I met Hare Krishnas, yoga freaks, witches, I Ching Taoists, and mystical Catholic teens wielding Ouija boards; I bonded with heavy-metal Satanists and born-again Christian surfers.

I had many dreams, trips, and experiences that bordered on the fantastic and occult, but it's pretty easy to write them off today as a morass of bubbling hormones, naiveté, and a drug-induced eruption of what psychologists call the primary processes of the psyche. In any case, the inevitable loss of that adolescent magic was hastened by the Ivy League college professors who initiated me into the deeply skeptical traditions of critical theory, deconstruction, and other post-everything razzamatazz. I was taught that neither science nor common sense nor Enlightenment categories of knowledge were fixed in stone; I grew to believe that all claims about reality took their place in an ambiguous and shifting network of language games, historical constructions, and political power grabs.

Though it took me many years to wed my younger seeking self with the East Coast intellectual I was coming to be, the postmodern house of mirrors also confirmed my already strong suspicion that reality can only be glimpsed through a kaleidoscope of overlapping and even contradictory points of view, an "aperspectival" sensibility first nurtured by psychedelics and the motley spectacle of California's spiritual culture. And so I came to see the world as a carnival of hybrids, of people and places and things woven from nucleic acids and epiphanies, money and Mind, sex and technologies. Though I found traditional religious claims as suspicious as any absolute truths, I understood that people's gods, myths, and everyday spiritual practices were irreducible strands in the webwork of the real.

After college, I found myself a freelance writer, covering the popular culture of the day: rock music, television, digital media. Like the religious historian R. Laurence Moore, who once wrote that he followed religion the way others followed baseball, I continued to track the spiritual and religious dimensions of our world, and I did so with the same enthusiasm and curious fascination I brought to the colorful subcultures that populate our age. Unlike religious traditionalists who bemoan rap stars and the horrors of heavy metal, I found that many of mass culture's fandoms, images, and electric rituals distinctly echoed the more populist and imaginative expressions of religious activity in earlier ages. And so I followed those echoes: *Star Trek* fans who held pagan rituals; Elvis devotees who found in the King the solace they no longer felt in Jesus; computer games that raided the occult; freaks who turned raves or Dead shows into psychedelic Eleusinian mysteries.

And the spirit never stopped tugging inside me, but exactly what that spirit was became more and more difficult to explain. The cultural trends I tracked spoke to spiritual needs unsatisfied by the secular techno-scientific world of late capitalism, but they hardly touched my own aches. What called me was something more intuited than described, more experienced than codified, more wagered than known. Books fed it, but those wonderful word machines weren't enough, and most spiritual groups I checked out seemed plagued with the mystical equivalent of office politics. I grew to suspect paths that depended on powerful teachers or an unleashed imagination, for those strategies often seemed to play off, in a different key, the same obsession with fantasy and celebrity that undergirds the so-called society of the spectacle.

Like a lot of overeducated people, I became attracted to Buddhism for the simple reason that it seemed to emphasize practice over belief. In other words, I could follow the bare-bones recipe of following the breath with the experimental attitude one approaches any intriguing technology — or drug, for that matter. The first Zen priest I met was a crazed Texan with a bad back who described himself as a Zen failure. As we talked, the topic turned to UFOs, and he showed me a videotape of Darryl Anka channeling an intriguing and rather amusing extraterrestrial being named Bashar. Six months later I met a monk at a Tibetan monastery in the Indian state of Karnataka, a diamond-eyed American man who had been practicing solidly in the Gelugpa tradition for twenty years. We talked about Philip K. Dick and William Gibson, and he showed off the laptop he used to prepare for the intense philosophical debates his monastery was hosting that month, an event he likened to a Buddhist Olympics. Returning to the States, I hooked up with my first serious meditation teacher, a Zen lesbian who taught multimedia at New York University. Then I met Taizan Maizumi Roshi, a diminutive Japanese monk who, rumor has it, may have partly inspired the *Star Wars* character Yoda. Definitely my kind of path.

So that's how I wound up staring at a wall on a mountain above San Bernardino, with a warm belly, aching knees, and an internal monologue that oscillated between a relaxed embrace of the passing present and a feverish spew of memes. As the days passed, I no longer paid much attention to the internal play-by-play, and my inner sportscaster gradually faded like the sound of a transistor radio carried away down the beach. Cresting into one particular heartbeat one particular afternoon, I felt myself expand and dissolve into a spacious and enormous web of interdependence. There was no longer a world *out there* that sent me information that I processed *in here*. Events simply occurred within a shimmering and bountiful field of lazy and luxurious becoming. A stomach rumble, a bird call, a flash of intense warmth in a knee, a warm breeze: they were like notes in an atmospheric symphony, organically related but freed from the linear rule of melody or the steady beat of clock time.

Of course, kindergarten satoris like this disappear faster than skywriting. But my experience that day helped me realize that meditation, which many outsiders see as an ascetic disengagement from reality, or at best a kind of relaxation exercise, can actually bloom into an awareness of the world far more crisp and, dare I say, information rich than our usual murky and multitasking consciousness can allow. Though I don't believe that my *zazen* did a damn thing for the kids in Bosnia or the stressed ecosystems that fringe L.A., I began to see that sitting practice can not only affirm the *binding* with things and beings that lies at the core of religion, but can train and nurture one of the most vital and highly prized commodities of our time: attention.

This lesson really hit home when I descended from the mountain a few days later. I still felt a serene balance, as if a gently whirling gyroscope was centered in my belly. But from the moment

I slouched into the SIGGRAPH convention, it was clear that the center was not going to hold. At least 35,000 people had traveled to the downtown heart of L.A.'s glittering strip-mall void to attend the event: company reps and computer geeks, Hollywood schmoozers and goateed digital hipsters, and hundreds of civilians who coughed up big bucks just to ogle the tech. And there was lots of tech to ogle: hundreds of games, software packages, virtual reality systems, media art projects, hardware platforms, Web technologies, and loads of digital eye candy. Add that to panel discussions on everything from artificial life to feminist critiques of the Cartesian coordinate system, and mere anarchy was loosed upon my mind.

For a wide-angle cultural observer like myself, conferences like SIGGRAPH provide convenient one-stop shopping for signs of the zeitgeist. In my sensitized state of mind, SIGGRAPH's frenetic hype, mind-bending machines, and garish color schemes began to take on the apocalyptic momentum and incandescent hubris of the information age itself. It was as if my newly hatched subtle body was loosed in some bad electronic Bardo, cacophonous and claustrophobic.

Like modern airport terminals or malls, the Los Angeles Convention Center is one of those abstract, weightless structures that belong in orbit. The poorly ventilated cavern serving as the main showroom floor was devoid of windows, because the game here — like the game at the Zen Mountain Monastery — was attention. Attention, after all, is the money of the information age, the one genuinely scarce resource in the false infinity of the Internet. Both on- and offline, the marketing engines of late capitalism have turned the capture of that attention into a science of psychological tease that rivals the fascist propagandists and religious mesmerists of earlier ages. Advertisements saturate the social field, as tag lines and slogans infect our speech and manufactured images organize our unconscious perceptions of the world.

Of course, hucksters and salesmen have been catching people's eyes in the dusty din of the marketplace for millennia. But at SIGGRAPH I began to feel like the machines themselves were attempting to lock onto my central nervous system and draw it in like a *Star Wars* tractor beam. And perhaps the best way for a machine to get your attention is to swallow your senses whole: in other words, virtual reality. Like the digital paint programs that specialize in simulating human flesh, virtual reality promises to translate our very bodies into the weightless condition of life inside the media. The old dream of angel flight, of rainbow bodies and astral doubles, has been electro-magnified into the virtual avatar.

The first virtual reality machine I test-drove at SIGGRAPH was a simulated hang-glider flight that used a full-body sling to provide a sense of floating as you navigated the twists and turns of the narrow red-rock canyon projected on the screen before your eyes. As with some other virtual reality experiences that have quick-ened my blood, the hang glider triggered a bit of the quicksilver serenity I've felt in lucid dreams. It's an odd and somewhat dis-turbing experience to have your most intimate forays into the oth-erworlds of the psyche recalled by an arcade game on a showroom floor, but there you have it. Moments like this have led me to take the connection between media technology and the archetypal imagination seriously. In this sense, SIGGRAPH was a savage temple of the electronic image, its booths and exhibits shrines for a cacophony of cults, whose terminal screens offer magical gate-ways into the surreal and tacky landscapes of the digital uncon-scious.

"See the Unbelievable! Witness the Unthinkable in 3-D!" the garish sign proclaimed. It was a StrayLight virtual theater and fea-tured a dozen blank-faced folks reclining on chairs that occasion-ally shook, each person outfitted with a bulky head-mounted display that projected a computer-animated 3-D video into their eyeballs. These folks looked like zombies in a liquid-crystal opium den, though I had to remind myself that I had just spent a week staring at a wall.

The video that so absorbed their attention was an intense, hal-lucinogenic spin on one of the most potent and infectious mytholo-gies of the modern West: the extraterrestrial encounter. The video's creator was Steve Speer, a brash and innovative computer animator who mixes scatological satire with archetypal splendor; his "Carl Jung's Dream" brilliantly fuses images of cathedrals and Norse gods with golden feces and giant wormlike penises. In this piece, a little kid gets sucked into an alternative dimension by a crew of the diminutive, almond-eyed gray aliens.

Strapping on a head-mounted display, I found myself somewhat underwhelmed with the ride, mostly because the point of view kept switching between first- and third-person perspectives — jarring cuts that ruined virtual reality's goal of psychic immersion. But when it came to the primal scene of UFO abduction lore, the piece became all too compelling. I lay on a surgical table in a flying saucer, and a group of impassive Grays leaned over me with buzzing surgical drills in their spidery hands. I shivered as their tools descended toward me, even though I do not usually fear psychic surgery at the hands of cartoon creations.

Perhaps what spooked me was the sense that this virtual reality experience symbolized the secret dream of contemporary media: to invade and rewrite consciousness itself. It drove home how insane technological culture has become. Unmoored from folkways, grasping after figments, addicted to the novelty and tyrannical demands of our hyperactive society, we drift in overdrive. Amidst all the distracting noise and fury, the hoary old questions of the human condition — Who are we? Why are we here? How do we treat others? How do we face the grave? — sound distant and muffled, like fuzzy conundrums we have learned to set aside for more pragmatic and profitable queries. Unless we open up clearings within the space-time of our lives, unless we take media fasts and dare to wander off the grid, such questions may never arise in all their implacable awe.

And so we recover our attention and draw it back toward embodied experience, toward real earth and the mindful now. We hear a lot about ordinary enlightenment today, about embracing our own ordinary equivalent of chopping wood and carrying water. Of course, this desire for authenticity, for reality and the natural, is also part of our popular culture, packaged and marketed in New Age catalogs and the shelves of beauty salons and health food chain stores. More paradoxical is the fact that we in the advanced West don't really live in a world of wood chopping and water carrying anymore, or even one simple enough to qualify as such. The processes that we call, variously, globalization, the information age, postmodernism, and the biotech revolution are now the backdrop of our seeking, but they have a nasty habit of stepping into the foreground. The fact that you can buy CDs of Siberian shamans or score a paperback copy of secret Dzogchen manuals by aiming your Web browser at amazon.com is only a trivial symptom of a far more tumultuous transformation in the world spirit.

Some fear that the relentless growth of global capitalism will dash whatever hopes we have of creating a sustainable future on the surface of this bleeding and tottering globe. Others fear that the new world order will lead to insidious forms of media surveillance and social control. And even if we dodge this multinational *1984,* we still have to face *Brave New World,* and its specter of rampant genetic engineering, happy pills, and an entertainment culture of soulless simulations. So how do we embrace spiritual practice in a world of digital capitalism, commodified DNA, psychopharmacology, and a steady stream of information about a planet falling apart at the seams? Though nostalgic and even reactionary sentiments have their place in a world intoxicated on novelty, I do not believe that a romantic retreat into old religious myths or Luddite primitivism is the answer. Though pockets of the gone world persist, there are no traditions that have not been marked by the peculiar dynamics of our time — not Tibetan Buddhism, not esoteric Christianity, not Native American ways.

Slowly, tentatively, a "network spirituality" suggests itself from the midst of yearning and confusion, a multifaceted path that might humanely and intelligently navigate the technological house of mirrors without losing the resonance of ancient ways or the ability to slice through the venality and delusion that court human life. Against the specter of new and renewed fundamentalism, free-thinking seekers both inside and outside the world's religious traditions are trying to cut and paste a wealth of teachings, techniques, images, and rites into a path grounded enough to walk upon. The mix-and-match spirituality derided by traditionalists is only the surface of a far more supple and dynamic synthesis in the making, one that demands a form of being we have only begun to intuit: open-ended and integral, embodied and viridian green. This path is a matrix of paths, with no map provided at the outset, and no collective goal beyond the lightness and grace of our step.

Such a networked path opens up an ecumenical space far more radical than New Age fantasies of global unity or the bland interfaith chats between liberal monotheists. We log on to this emerging "Indranet" when we accept that we will not transcend the sometimes agonizing tension between the world's various structures of belief and practice. Nor will we simply overcome more contemporary conflicts between faith and skepticism, the stones and the stories, the mundane absurdity of everyday life and the incandescence of the absolute. Instead, these tensions and conflicts become dynamic, calling us to face the Other with an openness that does not seek to assimilate the Other to our point of view. By replacing the need for a common ground with an acceptance and even celebration of our common groundlessness, network spirituality might creatively integrate these tensions while also learning when to let the gaps and ruptures alone. These are the spaces in which we simply breathe.

▼▼▼

**ERIK DAVIS** is the San Francisco–based author of *TechGnosis: Myth, Magic, and Mysticism in the Age of Information* (Three Rivers Press, 1998). He is a contributing editor to *Wired* magazine, and writes "The Posthuman Condition" column for the online magazine *Feed*. He has contributed articles and essays to *ArtByte, The Village Voice*, and *Spin*, and has lectured internationally on topics related to cyber-culture and the fringes of religion.

# ADVENTURES OF
# A NEW AGE TRAVELER

## BY MARIANA CAPLAN

**THERE WERE NO WELCOME BANNERS** at the entrance to
California as I had imagined from the way Joan Baez, Joni
Mitchell, and Kate Wolf sing of it. The Rainbow Family didn't
throw a welcome party just because I had arrived. Instead, I spent
my first weeks in Oakland looking out between the steel bars of a
dusty attic-bedroom window, wondering what the hell to do with
my life. Occasionally I would dare the walk between myself and
the BART subway, where I would pass the afternoon getting on
and off at random stops, trying to figure out where I was and
waiting for something significant to happen.

On a balmy September afternoon, while sitting on Hippie Hill
in Golden Gate Park with my journal, I divided my priorities into
four:

1. Find a spiritual practice that is practical and utterly ordinary.
2. Land a solid job.
3. Get a place to live.
4. Get myself into therapy to find out what the hell I have been running from all my life.

I did okay on the spiritual thing, landing myself as a *vipassana* Buddhist with a Jewish teacher from the East Coast. Pragmatically speaking, Buddhism meant that I'd sit my butt on a cushion every morning for a half hour trying to catch a glimpse of my breath between the entourage of visitors that frequented my mind. One evening a week I would attend dharma talks, during which my nice-Jewish-boy teacher who didn't know I existed would try to persuade us to act like human beings.

Twice a year I'd go to the desert in Southern California for a ten-day silent meditation retreat with a crotchety European meditation teacher. Hour after hour she instructed us in her shrill German-English accent about how to feel the flow of air as it brushed the hairs at the entrance to our nasal passages. She demanded round-the-clock practice, so when we used the toilet, we were requested to feel the texture of cheap toilet paper in our hand, experience the friction as it collided with our ass, and inhale the stench of the outhouse without turning away from it. Mindfulness, they said.

Watching an invisible breath for ten consecutive days without speaking to anybody can get pretty brutal, so my fellow meditators and I would deal with our frustration by doing things like dropping a fork during lunch so everybody would look our way or clearing our throats too loudly as we organized ourselves on our *zafus*. One day I purposely slit my finger while cutting carrots for lunch. It's not that I decided the moment before that I would cut myself, but the instant I did it I knew that it had been intentional, and I drank up the attention like a cool lemonade as people came over, fussed with my hand, and showed some concern for the fact that I was alive.

Seven days into the third retreat, I could no longer endure the inner workings of my mind. The teacher had refused my fourth request for a meeting to discuss my sanity, her German accent was driving me nuts, and when she asked which of my feet had touched the floor first that morning, I wanted to punch her.

In spite of my concerns of the karmic implications of ditching a meditation retreat, a spiritual teacher, and my own mind, I fled. At 3:15 in the morning, after all were sound asleep, I secretly packed my bags, crept over to the main building, left my good-bye note, and silently climbed into my white Honda with the green hood. After driving in first gear out the sand driveway, I cued my cassette player to Cat Stevens's *Wild World,* and blasted my way out of Joshua Tree at 90 miles an hour.

In spite of such rebellions, my spiritual practice was sound. God didn't punish me for breaking out of meditation jail, and through studying the Buddhist scriptures and beginning to familiarize myself with my own mind, I finally realized that my mind is no different than everybody else's. Therein I discovered I was not crazy.

Meanwhile, the home front became less and less conventional. Within days of moving into what appeared to be a sanctuary of goddesses, I discovered that I was living in a witches' coven. To befriend a witch is one thing, and to live with one, or many, is quite another. The presiding witch of the household called herself Luna. She had a tiny frame, huge breasts, tattoos all over her body, deep green eyes, and a different color hair every other week (ranging from bleached white, to psychedelic green, to bald, to black witchy braids). Luna ran a magic store in the city, but made her rent by working as a "sacred prostitute," tending to the sexual fantasies of a few wealthy donors. She painted her room forest green, covered the floor with soil, dragged in stolen trees, hung bones on the walls, and draped black fish netting from the red velvet canopy that covered her bed. Luna drank wine in the morning, smoked hash in the afternoon, and spent hours concocting witch potions, both to help those she cared for and harm those whom she didn't. A bona fide (and not too discriminating) bisexual, any gender, shape, or size individual might emerge from her bedroom in the late mornings.

But Luna's main squeeze was Jo, the other witch who lived down the hall in the dark blue bedroom painted like the night sky. People like Luna earn their title as witches through the beatific expression of wicked and demented attributes, whereas others are just witch wannabes. Still, Jo, a wannabe, could get away with just about anything she wanted because she was so cute.

She was young, barely twenty, and a flaming red lesbian. Freckles all over her body, a fiery mane of red hair (the kind people pay thousands for), ruby lips, a pink complexion, and arrogant as high hell. Jo had been raised by hippies, getting anything she wanted by screaming loud enough, and had left home and lived on the streets as a teenager. She did phone sex for a job, and we would often lie on her bedroom floor rolling around in suppressed giggles as she verbally masturbated faceless heterosexual men on the other end of the line with hilarious descriptions of herself as a six-foot, skinny blonde. Jo was a pussycat on the inside, but she wore a sheath of daggers.

There was one person, however, around whom Jo was as subservient as a willow tree, and that was Luna. Jo was Luna's servant — literally. Jo was Luna's backup lover whenever Luna didn't have somebody else in her bed. She was also her sister, friend, confidante, mother, and child. To say they were codependent would be an understatement, though together they created a chemistry that could light up a room. What finally got to me was when, in a fit of anguish over Luna's latest affair, Jo confessed that Luna had told her that Jo had been Luna's slave in a past lifetime and that this is how their relationship was to continue in this lifetime...and Jo believed her!

The third player in our scene was Kathy, an ex-surfer girl from Malibu. Bleach blonde, tight muscles, tall and confident, Kathy had quit surfing when she was diagnosed with Epstein-Barr virus and had moved to San Francisco to get over her surfer boyfriend, who had dumped her for a *Cosmopolitan* model.

Kathy and I liked to think that we were outside of the household psychosis, until Mistress Luna was on sabbatical to her native Nashville. That night as we three remaining coven mates lay on my black futon, presumably cuddling in my dark rose room with the large tree painted across the wall, we explored the fine boundary between an intimacy between women that is purely sensual and one that is erotic. We slowly experimented with the difference between loving one woman and loving two. We lived in that electric suspense for hours, not knowing what might happen from one moment to the next, until Jo finally broke out laughing. We all joined in, grateful, and got up and ordered in sushi.

Much as I enjoyed the status of bisexual on my increasingly self-aggrandizing spiritual résumé, I nonetheless began to feel an old familiar hunger: men. I figured a sexy, spiritualized man could provide an important training ground to test my newfound spiritual hypotheses. Plus, he would undoubtedly provide more raw material for therapy if things didn't work out. A no-lose proposition.

In this way I began to attract a new breed of men (or the same old breed disguised under a new set of clothes) that over time I came to call Zen boyfriends. I use the term *Zen* loosely here, because a man doesn't have to be a Zen Buddhist to fall into this category. He could be a Tibetan Buddhist, a Sufi, or even a practitioner of some obscure brand of yoga. The more rigid the tradition, the better for this type. What defines a Zen boyfriend is the manner in which he skillfully uses spiritual ideals and practices as an excuse for his terror of, and refusal to be in, any type of real relationship with a woman. He is both too identified with his balls to become a celibate monk and, at the same time, too little identified with the wider implications of them to take responsibility for them. The result: a righteous, distant, and very intelligent substitute for a real man.

Andrew was a great example of a Zen boyfriend. He was tall, bright, charming, and strikingly attractive. He was creative, well versed in spiritual scriptures, a great chef, and exceptionally funny — but he couldn't give in to a woman if his life depended on it.

This is how a typical morning went for Andrew and me:

At 4:30 A.M. his alarm sounds (not a simple ring or buzz, but the schizophrenic chirping bird type of alarm). "Andrew, your alarm is going off."

"Press the snooze."

I oblige. Then at 4:38 it goes off again. "Andrew, get up!"

"I'm too tired."

By the fourth snooze I was wide awake, while he dozed away like a baby in arms. When he'd finally open his eyes sometime around 5:30, I was undeniably and unspiritually pissed off. Without even a word or a glance in my direction, he would roll out of bed and head for the bathroom. I would listen with mounting rage as he gargled his Chinese herbs, did an hour of t'ai chi on the creaky hardwood floor, and then adjusted himself on his *zafu* to meditate. Often I would get up and meditate as well, but since I didn't practice the same form of meditation as he did, he said we couldn't practice together. Finally, just before 8 — approximately three-and-one-half hours after the alarm had first sounded — he would come in and tell me he was making breakfast. Yippee. During breakfast his rule was silence so he could read the paper over organic oats and mint tea, both without sugar.

The argument was always the same:

"Why do you set your alarm if you're not going to get up?"

"It's important to hold the intention to get up early. The energy for meditation is strongest between three and five in the morning."

"If it's so strong then why don't you just do it?"

And then:

"Andrew, it would make a big difference to me if you would at least say 'good morning' when you get up."

"I want my meditation to be consistent with the delta waves that are activated during sleep, and speech interferes with this."

"Even two words, 'good' and 'morning'?!"

"Yes, even two words."

"How about a hug then?"

"Same thing."

"Then why doesn't cold water on your face or flushing the toilet screw up the delta waves?"

"I need space. Conversation closed."

Men need space. All women know this. But some men need two parts space for one part intimacy, or even ten parts space for one part intimacy. But with Andrew, and other Zen boyfriends, it was more like ninety-eight parts space to two parts intimacy. What they really want to be in relationship with is a stone goddess, not a woman.

It was a lose-lose proposition with Andrew. Exactly why I wanted our relationship to work so badly in the first place is a worthwhile question, but I am a woman, and the more a man withdraws into himself, the more a woman chases him there to draw him out. Andrew told me that our relationship wasn't working because I wasn't spiritual enough. What a blow! He complained that I wasn't an experienced meditator and that my three short years of meditation practice didn't enable me to understand my mind the way he understood his mind, thus rendering me incapable of a "spiritual relationship." When he lamented that I only meditated a half hour a day whereas he meditated for an hour, I painstakingly began to meditate for an hour. When he complained that since I studied *vipassana* Buddhism instead of Zen Buddhism, that I couldn't really understand his true aim, I started reading Zen and altered my meditation. Finally, he said that even though I was starting to walk the path of Zen, that his teacher taught in a very particular way that was distinct from other schools of Zen. But when I told him I wanted to meet his teacher, he said that I had already taken over too much of his life and that he was entitled to keep the very thing he treasured most — his teacher — for himself (even though she taught publicly throughout California.)

Our relationship ended over a winter weekend at a rented condo on Lake Tahoe with his mother. I should have had the foresight to realize that for some men, having their girlfriend and mother in the same house is the very thing that takes them over the edge.

We began to fight over his special Zen knife — as if that is what we were really arguing about. He had this stainless steel knife he had bought from some Japanese samurai chef that he used to cut vegetables and fruits when we cooked. The knife had to be held a specific way, used at a certain angle, and could only touch the cutting board with a minimal degree of contact. He was proud of his knife and had given me special permission to use it as I was his girlfriend. That Sunday morning he came downstairs while I was preparing a fruit salad with a dull paring knife.

"You can use *my* knife if you're careful."

I nodded and continued chopping walnuts.

"Well aren't you going to use it?"

"No."

"Well why not?" he retorted, Zen compassion void from his voice.

I finally looked up from what I was doing. "There are so many damn rules attached to your Zen knife that I'd rather use a plastic picnic knife than bear the consequences of touching it the wrong way."

He told me once and for all that I simply wasn't enough yin to match his yang, I told him his spirituality was seriously deranged, and the relationship ended, though I missed him terribly for months.

Jake was another one of these scared guys who hid behind his spirituality. He was a Zen Buddhist when I met him but had become a Vedantic nondualist before we split up, which is as bad if not worse in terms of Zen-boyfriendness. We met at a narcissistic, eco-retentive, save-the-earth weekend workshop, but that's another story.

Two days after the workshop, as I sped off the Golden Gate Bridge and headed up 101 north toward my country home after a full day of seeing therapy clients, I noticed a tall man pounding on a drum while standing on top of a run-down VW hippie van alongside the highway. He looked familiar, but I couldn't be sure. I got off at the Mill Valley exit, drove back down the highway, turned around again, and pulled up behind his van. Sure enough, it was Jake. He told me that the workshop had inspired him to do a new form of political eco-protest. Once a week, he said, he planned to stand on his van alongside the highway and call out the list of endangered species while pounding on his drum. When I asked him what he hoped to accomplish by this, he said that he didn't know but that he was intuitively guided to do it. Strange as it sounds, I was impressed.

He asked me out on a date. The first night we ate vegetarian lasagna, Caesar salad, and Häagen-Dazs by candlelight in his living room, and then rolled around his balcony for hours while Mickey

Hart played on the stereo and Sausalito danced at our feet. The next morning, he told me he needed space. And in this way, our Zen relationship developed, in the small gaps between the large spaces.

Jake eventually left for India (a spiritually disguised intimacy escape plan I myself was to later emulate) and returned a year and a half later, looking very monklike in his white cotton Indian garb and ivory shawl. His long hair had been cut to shoulder length and had grayed, his skin appeared to have permanently tanned, and small wrinkles marked the corners of his eyes. He said he had thought about me a lot and would I like to go out for dinner? As I was between boyfriends (again), and as he was quite handsome in his new guru look, I agreed.

Jake thought he had become enlightened, though he wouldn't have dared to say as much. He had become a student of one of those Indian teachers who skillfully create mystical experiences in their groupies by momentarily cutting through their psychological blocks, and then declare them enlightened from the experience. In such a situation, the master gets a swollen head and an immense reputation for being able to enlighten people, and thousands of Western hippies who are afraid of really living life get to think that they have risen above it, and then proceed unsolicited to try to bestow the same boon upon others.

Jake was a living example of such a situation. The first night was all right, as far as Zen boyfriends go. I enjoyed hearing of his adventures over a cappuccino, only occasionally irritated by his references to having "seen through the nature of reality" or having "become one with everything." Of course by early evening he needed space, but that was to be expected.

The next day, however, as we walked in Muir Woods, he tried to do his spiritual number on me. As a definition of his spiritual approach in a sentence, nondualism is based on the tacit recognition of the oneness, or nonseparation, of all things. It means that "I" doesn't exist separately from you or any other animate or inanimate being or thing: all is one. However, there is a big difference between being able to spew these words (as I just did) and living as one who abides eternally in the truth of this reality.

"Jake, if we are going to hang out together I need to feel like you're really here with me and not always so detached," I opened the floor.

"But who is the 'you' who wants to hang out with the 'me'?"

"*I* am the me and *you* are the you!"

"There is no difference, so we can never really be apart or together — it's all the same."

"You're full of shit."

"But who do you think is the 'me' that is full of shit?"

"I think it is YOU!"

"Who's getting angry?"

"*I'm* getting angry."

"Look into my eyes, what do you see?"

"You."

"Look more deeply. Now what do you see?"

"I see a lonely man who thinks he's enlightened."

Extremely frustrated and teary eyed, I walked away and sat on a log by the stream trying to figure out why it was so important to me to try to get through to him.

"Why did you come all the way over here to cry?" he sat down beside me, fully believing in his own innocence.

I looked at him with that end-of-the-relationship look in my eye. "Because there is no one there to hold me if I cry, and I'd just as soon cry alone than cry with nobody."

And in this way came and went a couple more Zen boyfriends. Yet in the end, I blame not them but myself. For as distant, arrogant, righteous, and terrified as they were, it was I who sought them out, I who tried to open them in the ways *I* wanted them to be open, and ultimately I who re-created my childhood pattern of not feeling loved by eliciting the same response in my relationships. I could have just dated a nice Jewish boy after all.

Alas the internal quandary of spiritual intimacy that emerged through my relationships with the Zen boyfriends necessitated the accompanying emotional processing of those issues, and thus I sought out a therapist. Overwhelmed by the 986 listings under the category "therapy" in the San Francisco Yellow Pages, I remembered a business card I had been given at a bisexual women's gathering. In the recesses of my canvas army bag, I found the telephone number for a healer, named Iris, and called her up. The next day I was seated in a plush, baby blue armchair across from my projected New Age mother.

I had exactly two sets of feelings about Iris: I loved her and she drove me crazy. I loved her because she listened to me so closely that tears came to her eyes when I was in pain, and because she made it unquestionably clear that she cared about me far beyond her role of therapist. She drove me crazy with her New Age proclivities. From day one she was trying to push Archangel Gabriel and every other angel she knew on me. She channeled the Great Mother and every other known and unknown goddess into the room with us. She would give me weekly reports on the shade and size of my aura, and would trance out with rapid eye blinking as she received a psychic message from her spirit guides about what I needed to do about one dramatic situation in my life or another. She put crystals in my lap and insisted that I surround myself with rose, lavender, and effervescent lights.

I came into our second session and told her that if I was to do therapy with her, that I needed all angels, guides, gods, goddesses, channels, mediums, tarot decks, crystals, and auric cameras to remain outside of the room or I was out of there. In this way, Iris and I proceeded with our weekly sessions. Our agreement for normalcy generally held up, only occasionally being interrupted with conversations like this one:

"I hope you have a wonderful, enlightening, and profoundly peaceful holiday," she would say in her smoky voice as we parted before the winter holidays.

"Yeah, you too. What are you going to do for the week?"

"Well, tonight I'm going to finish wrapping presents for my kids, and hang their stockings on the mantel."

"You have kids? I can't believe I've been working with you all this time and you hadn't told me."

"Oh no, not *those* kind of children. I like to celebrate the holidays with my *inner* kids."

Our therapy was successful in spite of her undercover angelic interference, but still I wanted more, lots more. In fact, I have wanted more of any and everything I could get since I was four years old, and so I set out to conquer the therapeutic circuit. You name it: movement therapy, pseudo-Tantra, Rolfing, underwater massage, voice dialogue, hypnosis, encounter groups....

For therapeutic recreation, I took up contact improvisational dancing. Walking into the dance studio, I was met by four walls of mirrors, a jug of spring water, and all sizes, shapes, and colors of bodies swirling, undulating, shaking, and pulsating to world beat music. Couples who appear to be having sex with their clothes on in the middle of the floor are actually practicing contact dancing, which involves synchronizing yours and your partner's body such that you move as one person and surrender to the creativity that results from the connection. In other words: sex.

The basic rule for contact improvisational dancing is that anybody is free game. Couples who come together must be prepared to have somebody else crawling through their beloved's legs, and horny single people need to know that just because somebody slides down the front of them and wraps themselves around their feet, that this has no implications in terms of their wider relationship to that person.

In this way, many an evening was spent hanging on some man's back, being thrown into the air by some macho dancer, lying on the floor in pretend contractions with a group of women, or rolling about in a clump of people. Dance orgies were an ideal form of New Age foreplay, though the nights following it were often spent thrashing about my bed in yearning for a kind of orgasm that dancing just couldn't provide.

My internal mad scientist spared me no healing extravaganza until I reached the pinnacle of experimentation with Ariela and Ahmed, a Middle Eastern couple who were long-term apprentices of a Peruvian shaman. They had studied a brand of neo-shamanism that combined the intake of enormous quantities of organic and synthetic psychotropic drugs with music and sound. I must say that in spite of my initial skepticism and critical hindsight, these

guys were no fools. They had laser-sharp minds and the percep-
tivity of police dogs. They invited you to play on the razor's edge,
and if you were willing to show up, they would hang out with you
right at the brink.

Long days and nights were spent lying blindfolded in my
sleeping bag on the floor of their unfurnished "journeying" room.
I tempted the edges of Godliness and madness in the hopes of
catching the express train to enlightenment, as the stereo alternated
angelic symphonies with police sirens and funeral music in an
attempt to leave no inner arena untouched.

When all is said and done, I wouldn't recommend the process.
I am an experience junkie, and I got my experience, but what
changed in my life as a result? It is relatively simple to blast open
the psyche, and, more often than not, the person suffers no lasting
chemical or emotional consequences (ask me again when I'm
seventy-five), but sustaining such states can only happen over the
course of years and years of spiritual training. I was no different
than all the other people I knew who attempted to use drugs in our
shared hope that we could find some shortcut, some back door,
some easy way out of the necessarily arduous road to God.

Having said that, I credit Ariela as the springboard that threw
me into what was to come next.

When I showed up the following week at Ariela's conventional-
looking therapy office for my drug integration session, she asked
me how I was doing. I told her I felt bound by three hundred
pounds of iron chains, and that if I didn't break out of them, I
feared I might really go mad.

"So what are you going to do about it?" she said with a tough-
girl challenge in her voice.

I reiterated my now familiar story: I had finally settled down in
California. I didn't want to go anywhere or do anything (more)
outrageous. I had a fall job at a hospice and was going to help
people die so I could deal with my denial of my own death, and I
wasn't about to give up the first stability I had found since popping
out of my mother's womb.

Ariela walked across the room, kneeled down, and placed both hands around my neck in a grip that is uncharacteristic of a 105-pound woman. She repeated, "What are you going to do about it?"

She had succeeded in taking me by surprise. "Stay in California?" I squeaked.

"Fuck off. Are you going to sell out this early in life or are you going to do something?"

I was impressed. She had crossed a line of therapeutic formality that had been disturbing me for years, and had successfully commanded my respect.

"I want to follow my heart. I don't even know if I have one, or where it is if I do, but I want to follow it anyway."

She loosened her grip. "So, I repeat, what are you going to do?"

"I'm going to India."

"When?" she demanded.

"Next week."

Thus was launched what would become a long and not undramatic journey, but one that took me to my long sought-after Teacher. With less outer fanfare, he began to catalyze a slow and painstaking dismantling of the spiritualized personality I had so carefully constructed. My adventures until that point had forged grooves of longing in the soul and hints of deeper understandings, while at the same time they had strengthened my ego to a position where it could receive the first blows of the Master's great wrecking ball — sometimes with dignity, and other times far less gracefully. You use the ground to get off the ground, and in this way I became initiated into my eventual profession of spiritual bottom crawling. Those first years of New Age antics were an extended course in Spiritual Discernment 101: What Not to Do. Next to come was an eight-year sequel entitled "Spiritual Discipleship: Who and What You Are Not." The spiritual "highway" often more closely resembles a muddy path. The potholes and ditches change their location, and the legs of the discerning traveler grow stronger, but the road never ends. But I'm in it for the long haul, so I stumble onward, determined to walk until I fall off the cliff of the great void, or until the Great Mother sucks me back into her body, whichever comes first.

▼▼▼

**MARIANA CAPLAN** is a transpersonal counselor, seminar leader, and writing consultant in the San Francisco Bay Area. She is the author of six books, including: *The Way of Failure: Winning Through Losing* (Hohm Press, 2001), *Halfway Up the Mountain: The Error of Premature Claims to Enlightenment* (Hohm Press, 1999), and the forthcoming *Spiritual Authority: Navigating the Labyrinth of the Student-Teacher Relationship* (Thorsons, 2002). Her contribution is an excerpt from her book in progress, *Adventures of a New Age Traveler.*

# PART 3

# FRUITS OF THE JOURNEY

**AS A SPIRITUAL PATH ADVANCES,** something richer, more generous, and more sublime begins to emerge. That ineffable thing is the nectar produced by the flower, the kiss of a better world. In a remarkably consistent way, the peeling away of false accretions from our true nature leads to heightened creativity, a commitment to serve others, and a passion for justice. Yet these acts are held with considerably less angst and ardor than before. Justice is less a fiery slogan than a steady guiding principle for each action, each moment. Creativity does not happen through force so much as by grace and quiet inspiration. Service is no longer a game of exchange, cemented by guilt and obligation, but an expression of our fundamental nature, unconditional and pure.

The contributions in this section explore the nectar of a spiritual path, as well as the responsibility that it brings. It is important to remember that the contributors are ordinary people — no different than you — who are leading extraordinary lives by aligning themselves with the Spirit that caresses their hearts and by using their unique capacities to work for the greater good. Their contributions are, more than anything, about giving back. The graces of Spirit are without number, and, as we taste more of them, they ask only to be shared. So savor the succulence of the harvest in the following pages and allow some of their inspired surrender to permeate your own soul.

## THE SCULPTORS

BY **DENISE FUEHRER**

**WE ARE THE SCULPTORS**
  shaping the face of possibility
trying to mold tomorrow
  into something meaningful

The tools of our ancestors
lie dull and broken
  at our feet
as the clay of life
  hardens in our hands

An unfinished masterpiece
  stands taunting us

its ruinous and misshapen features
an excuse for our indifference

In rage and desperation
    we point the finger of blame
        at them

But then we notice our hands
    soiled with dry earth
we notice
        beneath our fingernails
            the remains of a hard day's work
and we realize...        we are them
Our hands
        are molding the future

And so we cry
    and laugh
    and live
with a passion forbidden to those
who passed before us

We pray
        although we know not to whom
for the strength
    the courage
to put aside
these molds of times past
so tight and clinging
    crumbling fast
        from the force
        of minds and hearts
            opening in desperation

On our knees we crawl
through shards of shattered illusions

collecting fragments
   of others' revelations
searching for useful remnants
among the scraps
   of yesterday's truth

Where do we begin?
  we ask ourselves
paralyzed by the same freedom
   we fought long and hard for
     in another lifetime

Where do we begin?

The question echoes
   through the hollow chamber
   of our soul . . .
           still no answer

And so we sit
     quietly
in the darkness
   haunted by the ghost
   of our imagination

We wait
  and listen
and eventually
we learn
  how to wait
   and how to listen

And just as the last grain of sand
  passes through our hourglass of hope
  we hear a voice . . .

The Muse has spoken:

Begin with the heart
        she whispers

Begin with the heart.

▼▼▼

**DENISE FUEHRER** received her master's degree in East West psychology with a concentration in expressive arts from the California Institute of Integral Studies. She currently resides in North Carolina, where she teaches improvisational dance and is working to create an expressive arts program for young women with eating disorders.

# LOOKING FOR GOD AND JUSTICE

## BY CLAUDIA HORWITZ

**LIKE MANY PEOPLE,** my life has been shaped by a quest. In the mythic tale of the hero's journey, we leave the world we know because we sense there is something lacking in our experience. And we hope that whatever we find will be radical and new and that it will have the potential to bring great changes to the world we left. There are wondrous precedents for this journey. The Buddha left the safety of his father's kingdom and found enlightenment. Moses went to the top of the mountain and came back with the Ten Commandments. And Jesus spent forty days in the desert before emerging with his truth.

Mine is taking a little longer. For over a decade, I have been searching for how spirit and justice can truly merge, across space and time. That is, I want to reconcile a deeply held belief that we are all one (if not in this material world, then on another plane altogether) with the reality that some have more power and privilege than others, resulting in tremendous pain and violence.

My own story begins, I suppose, with my awakening to the dire need for economic justice. I spent my first years out of college developing an understanding of economic injustice and rallying people around related activities. Mostly I worked to organize young people to address issues of hunger and homelessness in their surrounding communities. First this took the form of education and direct service, but after some time this seemed pretty pointless. When news of more shelter beds is greeted as a positive event, society's reality detector has clearly gone awry. So, I turned my sights to what I thought would be more effective: developing young leaders who could support low-income folks to organize their own movements. This period in my life was full of work and people and commitments. I learned from others what it means to be poor in America, how our economic system thwarts potential, and how communities achieve short-term victories. The work was all encompassing; there was no time for reflection, relaxation, or solid relationships. After many years on this path, I knew it wasn't exactly the right one, but I wasn't sure why.

I found my answer in the summer of 1993 when President Clinton's national service initiative brought fifteen hundred young people to Treasure Island naval base, just off the coast of San Francisco, to prepare for a "Summer of Service." I had been a strong critic of national service and quite skeptical about this particular program, devoid as it was of political analysis and hell-bent on championing young people over older folks who'd been quietly committed for decades. Still, I agreed to the invitation to be a trainer because so many of the peers I most respected were also going.

It was a complete disaster. More important, I was a disaster. During our final wrap-up meeting, I went outside and sat under a tree. Staring at the beauty of Marin County and San Francisco Bay, I recounted the failures of the week, mine and those beyond my control. The training curriculum had been developed in haste and with little input. Most of the national leadership had little experience with the program's primary constituency: young people of color from urban neighborhoods. The participants, ages seventeen to twenty-five, were stuck in military barracks and treated like children, asked to be in bed by 11:30 P.M. Cameras and the press stalked us at every turn. Many wondered aloud if this was merely a photo opportunity for the Clinton administration. Why else would we design a training program a thousand miles away from the actual communities it was designed to serve, without the expertise of the individuals who live and work in them?

Sitting under that tree, I realized that I had assumed a role I did not want and was not in any way prepared for. Where was the anchor that would have led me to make a different choice, that would have helped me remember my core values and my deeply held beliefs? Didn't I have a spiritual center of some sort? I was raised Jewish but did not find, growing up, enough sustenance in Judaism. Saying prayers out loud, en masse, did not feed me. The Jewish community felt too homogeneous to me, and my suburban synagogue put more emphasis on status than spirit. I had drifted from religion altogether. Was I now paying the price?

I began to weep. Then, mysteriously, I began to pray. I heard a different voice coming through, one that felt slightly familiar and entirely new at the same time. I asked for help from a powerful presence that I felt but could not name. I made a vow never again to be involved with something I didn't fundamentally agree with. And I committed myself to finding more sources of integrity, strength, and meaning.

Unsettled by this experience, I sought guidance from two mentors, who reflected back that what I really needed was a spiritual practice, though I was clueless as to what a spiritual practice actually *was*. I'd never heard that term before. But with their counsel, and the help of a couple of good books, I cultivated a daily routine of meditation, one that continues to this day. Within days, meditation brought a sense of calm detachment that I had never experienced before. I worried less about what other people thought and what I was missing in the world. My highs and lows weren't as gut wrenching. I watched as my attention to others and to myself grew.

For six years, most mornings have begun with fifteen to twenty minutes of quiet awareness, just me sitting and paying attention to my breathing. Through the breath, I am fed by the same energy that enables growth and death and everything in between. I often call this sustaining energy "god" because most people recognize that word. But that is just a word for what is ultimately unnameable. This essential part of my day instills a sense of peace and it reminds me what it means just to *be.* This state of being has a way of drawing important thoughts to the surface, while less useful thoughts recede. With so much of my day spent rehashing the past and anticipating the future, meditation lets me be in the present. I've found that it is hard to learn when the mind is frantic. In meditation, I train myself to be more mindful. And, the more aware I am, the more I can respond in a way that is truthful and wise. Meditation makes me a kinder person, somehow, and for that alone, it is worth it.

When I first began meditating, I felt isolated and wondered which communities supported individuals in their quest for that rather elusive quality I was unable to name. So, when I finished graduate school, I spent three months traveling, seeing old friends, and exploring the spiritual life. I visited holistic health centers, bookstores, and yoga centers. I read books and participated in workshops. Everywhere I went I found people who were considering questions similar to those preoccupying me: What does a life aligned with the spirit feel like? How can I bring more groundedness into my day-to-day life? What practices would help me feel less full of myself, more full of god?

For those three months, part of me was in heaven. I was surrounded by thoughtful, alive, intelligent people having the conversations I'd been yearning to have. An inner calm arose and I was able to sink into a comfortable sense of self that was new and yet vaguely familiar. I was discovering what it felt like to live life in the present, and I was incredibly grateful for it.

Soon, however, I began to feel uncomfortable. The worlds in which I was traveling were overwhelmingly white and well resourced: the homogeneity and privilege of my synagogue with a slightly new face. Many people seemed unwilling, or at least unsure of how, to see their lives in a broader context. There was heightened consciousness around the pain individuals had suffered in their own lives, but little conversation about the larger pain of a society thriving on violence and exploitation. The resounding message was, "The only thing you can change is yourself." I believed this, but at the same time I believed it was a cop-out.

Yes, my own spiritual practice enabled me to go out in the world each day as a calmer person, with more patience, and that made my work stronger somehow; it had some impact on the greater good, but only if I kept this greater good, this bigger story, in the forefront of my mind. Mostly, I felt torn between two worlds. My greatest commitments were justice based, but my ability to sustain those commitments, I now knew, would require the energy I was cultivating in this altogether different realm, the realm of the spirit. My daily experience of the divine was an individual one, but social justice required collective action. I was torn, unsure how to marry seemingly conflicting practices. I knew there had to be other people who were struggling with themselves as well as issues beyond themselves.

In 1995 I decided to formalize my quest to join spiritual practice with the world of social justice. I wanted to bring groups of people together to shed light on what it means to integrate one's personal journey with a collective struggle. I wanted to help activists develop tools to carve out time for their spiritual life. I wanted to find ways for community-based organizations to become more reflective, more conscious of their values, more able to live and work harmoniously from day to day. And I wanted to do it all in a way that would eventually bring a broader spectrum of faithful voices into the public square. I had experienced the gifts of a spiritual life, and now I wanted to share them with all of the brilliant but overworked activists who I had always worried might kill themselves before they'd saved anybody else.

I began by envisioning circles, small groups of activists who would meet regularly for reflection, renewal, and peer education. I saw these circles as supportive environments to explore individual vision, personal and political history, community building, and core values. Unsure of how to proceed, I asked people what they thought of the idea of a small group of activists, loosely defined, coming together for spiritual renewal. Would they come? Most people responded favorably, so I scheduled a potluck dinner at my house and sent out a letter with directions, stating my intentions.

Then a scary thing happened: people called and said they were coming. What was I supposed to do now? The day of the first gathering I stayed home and cleaned my house for five hours. This was about more than just sweeping and mopping. I was clearing the way for new people, new energy, and new ideas. In the midst of this ritual, the doorbell rang. I opened it to find two young men, missionaries from the Church of Latter Day Saints. A grin crept across my face.

"Good afternoon, ma'am," one of them said, "We'd like to tell you about a path that you might not have considered. You might have heard about us on television or something."

"Actually, I don't watch much TV...."

"Good, that's good," the other one said.

"But I certainly know who you folks are. I was in Salt Lake City once. Pretty beautiful." Now I'm starting to sound ridiculous, I thought.

"Yes, yes it is," they responded. "And we'd really like to share more about it with you."

"You know what?" I continued, calmly, "I'm on a path that I feel good about. I'm all about god; I just think differently about it than you guys do." They stared at me blankly for a couple of seconds, and then smiled again.

"Well, ma'am, thanks for your time. You have a great day."

"You, too," I answered. "Good luck."

I closed the door and resumed cleaning. Good luck? A nice Jewish girl wishing two nice Mormon missionary boys good luck? When I stopped to think about it, their activity wasn't all that different than mine. Wasn't I a missionary of sorts? This gathering at my house, wasn't it a way of saying to people, "Come on, put a little more spirit in your life. Get a little more god"?

Why did the promise and possibility of these circles matter so much to me? Because I knew that going out into the world every day to make some meaningful change was no easy task; it took energy, focus, and commitment. Every day, it seemed, I faced my own anger, anxiety, and insecurity. It took me a while to realize that these emotions were energy, the raw material of my life. Unexamined, this energy manifested as self-criticism, judgment, despair, pain, or paralysis. Through spiritual community, however, I knew we could transform this energy into strength, joy, serenity, compassion, and love.

And this is precisely what these circles provided for people. We gave each other ongoing support and built enough trust for real collaboration. We talked about money and Jesus and the Passover story. We created our own rituals to usher in the seasons and looked at baby photos while telling painful and joyous stories of childhood. We shared food and ritual and silence. We taught each other meditation and explored our greatest fears. And as a result, we built relationships that were more resilient to the tests of difference and time.

Small groups of spirited and faithful individuals coming together on a regular basis for a common purpose is nothing new. Seekers have always needed communities to reinforce their journey and to keep themselves authentic. They have a great legacy in forms old and new that continue to thrive: in the Jewish *havurah,* Christian mission groups, the tribe, twelve-step programs, Bible study groups, women's spirituality groups, and many others. I've come to think of these groups as circles of individuals who gather regularly, with intention, to support each other, to renew themselves spiritually, and to explore areas of common interest. Circles are communities unto themselves and, at the same time, they support the creation of community on a larger scale.

They seem particularly important to me now as I and many of my peers place greater emphasis on a spiritual path carved from meditation, ritual, yoga, writing, art, personal prayer, and other practices. Many of us are breaking with organized tradition, or at least attempting to counter its flaws with other experiences.

However, we forget too easily those aspects of religious traditions that have helped people both remember their social mission and find their way to god. Gathering weekly in traditional worship instills accountability and community, however flawed, that is harder to come by on an individual path. The Hebrew and Christian Bibles are full of stories and parables that nudge the faithful toward a larger sense of responsibility. They carry messages of faith and hope, reconciliation and redemption, love and justice. And religious mystics from both the East and the West have helped me believe a direct relationship with the divine is possible. I fear that in our quest for something that feels authentic, we often undermine the very traditions that have allowed us to come as far as we have.

When a photographer is taking a photograph, there is a moment in which he or she must decide how far to zoom in on the subject. Perhaps individuals get to a similar juncture when developing a spiritual practice. If our lens zooms in too close, and we see the work of the spirit as purely inner work, we lose the bigger picture, the sense of how we are connected to the world around us. If we pull back too far and forget about our own development, we are in danger of burning out or not honoring our uniqueness. If we focus just right, we see our own lives in a broader context. We are reminded that large-scale, societal transformations both require and inform our own transformation, and vice versa.

I believe some of the current trends in the world of spiritual development take us too deep within ourselves and too far from the rest of what matters. We cannot let the journey to spirit allow us to drift off into oblivion or isolation. We need to see how our journeys overlap. We need to create venues that elicit and celebrate the stories of inequity, oppression, reconciliation, and redemption, stories that inspire us to care for a larger circle than just ourselves. We need spiritual communities that will fulfill the individual longing for peace on the inside and further the social mission of justice on the outside. My experience is that such communities will allow us to weave both god and justice into the very fabric of our daily lives.

▼▼▼

**CLAUDIA HORWITZ** is the founding director of stone circles, a nonprofit organization based in Durham, North Carolina, that helps individuals and organizations to integrate spiritual practice, reflection, and faith into the work of social justice. Since 1995, stone circles has worked with change agents and activists all over the country through training, organizational development, and interfaith gatherings. Her previous work includes developing youth leadership, supporting struggles for economic justice, and strengthening nonprofit organizations. Her first book, *The Spiritual Activist: Practices to Transform Your Life, Your Work, and Your World* (Viking, 2002), is a practical guide to individual and social transformation through spirit and faith. Her work is focused where contemplative practice, creative expression, and social justice intersect. She is a Rockefeller Foundation Next Generation Leadership Fellow and teaches Kripalu yoga.

# THE SECOND COMING

## OUR SOUL'S JOURNEY
## OF AWAKENING

BY KIMBERLEE ANN KUWICA

**THE WORLD AS I KNEW IT COLLAPSED** in December of 1993. Driving in a car on a wintry road in Missouri, I started to switch lanes and suddenly saw a car in my blind spot. I overcompensated and sent the car flying off the bridge I was traveling on, tumbling over and over again onto a street far below.

As if in slow motion, in the moments of crashing, one world ended and another began: my very identity, hopes, and dreams all fractured in the twisted wreckage. In the twinkling of an eye the physical bridge I was driving on transmuted into an otherworldly bridge that connected the everyday, material world I knew to a luminous, divine realm in which I soon found myself. The twisted car and my damaged body dissolved within my consciousness, and another realm, suffused with love and incredible lightness of being, began opening.

I was graced with a Near Death Experience (NDE), and as if on celestial tour, I soared through myriad planes of reality, each pulsating with energy and all interwoven in a unified field of Being. The unity of these celestial realms was striking. Each plane and vibration had a unique and purposeful tone. Everything was connected in and as one body. This body was manifesting as substance and expressing as the whole field, All That Is. Nothing was separate and each element was playing its part in a celestial song. I then remember feeling gripped with an awareness of a distinction between two energy fields.

The first field was an endless sea of creative force, brilliantly and gracefully vibrating as pure light-power-potential. I cannot put into words its grandeur or its simplicity. It was like the substance of Bliss interwoven with the essence of math, expressing as a lattice energy web of light. The other field appeared microcosmic in comparison, a tiny container of energy that was continuing to be molded within the larger field. This more opaque energy I understood to be manifesting as the earth and its governing laws. I saw how the awareness or "mind" of this energy didn't see itself or know the enormity of love that was being directed to it and in which it was being sustained. It was in a filmed-over container that wasn't aware of its relationship to the whole field.

In an instant, another dimension of incredibly tender intimacy opened. I became aware of my individual soul essence being held sweetly and lovingly within this enclosed, intimate sphere. I was awestruck. In a flash all of the light substance that made up this field was there before me, as one expression. I received the message, "This is for you." This vast Presence then poured Itself into twelve distinct elements, each with its own essential energy and power. One by one, I could feel them approach me, gifting me with their unique quality.

While I was being blessed with this mystical journey, my physical body had, without my conscious knowledge, been transported to a hospital and lay in a coma. I was outside of time and unaware of the earth plane, reveling in cascades of light and grace, until a blur of awareness, a haze of incomprehensible bewilderment, grew into an idea of existence again. I found myself in an unreal and confusing dream state, blurry, chaotic, and thick, and with a few broken bones and a severe head injury. It was a harsh and abrupt contrast, nothing like the vividness and clarity of the celestial realms I had been traveling in and that now felt like my only true reference for Reality.

The head injury weakened my sense of an individual self, the self that experiences itself as separate from the All. I came to know this as a gift of grace, as my thinking mind was not able to insist on the idea that I was separate from God. I was like a child who had little identification with life lived on this material plane; I was a brain-damaged but God-intoxicated, mystically aware woman-child.

The road to recovery was arduous. Months of rehabilitation were required for me to do basic mental and physical things, and it took years to heal completely. As time went on, sketches of my former life surfaced, like odd fragments of a movie I had seen on another planet and in the distant past. Making matters even more challenging and confusing, that movie was randomly playing in another movie in which I was currently starring. Life was surreal but I was content, not feeling my life or my will as my own. I did not feel that I existed in my body, but more as an idea in God's head.

The deep presence of love that I experienced in the NDE and that now filled my heart was more real than anything in the material world. It was made very clear to me, like a command, not to give myself to the world's appearance, and to keep giving myself to that love. Obedience to this command felt like a life and death issue. Living with this intensity built in me the strength for weathering what was to come.

After four years of bumping around, somewhat reassembling my life, I began a committed relationship with a man named Manuel. The vividness of our relating included deep love and struggle. The level of intimacy and our practice of fierce truth telling helped me integrate more fully into my body again. Manuel took a stand with me in the intention to bring forward an artistic expression of the energetic transmission I received during my NDE. His committed stand for the relationship and the artistic intention supported my energy not to just fly out and around but to focus. Everything, including myself, was reflected back to me. It was like I met myself in my body for the first time. I began to understand more about the art and music that were tapping through my skin, eagerly awaiting birth, as well as important principles of how energy worked. I learned that, as I show up, feel my feelings, and tell the truth, I am always given the understanding I need for the moment.

The training course that began then has never stopped. Its main lesson has been to fully feel and give myself to love without allowing my thinking mind to take over. This wasn't so difficult in the earlier years, but as time went on, I had to work harder for it. As I healed and my thinking mind got stronger, it took more discipline to stay in the field of divine perception.

I took my newly acquired authentic relating skills and applied them in my studio, as I stepped up with a paintbrush in hand. While remaining empty of judgments, I would be present with myself, the circumstances of my life, and the world about me. With a prayer for God's will and God's good, I would be consistently met and guided to the next step of my healing and revealing journey. This act of full presence was the source for the painting and music that would come.

A complete transmission had been given to me in my NDE, igniting a spirit fire within me. Finally, after nearly four years in close to a rapturous frenzy, looking for someone to tell me what to paint, I came face-to-face with myself. I recognized that the work was within me. I just needed to start and guidance would come.

I felt like an overdue pregnant woman in labor, my spiritual and emotional body swollen with this tangible presence and its fierce desire to be made manifest. The immense love that I felt just naturally moved me. I was able and willing to give whatever I had, without limits; nothing else mattered. More than anything, I wanted to serve and cultivate this love. The intensity of my desire sustained the creative tension that has kept me on purpose through the twists and turns of life.

Telling the deepest truth was natural and simple. I abided in innocence, like a child, free of ideas, fears, and judgments. I was empowered by my life in God and the inner visions that I painted. My willingness to follow the energy in the moment to its depth each day was like medicine. I would feel myself again and again in the arms of God, loving, nurturing, and healing me. Engaged in this spiritual practice, I began working on *The Second Coming* painting.

Guided by the vision in my NDE, I started painting twelve canvases, each expressing one of the unique essences that I received in my NDE. The twelve canvases together created a panoramic 8-foot by 5-foot painting. I applied almost every thought, circumstance, and action inside and outside of the studio to its unfolding. I moved in deep reverence, loving God, contemplating God, serving God. I would sing, dance, pray, chant mantras, and perform rituals. There was nothing I enjoyed more than being in this spiritual intimacy. Even the act of painting became secondary to my soul's song of bliss.

In the studio my priority was to be completely given, to not move unless I was guided. My practice was simply to keep myself inspired and to remain in the field of divine perception. Many days I would feel myself on a wave, floating in love, then I would merge with and become what I was loving. I would be loving God, and then there would be no me. I danced between loving God and not having an idea of myself.

As time went on and my journey progressed, the images of *The Second Coming* became deeper in content and more interconnected with detail. I had very little conscious conception of what I was painting, or what the finished work would be. I would sing and listen to the images with my whole body, and a greater wisdom than what I started with would sing back. An understanding of the details coming forth in the painting would faithfully follow.

As my thinking mind became stronger, I would fall into the illusion that I was separate from grace and God. My practice then became to take whatever time I needed to center in my whole self. I would not paint unless I could know myself in God. I learned to bring everything to the canvas: tender intimacy, prayers of the heart, sorrowful mourning, eroticism, anxiety, confusion, fear, rage, jealousy, anger, a feeling of being overwhelmed. I embraced them all, and I surrendered them all. The images for the painting and understanding of their significance would come regardless of the thought or feeling I started with; they made absolutely no difference. I simply began to paint, and was always given what I needed.

As the months of painting progressed, I evolved a deeper understanding of the context and content of what was being given. It was a visual rendition of the Twelve Powers and Holy Spirit Regeneration as taught by the Unity Movement — the soul's transformation, regeneration, and return to whole life in Christ-consciousness. I understood that *The Second Coming* was not only giving a transmission and understanding of the universal self, but was also actually giving a teaching for awakening in the Divine Self.

*The Second Coming* portrays the creation of the world and the journey back to Source. It depicts our soul's journey from the Mortal phase, when we are lost in the physical senses, to the Metaphysician phase (God and me), when we attune to the domain of Spirit, to the Mystic phase (God in me), when we radically surrender to Spirit and transcend worldly cares, culminating in Master or God-realization (God as me), where we identify as the whole field of existence. The mortal-metaphysician-mystic-master journey of the soul is a teaching derived from the Unity Movement.

I believe every soul embodies the Second Coming and has a Second Coming stirring in them, a path of awakening sourced from our very Self. We are liberated as we follow the lead of our hearts in love and passionate action. We are both the vast field of spaciousness and the substance within that field, Spirit with body. The Spirit of God is in every atom of our being and in every breath. We're awakening to the full state of the unified field, the full state of God-consciousness, the field of love that is drawing all of humanity into the One.

I now travel to New Thought churches and conferences around the country, showing *The Second Coming* painting and sharing the music it has inspired. It is a joy to witness people's experiences with the painting, because many are touched so deeply.

Since crashing from that wintry bridge in Missouri, bridges have become a metaphor for my life work. I am blessed to share art that bridges the material and celestial worlds, piercing the veil that separates heaven and earth to reveal in words and images that we are the Universe in expression, existing in and as an infinite field of possibility.

*To know the breath as grace, I need only be present.*
*To be present, I need only tell the truth.*
*To tell the truth, I need only courage.*
*To have courage, I need only know how much I am loved.*
*To know how much I am loved, I need only quiet the mind.*
*To quiet the mind, I need only sing the name of God.*

▼▼▼

**KIMBERLEE ANN KUWICA** is a visual and vocal artist who resides in the San Francisco Bay Area. With the support of her art and music ministry, Unity Way, she speaks, exhibits her work, and offers music and chanting events throughout the country, bringing forth the teachings and inspiration of *The Second Coming.* She can be contacted at unityway@aol.com to schedule speaking engagements or to purchase her artwork.

BY **STUART DAVIS**

## MEDITATION AND CREATIVITY

Three A.M. Though I'm lying in bed next to my zonked-out girlfriend with my eyes nearly closed, I'm wide awake. Or maybe I should say wide aware. This year, in addition to sitting meditation, I've started meditating in bed before and during sleep. I use simple practices focused on breathing in order to move my awareness to a place where I witness events (internal, external, physical, cerebral, et cetera) without identifying with them. Other times I'll use a mantra. I've only been meditating for a couple years, so I'm a beginner, but I've noticed some differences already, most notably in my creativity. The way I write songs, their content, and how I perform them have been changing right along with the way I've been changing as a person. Tonight, my creative and meditative dimensions are intermingling more deeply than usual.

As I lie trying to follow my breath and witness things with equanimity, something unusually compelling pops into my mind. It's a song. A new song. What makes it so unique and intriguing is that it has appeared complete and instantaneously, right out of nowhere. As a songwriter, I know this moment is like hitting the artistic jackpot. As a meditator, I know this moment may be a distraction that can yank my awareness out of hard-won focus. Conflicted this way, I run the same silent debate I've had a hundred times: should I break my focus to get up and write down this creative burst? If I don't, I may lose a special song. If I do, I feel like a bad meditator, a scatterbrain who meanders off the path whenever something beguiling appears. But then, part of me argues (or perhaps rationalizes) this song is about spiritual seeking. Rumi created thousands of poems while spinning in an ecstatic state. My lyrics may not compare to Rumi's poems, but maybe it's okay to explore a creative flow that comes during meditation. Discernment is key: I can't just jump up every time my brain generates an idea while I'm meditating. But this song feels like it came through my brain, not from my brain. This sort of creativity is new to me, but my intuition tells me I won't be spiritually AWOL if I get up to write down the song. So, I do. It is simply this:

> It was easy
> when I thought I had to go somewhere
> to find You
> now I learn
> that I must attend to my own funeral
> while this body still works
> so that You may look through these eyes
> and draw breath through this nose
> and reach with these fingers
> and pulse with this heart
> who am I
> to keep You from Your house?

When these words appear, they are without music. But, as I write them down in my dream journal next to the bed, a melody arrives too. There it is, a new song, but I feel as if I haven't done any writing. It's more as if by meditating I created an internal setting that precipitated the creative burst. Later, I write more lyrics to it, to "finish" it (with a discerning artistic eye?), and then give it to my Sufi teacher. Without knowing any history of which lyrics were written when, my teacher circles the original lyrics that came in meditation and writes the comment "wonderful." He also underlines exactly my later additions and writes, "Is this material necessary?"

Reading his comments, I burst out laughing. Caught red-handed! Over time, I've started to get the hint that in some cases my most important job as a songwriter is not to write but to learn to open an inner space for things to come through, and then to know when I shouldn't meddle with the results. I can't say precisely where or what such lyrics emerge from, but I think it's safe to rule out the ego.

I can sense where a song comes from by what part of me is moved when I write and play it. The above song is about the ego lying down so that something greater can move in. It appeared when I was in a more open, aware state, and when I play it, I feel a softening and expanding take place within me. These are all good indicators that its genesis was somewhere beyond the ego. I can check any of my songs in this way and trace their roots. I have lots of songs that I know come from my intellect, emotions, or wit because that part of me was buzzing when I wrote them, and the same part is gratified in playing them. The smart-ass in me gets a kick out of writing something like:

*Stephen's exhibition is a masterpiece to see*
*it's a series done in oil of his wife in bed with me*
*in really wild positions, all throughout his home*
*we cluttered every room with empty tubes of paint and foam*
*he's done good work before, but this is closer to his heart*
*I'm glad that I could help out my friend Stephen with his art*

But such a song never comes out of a meditative state. Work like that comes out of my brain, and takes a lot of thinking to write. For a long time thinking and egotistic emoting were the only way I created, but meditation has brought more to the way I write songs, what they're about, and how I perform them. Although having a song appear completely finished is still a rare event, it has become very common for me to write songs with tools other than just my brain.

Many of my creative blocks are now resolved by meditating for a while and stilling the thinking part of my mind. Whereas I once would sit for days on end pulling out my hair (most people still think I *shaved* my head) trying to come up with the next witty, intellectual zinger for one of my verses, now when I become blocked I often choose to lie back and focus on my breath and open an inner space. I still write songs using my intellect, but it's no longer the only way I write. Of course, blending creativity and meditation doesn't mean that whenever I meditate I get a song out of it, or that God is writing songs for me and then dropping them in whenever I open up enough. But I think it does mean that I have access to parts of my self that run much deeper than my intellect, and that those dimensions can be every bit as active in the creative process as my brain has been. For me, this means developing intimacy with Spirit, and when the intimacy is there (even a little bit), it has a great deal of influence on my creativity. There are artistic drives present in the subconscious, conscious, and super-conscious awareness, and meditation enables my creativity to move more freely among all three. Exploring this new creative terrain not only changes where my songs can come from but what they're about.

## AND IS THIS MY BEAUTIFUL HOUSE?

When I took up esoteric spiritual practices, it was because of an ache that was tough to describe, but unmistakably real. I felt a need for closeness with God, through something more than just beliefs. Reading or hearing people talk about God just made me sick, like I was being shown pictures of food to treat my starvation. What did seem to help was prayer/meditation, and my creativity. In retrospect

I think that my art was a mystical start-up kit. In fact, all the time that religion was empty for me, art kept my soul going. I started using songs to help create a closeness with Spirit.

The Sufis say that if you take one step toward God, God comes running toward you. Soon after I started exploring my spirituality through songs, that became the only thing I could write about. It went from me wanting to take a closer look at spirituality to me looking at everything from a spiritual perspective. Opening a different kind of awareness in prayer and meditation carried over into and colored the rest of my life. Everything from sleep, sex, and eating to driving, watching TV, and especially songwriting looked and felt different. And if I wrote a song about sleep, sex, eating, or whatever, Spirit would show up there every time. I would write a song about a cowboy, and it would come out like this:

*They say I'm how the West was won*
*that's a God-dammed myth*
*the West is what I'm One with*

I'd write a song about sex and it would end up like this:

*Every body wants to taste*
*a little something carbon based*
*sex is proof the Holy Ghost*
*crawls around in stuff that's gross*
*yea!*

If I tried to go for the opposite and write about the Devil, I ended up with this:

*God is Spirit*
*Spirit is everything*
*even the Devil*

And war:

*Right now they're building Gandhis*
*they're gonna bomb our ass with Love*
*and bring us to our knees*
*just using what we're made of*

Even when I didn't want to write songs about Spirit, I would end up writing songs about how I didn't want to write songs about Spirit:

> *What I refuse*
> *You will use to surround me*
> *I spit out Your seeds*
> *and You grow all around me*
> *even my poison flowers in You*

Since then I've been getting what I've asked for, which is simply some One awakening in my heart, which changes my inner and outer worlds. It doesn't mean that I've magically had all my faults removed. Far from it. I still have all the same laziness, lust, greed, arrogance, fear, and on and on. But the difference is that now there's Something Else present in addition to all those things. I'm able to witness, to observe those aspects from a place that both acknowledges their reality *and* their impermanence. Very slowly, my sense of identity is moving into that place, where *I* am the awareness of the stuff that comes and goes, but ultimately, I'm not the stuff that comes and goes. My personality is finite and impermanent, but my awareness does not have to be finite and impermanent. Songwriting is one way I can move into that witness, one way I can observe the qualities without clutching them. The old baggage is still there, but my relationship to it is changing. My relationship to everything is changing, including how I approach giving concerts.

## LIVE FROM BUDDHAKHAN...

Because I can get stressed out before a show, I often hide in the greenroom (when there is one) and meditate or repeat a mantra before I go on. On one tour, I started repeating the words to a song I had recently written like they were a mantra:

> *stretch this thread into Your loom*
> *pick this rose to scent Your room*
> *boil this leaf to make Your tea*

*boil me*
*mold the bones that form this face*
*break the dam that holds Your grace*
*burn a wick so Light can be*
*burn me*

The message was simply offering all parts of myself in hopes that God would reinvent them. It worked. It worked a little too well. Because when I did go onstage, I found myself no longer able to automatically slip into my "entertainer" stage persona, and if I did, another part of me was observing it for what it really was: vanity. From this new perspective, I could see how my ego craved to get up and be the center of attention, and how shows could often just be a vehicle for the gratification of *me! me! me!* As the tour went on, I started to become less and less fulfilled by doing shows where I was mostly being smart, witty, shocking, or entertaining. I needed something more out of them.

A tension formed between my inner world, where I had been seeking closeness with Spirit, and my outer world, where I was still the outrageous performer. I was writing tender songs about God in private, and then doing shows where I would fall right into my old routines of being the guy with the big brain and crazy antics. I began feeling untrue, being touched by Spirit in meditation and writing and then getting on stage and forgetting all about it. I was trying to have my metaphysical cake and eat it too. But those tidy compartments were starting to merge, and boy did my ego piss and moan when it realized that its free ride was about to end.

Over one hundred times a year for seven years I have gathered with strangers who offer their attention for over an hour. Only now have I started consciously asking, What do I want to do with that attention? For much of my performing life my ego has soaked it up like the sponge that it is. But, just as meditation has taught me that sometimes my job as a songwriter is to create a space, and not to fill one, it has also shown me that my role as a performing artist includes putting people's focus on things beyond just the performance. Nothing else can be the center of attention as long as my personality is inflated like a big balloon on stage. But if I deflate it from time to time, some beautiful surprises can then arise. There is a place for both actually, the balloon of my personality and the space for something more. Both can be part of the same evening. It isn't a matter of either/or, the ego versus the soul, it's more about knowing how to coordinate them so that they work together.

And they can work in harmony. In fact, ego is actually an asset in increasing the depth of a show. It can be a crucial set-up tool. For instance, I use entertaining or accessible material as breathing space between songs with deeper messages, so that the evening keeps moving through different layers. And I often find humor to be an ally when sneaking into a delicate subject. Knowing how to pace this dance, where personality grabs people's attention and then steps aside to make space for something greater, is a skill I'm still learning. Of course, sometimes it's impossible to get beyond the surface, but that's almost always because everyone in the audience is drunk. Then I either stay on the surface or annoy the hell out of a hundred drunks with songs about spiritual intimacy. Trust me, that can be dangerous in some parts of America.

Even when an audience is amenable to going deeper, it's still the hardest part of my practice to resist playing on the surface where there's an easy payoff for just being entertaining. It's tough to surrender the show to the Heart when it's so safe and fun to stay in the brain. But frolicking in the brain all night gives me a metaphysical hangover after the show, and those are even harder to deal with than surrender is. Luckily, if I say a mantra long enough, it keeps going even when I'm not trying to repeat it, and that reminds me during a show that I should be steering things toward the Heart from time to time. One thing is for sure: if I don't surrender and open up, the audience won't either.

Being a performer is like being a tuning fork. I try to get people to vibrate at the same frequency for a while. When I'm able to become totally unselfconscious playing certain songs, the audience sometimes opens up in similar ways. People's boundaries will drop from time to time during a show, without them even realizing it's happening. The best part of giving concerts is simply being in a room when this happens, and right out of nowhere (again!) a bunch of strangers suddenly all forget their *selves* and fall into a shared, contemplative stillness. It doesn't happen all that often, but often enough to keep me waiting for the next time. That's what I always wanted church to be like: unacquainted people letting down their walls and connecting through what is common to them all, Spirit. Concerts are another kind of church, a setting that encourages raising the consciousness of a group of people through inner and outer activity. A perfect blend of the exoteric and esoteric.

While I know that greater awareness is available to me at all times, the reality is that I'm only able to tap into it intermittently. My hope is to find "on" more often and have "off" become more infrequent. I also realize that the way meditation has changed my songwriting and performing is really just a happy by-product of the real blessing, which is being more aware of Spirit. The Heart is the gem, and art is the play of Light shining through it.

On tour a few weeks before I wrote this, I was meditating before a show. I had a very strong notion pop out of nowhere that said I should change the way I perform one of my new songs, "Infinity Hymn." Typically I play it like I do all my other songs, just me and my guitar. But this impulse said to change it so the audience had the more important part. The song uses a single note to represent the presence of Unity throughout all manifest and unmanifest reality. Normally, I sing a verse, then sum up its message by simply humming one note, the note that stands for God. But instead, on that night, I changed it so the audience and I sang together after every verse, so that each of us was in the role of God. With a couple hundred voices humming the same note in one room, I was reminded how each of us really is God, that our essence is that unifying hum from which all else issues.

*Every atom plays the hymn*
*every echo is from within*
*every eardrum makes a map*
*and it sounds like this when one hand claps:*
(audience hums the note in unison: hmmmmmmmm...)

▼▼▼

**STUART DAVIS** is a performing songwriter with international recognition and ten albums to his credit, including *Bright Apocalypse, Kid Mystic, Nomen est Numen,* and *16 Nudes.* He tours extensively, doing more than a hundred shows each year. Stuart's Web site can be found at: www.stuartdavis.com.

# MEDITATION IN JUVENILE HALL

## BY SOREN GORDHAMER

**IT TOOK EIGHT MONTHS** to begin meditation classes at the local juvenile hall, seven months of talking about it and one month of letters, phone calls, and meetings. The director was not sure the kids would go for it. He said that if we expected the kids to sit down, cross their legs, and watch their breath for forty-five minutes, we were mistaken. My coleader, Jason Murphy, was a former resident of the hall and worked as a drug rehabilitation counselor with a similar population. He said, "We could teach basket weaving and, if we are genuine, they will go for it. They watch you, not what you say." The director warned us: "You need to be a master of your art. If you show signs of weakness or doubt, they will see it and blow you away. They won't hold back."

The first night, we walked through three locked gates and a quad to arrive in an all-purpose room that would serve as a meditation hall.

As we put the chairs in a circle, a worker asked, "We got some kids who misbehaved and are in lockdown. You want them in here?" "Sure," we responded. "Also, Johnny is planning on coming. He has the attention span of a fly. You sure you want him in here?" "Yes, of course."

Ten boys and girls finally meandered through the door. Some had tattoos, others had funky hairstyles, and all had a particular toughness about them. The kids were in for everything from skipping school to murder. We introduced ourselves, went over the guidelines of the class, talked about respect, and then spoke in simple terms about meditation: finding what is true, being with the moment as it is, developing mindfulness. We then went around and asked what they wanted out of the class. "An ability to levitate," said the first kid. Everyone laughed. Most talked about wanting to better control their anger. Juan leaned back in his chair and announced, "I love two things in life: marijuana and violence. But violence gets me into trouble. I know when I get out of here it will be easy to get back in a gang and start busting people up. I don't want to do that anymore." Anger thus became the primary theme of the class.

We guided them in a silent mindfulness of breathing meditation. No one walked out, yelled, or made too many wisecracks. A decent start. Johnny, with the fly's attention span, nervously shook his leg the entire time, but hung in there. Most of the kids kept their eyes closed and did their best. Sitting still was probably the hardest activity many had ever done.

Next we conducted a short loving-kindness meditation, focusing on sending love to oneself then spreading it out into the world. This seemed much easier. Since this was the first class, we did not ask for comments about their experiences. We wanted to let the kids keep the experience to themselves. However, after the loving-kindness meditation, Audrey looked up and spontaneously said, "That was tight." "You mean you were tense?" I inquired. "No, it was tight. That means it was good; it was cool." "Oh."

Our class certainly had its difficult moments. Johnny, in particular, made a lot of wisecracks and disrupted the group occasionally, and I was not experienced in dealing with such behavior in a meditation class. Finally, Audrey had all she could take of Johnny's antics. During one supposedly silent meditation, Johnny decided to eat an orange loudly. I thought of the Vietnamese monk Thich Nhat Hanh and his tangerine meditation and said nothing, but Audrey was fuming. After the meditation, she glared at him across the room. Then forcefully shaking her finger at him, she shouted, "He's fucking up my meditation." I was dumbfounded. I had never previously heard the F word and the M word used in the same sentence. No one had ever cussed or shouted in any meditation group I had been in. Should I get mad at her for cussing or at him for making noise? I did the only thing I could think of at the time: sat there with my mouth open. Audrey gave him an ultimatum: "Fucking take this seriously or else fucking leave." He left. A great weight lifted from the class. Everyone seemed much more committed and focused. I was confused by this, though happy that Audrey cared enough about her meditation to defend her right to sit quietly.

Another night, when I led a meditation on kindness, I asked everybody to remember a time when someone was kind to them. "What did it feel like to receive this kindness? Can you feel it in your body?" Then, I asked them to remember a time when they were kind to someone else, even if it was something really small. Next, I said to send this kindness to all the people in the room, then to others outside.

Afterward, we asked them how it was. "Could you bring to mind times you both received and gave kindness?" One guy answered, "I could picture it. For the first one, I thought of my mom, who has always stood by my side through my court appearances. She always shows up to court." He lowered his head, a bit shy. "Then for the other one, I remembered how I used to let my homeboys sneak into my house and sleep when they needed a place to crash. Even if everyone else was on their case, I would let them in and feed them." Then he looked to the other guys in the room, first at a guy across from him: "I wished you happiness and hoped you would get to see your child soon." Turning to another, he said,

"I wished that your court appearance next week goes well." And to another, "I wished that your relationship with your parents improves." Around the room he went. All the other kids seemed to take in the good wishes. The room was filled with a feeling of trust and support.

The classes were rarely what I expected. Once during guided meditation, we encouraged them to see their thoughts arising and passing away as if watching train cars pass by. After the meditation, Juan said, "That was great. I was just sitting there smoking a joint and watching a train go by." Not exactly what I had in mind, but what do you say? Strangely, Juan seemed to get more out of the classes than anyone else and expressed the desire to continue the practice after he got released. He had spoken about the benefits he was receiving and was very curious about books and practice centers in the world beyond juvenile hall. He seemed touched by the practice, and I was happy and excited for him.

Later in the year, though, I was saddened to see Juan walking through the hallway in the juvenile hall. Back behind bars. Perhaps, though, he might be interested in coming to the meditation class that evening. I said hello and invited him to the class. "Man, not tonight," he said, lowering his head. "Too much is going on. I recently got my girlfriend pregnant, and I have been charged with attempted murder." He turned away.

"Attempted murder!" I thought to myself. "I teach you to meditate, then you go and try to kill someone! What on earth were you thinking? Go back to your breath, for crying out loud. Soften, and calm yourself, damn it!" But at that moment, I was the one who needed to calm myself. I tried to soften around my reaction to Juan's words. The last thing he needed was for me to vocalize such thoughts, so I told him that I understood and would look forward to seeing him the following week.

Juan's news made me question the reason I was showing up at the hall each week. I wanted to make a difference to the kids, to teach them skills that would help calm their bodies and focus their minds. I wanted to show them an alternative to drugs and violence. But I realized that I had presumed an unstated agreement: I will show up if you agree to act in a certain way. Juan had broken the agreement, and my first impulse was to give up the classes all together.

Looking more deeply, I saw that he forced me to explore my intentions in working with this group of kids and raised some basic questions for me about meditation practice. What is the heart of the practice, anyhow? Am I offering this heart to these kids or just teaching meditation techniques? How do we share our practice with those who are not seeking it, our judgmental aunt, our hyperactive child, our depressed neighbor, or a tough kid at juvenile hall? A Zen master gives students paradoxical questions called koans on which to meditate, eventually leading to a flash of enlightened understanding. Questions like these continue to serve as my koans.

It's now been almost six years since I taught those first classes in juvenile hall. Through the Lineage Project, a nonprofit I started with my friend, Andrew Getz, I currently teach about eight classes a week for incarcerated teens in New York City. These facilities hold the toughest, poorest, and most troublesome teens of all the boroughs. Many of them are in for very serious offenses, like armed robbery, attempted murder, and murder. Classes over these years have gotten easier as more and more of the kids have become accustomed to our program. The kids who end up in juvenile hall come in with enormous stress, and both desperately want help and are extremely suspicious of everybody. Whenever I start a new class, there is usually a "feel out" stage. This involves the kids insulting both the practices and me, then watching how I respond. "You ever been told you look like that guy from *Ghostbusters*, Egon? Nah, you look like Slinky Man. This meditation stuff is dumb. People really like to do this? I can't believe how stupid this stuff is." Sometimes these comments express legitimate doubt about the class, but mainly the kids are putting me through an initiation. Can I be insulted? How do I respond when the practices I hold to dearly are criticized? Their central question seems to be, "Do I care about them more than I care about them doing meditation or yoga? Where is my true commitment?"

I have also gone from introducing practices like meditation

and yoga as something new and different to something that in some ways they already know and do. I often ask them, "What is the difference between meditation and 'chilling'?" After I ask this, I often follow it up with, "What is the opposite of chill?" Most the kids respond with the word "hyped." I then ask, "Would people rather be chill or hyped?" Everyone agrees that people would rather be chill. So this is our common ground, our common denominator, no matter our age or skin color. Then the question is, "How do we help each other reach this goal? And how do we live in a way that makes it better for others, to create less pain both for ourselves and others?"

I've also learned that how I relate to the guard as I enter the center is as important as whatever I say in the class. The same is true with how I relate to the other staff and to the kids who are not into the practices. Do I relate to the kids who are not into it with frustration and anger, or is there a larger teaching here? A number of months ago a kid named Jamal used to come to my class every week. Though he showed up each week, he never really tried to do the yoga, and during the meditation, he would keep his eyes open and look around like he was bored. However, after the class, he always gave me a big hug and said thank you. I later learned that he was on trial for a gang-related murder. I started to get frustrated with Jamal because I thought, "Why keep coming to this class if you are not interested in the meditation or yoga? What's your problem?"

It then hit me one day: he didn't come to the class for meditation or yoga; he came for a hug. He did not have the problem. I did. It might be the only hug he got all week. If he was not being disruptive, why not come to the class for a hug? I began to see how limited my views were of how love should be expressed. Gradually Jamal was able to close his eyes for a short time during the meditation, and he seemed a little more engaged in the yoga. But if my devotion was strictly on youth doing meditation or yoga, I would have given up on Jamal a long time ago. I began to see how I could use even spiritual practices as another thing for the kids to feel hard on themselves about instead of as an expression of care and compassion for themselves. While certain guidelines need to be followed in class and I sometimes ask disruptive students to leave, the kids need to feel genuine care from me or nothing is going to work. If my care and devotion are not for them as people, then I'm just one other person with an agenda for them, just another person trying to fix them, and they want no part of it.

I've also realized that there is an amazing amount of compassion and love underneath their tough exterior frames. During a recent class, we got in a heated discussion about whether it is a good thing to help people. Several people thought helping people was a good idea, but a kid named Michael did not want to hear it. "I know it don't work to help people," he said, sitting up in his chair and speaking with great sadness and intensity. "You know why I'm in here? I'm in here 'cause I tried to help out a friend. My friend, who is like a brother to me, tells me that his momma just got laid off and that he wants my help getting them rent money. He wanted me to rob this store with him. I knew it wasn't right, but I wanted to help my friend and his family, so I told him that I would do anything he wanted. And I knew I was putting my life on the line for him. Anytime you do a robbery, you know you're putting your life on the line, but I was ready to do it. So we both got guns and walked in the store. We pulled out our guns and said give us the money. Then the manager comes from the back of the store with a fuckin' shotgun pointing right at us. I was like, *Shit!* I put down my gun and put my hands in the air, but my friend takes off. He left me there standing. So now I'm probably going to do several years and all I was doing was helping out my friend." He was right at the edge of tears. I was speechless. I looked around, and everyone seemed to relate to the pain of thinking that you are helping out a friend, and that friend leaving you, and you having to do the time.

A kid then asked, "Where is your friend now?"

"He's on the streets," Michael said.

"I would pop that mother fucker if I was you."

"I ain't going to pop him. He is like a brother."

On one hand, Michael made a very bad decision that could

have resulted in someone getting hurt or killed. On the other hand, he had enormous compassion for his friend's situation and great courage to put his life on the line to help out his friend. Many of the youth like him have such love that yearns to be expressed but too often gets acted out in painful ways, because the situation they are in offers them few alternatives. While they are responsible for their actions, we all share some responsibility for the situation. If I had grown up in the conditions of the kids with single or no parents, crime-ridden communities, and intense poverty, I would have likely resorted to some of the same crimes. It's a system in which we all play a part. We are all a part of this problem and the solution.

We will now spend roughly $150,000 in two years locking Michael up, when all he and his friend needed was $200 to cover rent. But as kids from the inner city, they had few other options. He will likely come out after his time with few skills, more anger, and with a resolve to never try to help anyone ever again. Our challenge should not be just to punish youth but to give them a bigger challenge, to show them ways they can use their natural caring for community, which often gets played out in gangs, and their desire for altered states, which often gets played out only through drugs, in a way that truly benefits the world. Too often we give young people the vision of "stay out of trouble" when we need to help them make "good trouble," to use that rebellion to make important changes in our society. The greatest sadness I see on boys' faces is when they find out that their kid brother has been arrested. They can suffer for their own actions, but when they realize that their actions and example helped lead to the suffering of the person they should be helping, they can't hold back the sadness. The care they have is enormous yet so rarely recognized or acknowledged.

The challenge seems to be making the space where the deeper care and longing for meaning can come forth. For some youth, they say the only time they feel truly alive is when they are running from the cops or doing a drug deal. Telling them not to do crime is like telling them not to feel fully alive. Instead, we need to find other ways to meet their need for aliveness and meaning. How we begin to address these issues, whether through meditation, nature walks, singing, or something altogether unique, is not so important, but that the subject is addressed and that space is available for youth to openly explore their inner world — this is paramount. We need to give them other ways to feel the aliveness that they seek. As one guy said after a meditation, "That was weird. I usually only feel this good when I am doing something illegal!"

▼▼▼

**SOREN GORDHAMER** is author of *Meetings with Mentors* (Hanford Mead, 1995) and a meditation book for young adults called *Just Say OM!* (Adams Media, 2001). He is cofounder of the Lineage Project, a program of the Tides Center, focused on offering awareness practices like meditation and yoga to incarcerated teens. He is currently executive director of Lineage Project East and teaches meditation at numerous places in New York City, including the New York City Juvenile Justice System.

# COMMITTED: LOVE IN ACTION

### BY JULIA BUTTERFLY HILL

**I WAS BORN INTO A DEEPLY RELIGIOUS FAMILY.** My father was an itinerant preacher and we traveled across the country offering our service to rural communities. My father would preach, my mother would sing, and my brothers and I would perform puppet shows to entertain the young ones. My early life lessons were to respect my elders and to offer myself to the greater good.

In our family we placed God first, community service second, and our own personal concerns last. Like many teenagers, I rebelled against my upbringing and questioned the way I was raised. Because we were extremely poor and religious, I rebelled by valuing money and deviating from organized religion.

I graduated from high school at sixteen. I decided to study business in college because I truly believed that our value in society was measured by our financial wealth. Because I am someone who prefers experiential learning, I left college and opened my own restaurant when I was eighteen. I am a hard worker, and the next two years of my life were devoted to this business. I even helped others run their enterprises. My life revolved around saving for the future. Yet like most young people, I liked to party and have fun.

In 1996, I was out late with some friends, and I was the designated driver. I was driving a small two-door hatchback and was rear-ended by a drunk driver in a Ford Bronco. The steering wheel jammed into my skull, causing brain damage.

The accident affected my short-term memory and my motor skills. I underwent nearly a year of cognitive and physical therapy. During this period, I had time to contemplate the possibility that I might not fully recover. What if I could not function normally again and what if that impaired my ability to work and earn money, the way I had become accustomed? This possibility struck a chord in me that forced me to question my perceived values. I realized that my value as a human being was certainly greater than my ability to earn money. I began to ponder what my true meaning and purpose on Earth were.

When your way of life is threatened, nothing is ever the same. I suddenly saw everything in a new light. All the time and space I had taken for granted became precious. I realized that I had always been looking ahead and planning instead of making sure that every moment counted for something. Perhaps because I had injured the analytical side of my brain, the more creative side began to take over, and my perspective shifted. It became clear to me that our value as people is not in our stock portfolios and bank accounts but in the legacies of life that we leave behind.

My parents' legacy began to take hold. I guess I really am the daughter of a preacher. Having survived this horrible accident, I developed a greater appreciation for the sanctity of all life. I resolved to change my life and follow a spiritual path. If I was to become whole — and that meant body, mind, and spirit — I was going to have to find out where I was meant to be and what I needed to do. I decided that, when I was well enough, I would go on a journey around the world. I would visit places that had deep spiritual roots. In those roots, in that common thread of spirituality, I felt, I would find my sense of purpose.

Once I had recovered sufficiently to travel, I jumped at the first opportunity for adventure that presented itself. Neighbors were heading west to California, and I joined them. Along the way, we had a chance encounter with someone who raved about the beauty of the Lost Coast of California and the redwoods.

On the way to the magnificent shore, we entered Grizzly Creek State Park to see the California redwood giants. Upon entering the forest, I felt something calling to me. I started walking faster and experiencing an exhilarating energy. I broke into a run, leaping over logs as I plunged deeper into the forest.

After about a half mile, the beauty of my surroundings started to hit me. I slowed down for a better look. The farther I walked, the larger the ferns grew, until three people with outstretched arms couldn't have encircled them. Lichen, moss, and fungus sprouted everywhere.

The trees were so big that I couldn't see their crowns. Their trunks were so large that ten individuals holding hands would barely be able to wrap around them. Some of the trees were hollow, scorched away by lightning strikes and forest fires. Wrapped in the fog and moisture that they need to grow, these ancient giants stood primordial and eternal, a long line of sentinels stretching back to the age of the dinosaurs. My feet sank into rich earth with each step. I knew I was walking on millennia of compounded history.

As I headed farther into the forest, I could no longer hear the sounds of cars or smell their fumes. I breathed in the pure, wonderful air. It tasted sweet on my tongue. Everywhere I turned I could see, smell, hear, taste, and touch life force. For the first time, I really felt what it was like to be alive, to feel the connection of all life.

The energy hit me in a wave. Gripped by the spirit of the forest, I dropped to my knees and began to sob. Surrounded by these ancient giants, I felt the sensory film caused by our fast-paced, technologically dependent society melt away. I could feel my whole being bursting forth into new life in this majestic cathedral. The tears turned to joy and mirth as I drank in the beauty of it all.

Two weeks later, I learned that if I had walked a little farther

along the path, I would have been dumped into a clear-cut cour-
tesy of Pacific Lumber (PL)/Maxxam Corporation. When I first
saw a photograph of a clear-cut, I thought that a bomb had been
dropped in the forest because the land looked devoid of all life,
charred and desolate. The photos depicted a horizontal forest
where ancient trees criss-crossed the landscape like scattered bones.
"How could redwoods that could thrive for thousands of years be
felled by chain saws in less than an hour?" I grieved that our culture
could destroy such a precious gift of Creation.

Learning about the clear-cuts made me feel like a part of myself
was being ripped apart and violated, just as the forests were. For
me, these redwood cathedrals are the holiest of temples, housing
more spirituality than any church. I desperately wanted to do
something positive to help protect these ancient beings that are the
lungs of the planet.

I returned to the Lost Coast to pray for guidance. I believe in
prayer, but ultimately the biggest power in prayer for me comes
from the willingness to accept the answers. So I added, "If I'm truly
meant to come back and fight for these forests out here, please help
me know what I'm meant to do, and use me as a vessel."

On December 10, 1997, when I was 23, I climbed into the
canopy of a thousand-year-old redwood tree named Luna to try to
save her life and to help make the world aware of the plight of
ancient forests. From my perch 180 feet above the ground, I was
able to see the Pacific Lumber mill where redwoods are turned into
lumber. I could see the Eel River swollen with mud from defor-
ested slopes. I could see the town of Stafford that was destroyed by
a mud slide caused by PL's/Maxxam clear-cutting practices.

When I lived in the branches of Luna, I withstood El Niño
storms, helicopter logging that ravaged the forest canopy, and the
tremendous sorrow of witnessing the family of trees surrounding
Luna cut to the ground. Each time a chain saw cut through those
trees, I felt it cut through me as well. It was like watching my
family being killed. And just as we lose a part of ourselves with the
passing of a family member or friend, so I lost a part of myself with
each fallen tree.

Like any threatened animal that is torn from its habitat, my first impulse was to strike out at the forces that were killing the forests. I wanted to stop the violence, pain, and suffering. I wanted to stop the men who were cutting the hillside in complete disregard for the forest and the people's lives in the town of Stafford below. I had hate for everything, including myself, because I was disgusted to be part of a race of people with such a lack of respect.

I knew that if I didn't find a way to deal with my anger and hate, they would overwhelm me and I would be swallowed up in the fear, sadness, and frustration. To hate and strike out was to be a part of the same violence I was trying to stop. And so I prayed: "Please, Universal Spirit, please help me find a way to deal with this, because if I don't, it's going to consume me."

I have seen a lot of activists overcome. The intense negative forces that are oppressing and destroying the Earth wind up overcoming many of them. They get so absorbed by the hate and anger that they become hollow. I didn't want to go there. Instead, my hate had to turn to love, unconditional Agape love.

One day, through my prayers, an overwhelming amount of love started flowing into me, filling up the dark hole that threatened to consume me. I suddenly realized that I was feeling the love of the Earth, the love of Creation. Every day we, as a species, do so much to destroy Creation's ability to give us life. But the Earth continues to give us life anyway. And that's true love.

If the Creation source and Mother Earth keep giving us the gift of life, then I had to find it within myself to feel and express unconditional love for the Earth and humanity, even for those destroying the gift of life.

Through a series of challenges, I was able to experience and transform feelings of frustration, rage, and grief into perseverance and positive action. I was broken on every level, physically, emotionally, mentally, and spiritually. It was only after living in the face of destruction and being pummeled by the elements that I could rise to my highest potential: a being inspired by love of the Earth and humankind.

When I almost died in a torrential storm, tossed about like a rag doll for sixteen hours in ninety-mile-an-hour winds, I lost my fear of dying, which proved to be the last attachment. Letting go of fear and embracing love freed me, like the butterfly frees itself of its cocoon. I began to live day by day, moment by moment, breath by breath, and prayer by prayer. I had come through darkness and storms and had been transformed.

True metamorphosis occurs only when we face our attachments and inner demons, free from the buzz of commercial distraction and false social appearances. At some point in our lives we need to leave the comfort and security of our cocoons and emerge as creatures with fragile wings and a strong resolve to survive life's hardships.

The image of the butterfly has been with me since childhood. When I was a child, I was often melancholy and despondent because of difficulties in my life. During times when I felt alone in the world, I often found solace in nature. When I was seven years old, a butterfly landed on me and stayed with me for hours while I hiked in the mountains of Pennsylvania. Since then butterflies have always come to me in times of need, sometimes in reality and other times in visions and dreams. At one point, a vision came to me of a butterfly poking out of a cocoon. When it finally broke free it was a magical butterfly with prismatic colors. As the butterfly emerged, the cocoon's brown shell turned into a shimmering ribbon that unwound. The message that came to me with this vision was, *Through life's trials and hardships we arise beautiful and free.*

That was when I began to learn how to internalize the process of the butterfly, which is all about understanding and letting go of our attachments. There were many times in the course of the two-year Luna vigil that I had to let go of my attachments, including my attachment to my own life and personal comforts.

There were moments when it would have been easy to feel too comfortable in Luna. Connecting to her in such a strong way was a heady experience. But when we feel too comfortable, we make careless mistakes. And at 180 feet off the ground, a fall, or even an accident, could have killed me. So even when I slept, my senses remained attuned, because a creak or a groan could have meant that something was breaking that my life might literally depend on.

I couldn't afford to ever really relax, because I couldn't afford to make a mistake. And not just on the physical front; I had to be on guard spiritually as well. Because my actions, increasingly spotlighted, affected people's perceptions about the forest, environmentalism, and direct action, I felt that I needed to be careful about my every word and deed. The timber industry and corporate government could attempt to exploit and discredit me, and I was concerned that that could strip other activists of their credibility. I often felt exhausted and drained by the responsibility of being a spokesperson and the struggles of living without everyday comforts.

Yet each time that I'd start to feel the fire within me wane and that I couldn't face another day, the great spirits of the universe would send something to fan those flames into the bonfire I needed to renew my strength. When I felt overwhelmed by demands and pressure, I would remind myself to take time and remember to breathe. That was part of the lesson that Luna taught me: to be still and listen, even in the chaos of my life.

Prayer had taken me to the Lost Coast, prayer is what guided me to the redwood forest, and prayer is what led me to Luna. Prayer is what had given me the strength to continue all this time. And someday, I knew, prayer, patience, and an open heart would guide me down.

Prayer taught me to practice compassion, understanding, and acceptance of our perceived differences. The common thread that humanity shares is that we are all children of the Earth. We all need clean air, food, and water for our survival. We are all planetary citizens, and the ancient trees are living, breathing elders that remind us to respect and honor what we cannot replace.

Every religion in the world builds shrines, temples, and churches so people can worship and feel connected to Creation. The ancient forest cathedrals are also places of worship where we feel connected to the Creation source. Yet they are continually desecrated by industrial logging practices. The desire to protect these sacred forests can unite all denominations, because protecting the remaining ancient forest ecosystems is a moral imperative on behalf of all life.

For millennia the two-million-acre redwood ecosystem thrived and sheltered myriad species of life. In the last 150 years, 97 percent of the original redwood forests have been destroyed by timber corporations. With only 3 percent of these native forests remaining, species like the marbled murrelet and coho salmon are on the brink of extinction; at the same time, people fear that they will lose their jobs and futures. Big business cut-and-run logging operations have instilled a false dichotomy: jobs versus the environment. As long as we label each other "loggers" and "environmentalists," it is difficult to find our common ground and restore the forests and diversity that are our true legacy.

During the tree sit, I dialogued with loggers in an effort to reach common ground and gain a deeper understanding of the issues. I developed a good rapport with the workers, but the spokespeople of Pacific Lumber continued to dehumanize me. After awhile though, PL/Maxxam realized that their threats and actions were not forcing me down from Luna. Because I had learned to speak out from a place of compassion and love, higher-ups within PL started to treat me like a person rather than an "eco-terrorist."

I was like water wearing away at the stone. Water acts differently than a hammer and chisel, which chip away at something. I was just a constant presence that sooner or later would be heard. Not because I'd pounded in the message, but because I was always there.

I began talking with John Campbell, the President of PL. He actually came to a clearing across from Luna so we could meet and see each other as people rather than adversaries. He brought me a six-pack of Pepsi as a gift and I gave him a crystal from a powerful mountain in Arkansas. He was giving me something that he thought I might miss and I was giving him a gift from the Earth that I hoped would open his heart. Our funny gift exchange exemplified how although we come from two different perspectives and had different values, we could still communicate.

Talks eventually led to negotiations to protect Luna and a buffer zone around her. Reaching an agreement was a nearly year-long process with many stumbling blocks and stalemates. During the course of the negotiations, Pacific Lumber wanted me to denounce treesitting, civil disobedience, and forgo my freedom of speech. I was unwilling to compromise my beliefs, morals, or values, or to sign away my First Amendment rights. I was determined to not come down until I had done everything in my power to protect Luna. I wanted to protect Luna for the thousands of people across the country and around the world for whom she had become a symbol of hope, a reminder that we can find peaceful, loving ways to solve our conflicts.

Another sign of hope was the alliance that was forming between labor and environmentalists. One of the most exciting alliances in recent history is the Alliance for Sustainable Jobs and the Environment (ASJE) that was formed by striking United Steelworkers of America and environmentalists who found common ground fighting against Maxxam Corporation's destructive practices. At a time when the negotiations fizzled and I had to let go of my hopes of resuming my life on the ground, a locked-out U.S. steelworker named John Goodman entered the negotiating ring. John had worked for Kaiser Aluminum, a subsidiary of Maxxam Corp. John, a Texan like Maxxam CEO Charles Hurwitz, was a stalwart negotiator along with several key environmental activists.

In reality, the support of thousands of people around the world helped turn the tide and create an environment where the corporation was compelled to do the right thing and protect this incredible being that came to represent hope and the power of committed love in action.

Finally, after 738 days living in the canopy of an ancient redwood tree, the Luna Preservation Agreement and Deed of Covenant was recorded, protecting Luna and a 200-foot buffer of her family around her in perpetuity. We succeeded.

Sometimes, people ask me, "What next?" and I have to laugh because living in Luna's embrace was not a stunt that I need to top. It was an experience that I will build upon in my life of service. The magic of living with Luna is an experience that I relive every day as I share the messages and wisdom that she lovingly shared with me.

I will continue to stand for what I believe in, and I will refuse to back down and go away. No person, no business, and no government has the right to destroy the gift of life. No one has the right to steal from the future in order to make a quick profit today. It's time that we as humans step back into living only off the Earth's interest, instead of drawing off the principal. And it's time we restored some of the capital investment we've already stolen.

It is our responsibility to stand up for the life that we've recklessly squandered, no matter the consequences. So I'll continue to hold the light strong even in the midst of darkness. I will continue to believe in the power of prayer and love as guiding forces in this time of global transition into the next millennium. By living in a respectful and sustainable way we enrich our lives and make the world a better place for all species.

▼▼▼

**JULIA BUTTERFLY HILL** lived in an ancient redwood tree called Luna for more than two years to protect the tree and to help make the world aware of the plight of ancient forests. Her courageous act of civil disobedience gained international attention for the redwoods as well as other environmental and social justice issues and is chronicled in her book *The Legacy of Luna: The Story of a Tree, a Woman, and the Struggle to Save the Redwoods* (HarperSanFrancisco, 2000). Julia came down from her perch after successfully negotiating to protect Luna and a three-acre buffer around her. In November, 2000, an unknown perpetrator made a critical cut to Luna that went through a significant part of the tree. A team of specialists came to her rescue and it is believed this magnificent beauty will survive. Julia continues to reach out to religious leaders, schoolchildren, labor unions, indigenous people, celebrities, politicians, and millions of everyday folks. Julia has been able to appeal to diverse audiences because she speaks from the heart with a moral conviction that brings people to tears and calls them to action. She currently resides in Redway, California. For more information on Julia and Luna visit www.circleoflifefoundation.org.

# BREAKING THE CYCLE OF FEAR AND VIOLENCE

## BY OCEAN ROBBINS

**I COME FROM AN UNUSUAL BACKGROUND.** My dad, John Robbins (author of *Diet for a New America,* and an inspiration to millions) and my mom, Deo, are not just parents to me; they are also my dear friends. From an early age, they helped me to look at problems in the world not as monsters to fear but as opportunities for healing. "However bad things are," my mom used to tell me, "is exactly how much better they can be with a change."

I remember walking with my dad at the beach on a cold winter day in Victoria, Canada, when I was about six years old. We came to a woman and her little boy (who must have been about three) standing on the sand fifty feet ahead. She was hitting the child and shouting: "Don't you *ever* talk back to me again!" The boy was screaming, a look of terror in his tear-filled eyes. I felt my face becoming pale, and I clutched my dad's hand. He held my hand firmly and said something I will always remember: "When you see someone hurting another person, it's usually because someone hurt them once. People get hurt, and then lash out at others. The cycle of pain just keeps on going, until someone says 'enough.' Well, this is enough."

The woman didn't seem to notice us as we approached, my dad in the lead, holding my hand as I followed about a step behind. The boy was wailing at the top of his lungs, his cries broken only by shouts from his mother and the occasional slap. The woman was so absorbed that she was oblivious to our presence as my dad came alongside her. Then, in a strong yet gentle voice, he said: "Excuse me." She spun to face him, a look of shock on her face. "I'm sorry to bother you," my dad continued, "but it looked like you were having a hard time, and I wondered if we could help." She stared back at him, and her mouth dropped open incredulously. "It's none of your business," she snapped. My dad's eyes were steady and soft, and his voice gentle, "I'm sorry to see you hurting so much." For a moment, I thought she was going to lash out again, but then a look of shame passed over her face, and she said: "I'm sorry. I'm not normally like this. I just broke up with my boyfriend — his dad — and it just felt like everything was falling apart."

As they continued talking, I introduced the boy, whose name was Michael, to a toy car I carried in my pocket. Michael and I played together on the beach for a little while, as his mom and my dad conversed. After a few minutes, they came toward us, and I could hear Michael's mom thanking my dad. "It's amazing what a difference it makes just to have someone to talk to." And then, reaching to pick up Michael, "It'll be okay now. We're in this together, and everything is going to be all right." Michael looked at her, as though not sure whether to believe or trust her. "Here," I said, handing him my toy car, "this is for you." He smiled at me. "What do you say?" His mom was more commanding than asking. "Thank you," Michael replied. I told him he was welcome, and then my dad led me on down the beach, turning to wave as we walked. The mom waved back, and as she said "Thank you," a faint smile came over her face.

I never forgot that moment. For I had been introduced, at the age of six, to the power of meeting hatred with love. I had learned that there aren't really any monsters, just people who have been hurt and then take their hurt out on others. Just people who need love.

Now I am twenty-five years old. I'm part of a generation of youth who have, for the most part, grown up watching five hours of television a day, with microwaves, rap music, and parents who both work at least forty hours a week. A generation with skateboards, gangs, Nike shoes, and Internet access. A generation of youth who have lived our whole lives under a nuclear shadow, with environmental problems mounting and the fabric of community fraying.

Roughly 95 percent of the high school students in America today believe the world will be a worse place in thirty years, with more violence and more pollution. Some of us feel so overwhelmed by the problems, and so depressed by our planetary mess, that we've turned cold. It's hard not to turn cold in the face of it all; especially when that's exactly what so many people around us are doing.

It was often hard for me to be growing up in this generation. I felt deeply concerned about the state of our world, and had been raised to think of service as a fundamental part of my life. Questions of the arms race, homelessness, ecology, and planetary survival were discussed in my family daily, and I learned early to consider myself and my actions in relationship to the great issues of our time. Most important, I was raised to think and feel that the choices I make and the way I live can make a difference. Most of my peers did not feel so empowered and supported by their parents. They seemed more interested in shopping malls and MTV than stopping global warming and feeding the hungry. I often felt isolated among people my own age, for few of them seemed motivated to do something about the problems and pain of the world.

When I was fifteen, I attended a summer camp sponsored by an organization called Creating Our Future. There, for the first time, I met other young people willing to really talk about the state of our world, young people who wanted to work for positive change. It was exhilarating for me to realize that there were in fact many young people all over the world who cared. We explored issues ranging from saving the rain forests to healing sexism and racism, and looked at how we could bring peace to our families, our communities, and our world. One of the people I met at that camp was Ryan Eliason, then age eighteen.

Ryan and I quickly became good friends, and we decided that we wanted to work together. We knew many young people were lost in apathy and despair, and we wanted to let them know they could make a difference and help them to learn how. So in the spring of 1990 we started Youth for Environmental Sanity, or YES!. EarthSave International, the nonprofit organization my dad had started, took us on as a project and gave us office space and a computer. My dad's work had inspired many people, some of them wealthy and prominent. So with help from him and the people with whom he put us in contact, combined with the hardest work of our lives, we were able to raise money, find other young people to join us, and start an organization.

Our first assembly presentation was at Galileo High School in San Francisco. An inner city school surrounded by a barbed wire fence, Galileo is one of the tougher schools in Northern California, with a significant gang population and a high drop-out rate. Upon arrival at the school, we realized we had forgotten to ask for a sound system. No problem, the principal said, handing us a megaphone. So there we were a half hour later, standing in front of three hundred kids, half of whom didn't speak English well, with a battery-powered megaphone amplifying and distorting our words, in an enormous gym that seemed to keep each sound echoing off the walls for at least ten seconds. Annoyed by the strain of trying to hear us, the students began to chatter among themselves, while we stood there like a bunch of fools and lectured them on the virtues of living in harmony with the Earth. I don't think many of the students could have heard us even if they had wanted to. We hadn't yet arrived at the end of our presentation when the bell rang. The students got up and left, without waiting for us to finish, or even clapping. I asked one departing girl what she'd thought of the assembly. "Bo-ring," was her only answer. At that moment, I wished I could crawl into the nearest hole in the ground and never come out. We had so many hopes and dreams invested in the YES! tour, and now I wondered if it might all be for naught.

As we left Galileo, we were one dejected bunch. We might have canceled the whole tour and given up on changing the world right then, except for the fact that we had an assembly at Los Altos High School already scheduled for the following morning. We went out to a restaurant that night and made a list of everything we had done wrong in our presentation. The list went on for eight single-spaced pages. The bottom line was that we had talked, and given statistics, but we hadn't related to the people in the room. Our presentation had lacked humor, music, visuals, entertainment, and perhaps most important, personal depth. We stayed up all night brainstorming ways to improve our presentation and then talking about how to implement them. When we arrived at Los Altos the next morning, we were nervous, exhausted, and yet excited to see how our ideas would work. The response was outstanding, with dozens of students coming up to us after the presentation to thank us and tell us how much the assembly had meant to them.

As the years went by, our presentations improved. The more we did it, the better we got at reaching diverse audiences. The YES! tour has now reached more than a half million students through assemblies in thousands of schools. We've conducted hundreds of day-long workshops in thirty-five states. And realizing that assemblies aren't enough time to really change lives, we've organized fifty-four weeklong summer camps for young environmental leaders from thirty countries, camps that have taken place in not only the United States but also Singapore, Taiwan, Australia, Canada, and Costa Rica. YES! camps bring together diverse young adults who share the vision of a better world and offer support and skills for compassionate and effective action.

Working with youth, I notice with sadness how often tension and misunderstanding arise between the generations. The so-called generation gap often seems to be a chasm. I find little respect among my peers for the generations that have come before us. Perhaps it's because previous generations have made such a mess of things. But I think it's also because we tend to model how we've been treated. Young people who have been treated with little respect by adults will rarely feel much respect for them. Most young people frequently experience adults who dismiss their thoughts and feelings on account of their young age.

In light of this, I was intrigued when I heard that the Dalai Lama was coming to San Francisco in June of 1997 for a conference that would include people of all ages, from many different cultural backgrounds, for a common exploration of peacemaking. The conference, titled "Peacemaking," was to include speakers who were working for peace and social justice all around the world, including the jungles of Guatemala, the forced labor camps of China, and the American inner city. I was particularly fascinated to learn that the Dalai Lama had specifically requested a meeting with the youth participants of the conference, a meeting that would not include any participants over the age of twenty-four. When asked why he wanted to have this meeting, the Dalai Lama had replied: "Youth are the future. All ages are important, but it's young people who have to carry the burden if the world's turned over in a bad state." Somehow it seemed appropriate that the Dalai Lama, one of the great elders of our times, would respect young people enough to have a special meeting with us. I knew I had to be there.

The atmosphere was intense and charged with excitement as five hundred young people poured into the room. They represented every major race and religion in the world. Young people from Hawaii to Harlem, from communes, gangs, high schools, and homeschools; punks, skaters, social activists, environmental leaders, farmworkers, students, and school dropouts. To my left sat an African-American teen with long dreadlocks, perhaps eighteen years old. He came from Compton, where he was part of a school club that combats racism. His T-shirt said: "Fight the Machine." Why did he come to the conference? "Because I'm sick of the way things are going, and I wanted to learn how to do something positive."

To my right sat a seventeen-year-old Caucasian girl with light brown hair. She was preparing to study journalism in college and hoped to gain ideas that would stimulate and inspire her. In that one room sat young people from inner city gardens, suburban recycling programs, gang prevention projects, groups that teach conflict resolution skills, and organizations working for the homeless, for prison inmates, for social justice, and for the environment. The feeling was electric. As I looked around, I wondered: Would these young people, from so many different backgrounds, be able to find common ground? A noisy, expectant chatter filled the room. And then a clapping started, and spread, as one by one we rose to our feet to greet the Dalai Lama, who was just entering the room. Though our backgrounds varied greatly, we would all soon be united in our respect for a great peacemaker.

In his maroon and yellow robe, the Dalai Lama looked anything but intimidating. Yet though he spoke gently, his words and sweet amiability carried with them a sense of a deep humanity, and of a peace unruffled by the violence and genocide his people have endured.

It was announced that anyone who wished to ask a question could come over to the microphone, and within seconds there were twelve people waiting in line. The first person in line was a young woman who started shaking when she began to speak. Finally she managed to say how moved she was to see the Dalai Lama, and that he was her greatest hero. Then she asked: "Is it possible to be in a state of oneness and peace all the time?" The Dalai Lama smiled, and then burst out laughing, as he answered: "I don't know myself! But you must never stop trying." A bright smile danced across his face, and she returned to her seat glowing with excitement to have spoken to her hero.

One young man from a gang coalition in Mexico spoke through an interpreter: "Many of us in gangs are tired of waiting. We've come together to denounce violence. We don't want to be the bad guys anymore. But still we face much racism and struggle. What do you think of urban Mexican guys like us?" Loud clapping filled the room, and someone else spoke before the Dalai Lama could answer. But a short time later, perhaps in response, the Dalai Lama spoke of racism and said in his uniquely simple way: "We all have two eyes, one nose, one mouth. Internal organs also the same! We are people." Then he broke into a peal of laughter, as if he found the whole notion of racial prejudice rather absurd. Later, he again touched on the subject: "If you have only one type of flower, over a big field, then it looks like a farm. But many different types of flowers looks like a beautiful garden. For a beautiful garden, we must take care of each plant. I think the many different cultures and religions of our world are like this garden."

Knowing a bit about the plight of the Tibetan people, I would have understood if the Dalai Lama was bitter. After all, he was forced to flee his country under the onslaught of the Chinese invasion in 1959. Since then, he has seen hundreds of thousands of his people tortured and murdered by the Chinese government. He has helplessly endured the wholesale clear-cutting of Tibetan forests and the dumping of countless tons of hazardous and nuclear wastes on Tibet's fragile and pristine ecosystems. And he has been in exile, unable to return to the land over which he still presides. Yet a remarkable peace emanates from this man. A man who, remarkably, does not hate the Chinese. A man who clearly feels great compassion for them.

What, I wondered, gives him such tranquility in the face of the horrors he's seen? How does he persevere as the revolutionary leader of a conquered land he cannot even visit while holding an inner peace at the core of his being? Then I realized with a flash of excitement that the Dalai Lama was able to persevere in the face of so much suffering precisely *because* he had a deeper spiritual base upon which to depend. If he thought the only thing that mattered was Tibetan politics, he would have long since been lost in despair. But he has learned to take root not in external results but in a peace that comes from within.

One of the people at the Peacemaking conference was Thrinlay Chodon, a thirty-year-old Tibetan woman who was born and grew up in northern India after her parents fled Tibet. They both died while she was young, and Thrinlay's life has been that of a refugee, living in tremendous poverty. I asked her how she kept from hating the Chinese. "The Dalai Lama reminds us that the Chinese have created much bad karma for themselves, and the last thing they need is our hateful thoughts. If we hate them, we will have lost.

Love will have lost to hate. So we must keep them in our hearts if we are to persevere in the struggle."

Political and social activism, I realized, are not separate from spiritual work. They need each other. We cannot expect to get anywhere preaching a doctrine of peace while hating the warmongers. We will never free Tibet while hating the Chinese. Because freeing Tibet and bringing peace to our cities and our world are not just about politics, but about values.

I'm only twenty-five, but I've had the opportunity to be around many people who have given themselves to the goal of fostering positive change. Yet the forces of destruction are so great that they can sometimes feel overwhelming. How are we not to get lost in the despair and pain? The Dalai Lama, and the whole movement for the freedom of Tibet, teach me something profound. For in them I can see that, in the final analysis, what matters most isn't that our efforts meet with success, it's that we give all we have to the causes we hold dear, trusting that in the greater panorama that lies beyond our perception, there is a profound meaning to all the love we share. I believe the struggle for the liberation of the human spirit is taking place on many levels, including some we cannot always see or hear. If we are to persevere in our work in the world, we cannot depend only on external results. We need a spiritual foundation from which to gain perspective, act, and draw nourishment. If we want to bring peace to the world, we must also strive to have inner peace. As the Dalai Lama said at the Peacemaking conference: "The same is true in reverse. Peace in the community helps make peace in the individual. Peace anywhere helps make peace everywhere. That's why we need more peace."

Some young people at the conference found talk of peace hard to swallow. Many of them came from inner cities, where drugs and drive-by shootings are prevalent and homelessness common. "I don't want peace," said Philip, a teen from San Francisco, "I want change. Fast. I'm mad, and I'm not going to just sit back and pretend everything's nice in the world." I have heard these kinds of sentiments again and again. Many young people are angry about what's going on around them. Bottle that anger up and it will become destructive. Give young people a meaningful outlet for our energies, and we can accomplish extraordinary things.

"Peace" sounds passive to some youth, like a cop-out in a world desperately in need of action. Yet during the Peacemaking conference, lifelong activists in the fields of human rights, social change, ecology, and racial healing sounded a different chord. Harry Wu, an exiled Chinese dissident who has spent much of his life in China's forced labor camps (which he compares to German concentration camps) told the conference: Peace is not the denial of injustice, nor is it merely the absence of violence. In a world torn apart by war and separation, peace is revolutionary. In a world where abuse of people and the Earth is normal, working for peace means directly challenging the status quo.

Sometimes, as many of the conference presenters could attest to from personal experience, working for peace means placing ourselves at great personal risk. But to do anything else is to risk our souls and our world. No real peace will ever last without economic and social justice. Harry Wu ended one of his speeches with a profound message: "The power of nonviolence is to tell the truth to all the people. The power of nonviolence is to never give up the ideal of justice."

Toward the end of the conference, a large group of young people noticed the irony of noble peace talk inside the convention center while dozens of homeless people sat hungry on the street outside. They made up several hundred sandwiches, then went out and gave them, free of charge, to all who wished to partake.

▼▼▼

**OCEAN ROBBINS** is founder and president of Youth for Environmental Sanity (YES!) in Santa Cruz, California, as well as author (with Sol Solomon) of *Choices for Our Future* (Book Publishing Co., 1994). YES! sponsors assemblies, programs, and summer camps to educate, inspire, and empower youth worldwide. For more information, see www.yesworld.org.

# FROM HOLLYWOOD TO THE HOLY WOODS

## BY SADHVI BHAGWATI

**"GRAAANDMAAA, BUY ME A PAIR OF JORDACHE JEANS,"** my voice would sing out in a whine as we stepped through the wide glass doors of the department store. My dad used to joke that I was the only person he knew who called her jeans by name: my Guess jeans, my Jordache, my Calvin Kleins. I knew when Esprit was in and I wore Esprit matching outfits, starched cotton shirts with pleated shorts, joined at the center by the essential thin leather belt. It was, in fact, too time consuming to figure out what to wear each morning; thus, I would scour my closet the evening before, picking out just the perfect clothes for school the next day. Back then, every season demanded new clothes: back to school clothes, summer clothes, spring clothes, birthday clothes. . . .

Now I live on the holy banks of the Ganges, in Rishikesh, India. I sit each evening as the sun's last rays dance off Her waters, a child's soft, dirty arms wrapped around my neck, dozens of others vying for my hand, finger, or a place on my lap. We are gathered together with hundreds of others to offer our prayers, our thanks, and our love to God in a fire/light ceremony called Aarti. The stress, the tension, the pains of the day melt away into the heat of the flames and are carried swiftly away by the purifying current of Mother Ganga. The children, children who live well below the Western standard of poverty but with an unmistakable glow of joy in their eyes, sit and sing with their heads on my lap, their voices loud and out of tune. In their young innocence and piety, they are oblivious to any sense of self-consciousness. The evening wind blows gently across our faces, carrying misty drops of Ganga's waters onto our cheeks, already wet with tears of divine surrender. Ganga flows quickly, dark as the night yet as light as the day. I am surrounded by people singing, singing the glories of God, singing the glories of life.

I wake each day as the sun peaks over the Himalayas, bringing light and life and a new day to all. I sleep each night in the shelter of Mother Ganga as She continues Her ceaseless journey to the ocean. I spend the day working on a computer as spiritual songs play in the background throughout the ashram on which I live, an ashram not dedicated to one guru or one sect but whose name is Parmarth Niketan, meaning an abode dedicated to the welfare of all. My days are filled with *seva,* Sanskrit for selfless service. I work for schools, hospitals, and ecological programs. Now I never wear jeans at all, except on rare occasions when I am back in Los Angeles with my parents, and my mother insists that I look "normal." Today, I give away my nicest clothes to others, knowing how happy it will make them. Today, all the possessions I own (mainly books, journals, and a filing cabinet) fit on the floor of a closet at my parents' house.

My parents came to visit me in Rishikesh last Christmas. Christmas had always been a time for extensive wish lists, arranged and rearranged in meticulous order of preference. The anticipatory excitement of waiting for Christmas morning was matched only by the thrill of tearing away wrapping paper to reveal what treasure lay beneath. When my parents came this year, it was the first time I had seen them in four months, and it would be another four months before I saw them again. On their last day, they were generously preparing envelopes filled with the equivalent of more than a month's salary for each of the boys who had cared for them during their visit, boys I call *Bhaiya* (brother): the cook, the driver, the cleaner. After the envelopes had been stuffed, my mom looked at me, wallet open, and said, "Okay, now you. What for you?" "Nothing," I said without a moment's hesitation. "Oh come on," she said, as though my life of simplicity were simply a show for others. "We're your parents." "Well," I replied, "If you really want to give something, you can make a donation to our children's schools."

What happened? How to go from calling my jeans by name, from being unable to begin the day without a double latté, from a life in Hollywood and Beverly Hills to the life of a nun on the banks of the River Ganga? How to go from being unable to work for more than two hours at a time without a break, from spending more time complaining about my work than actually doing it, how to go from this to working fifteen hours a day, seven days a week for not a cent, but with a constant glow of joy? How to go from being an avid movie fan, to being someone who would rather work on the computer or meditate? How to go from being someone for whom a "perfect evening" meant a nice, expensive dinner out and a movie to being someone who would rather drink hot milk at home?

How did this happen? The answer is God's blessing. My ego would love to say, "Oh I did it. I decided to make myself a better person. I became spiritual and worked to free myself from the constraints of the Western world." But that is only my ego's fantasy. It is not true. The truth is that God picked me up in His arms and carried me forth to the life I am supposed to live.

People ask me frequently, "Wasn't the transition difficult? Boy, you must have had to really adapt. Don't you ever miss the Western life, the life of comfort?" To them I say,

Imagine that you have size eight feet. However, your entire life people have told you that, in fact, you have size five feet.

They were not being malicious or consciously deceptive. Rather, they really believed that your feet were size five. Thus, for your whole life you have worn size five shoes on your size eight feet. Sure, they were uncomfortable and tight, and you developed chronic blisters and corns, but you just thought this was what shoes were supposed to feel like; whenever you mentioned it to anyone, they assured you that, yes, shoes always feel tight and always give blisters. That is just how shoes are. So, you stopped questioning. Then, one day, someone slips your foot into a size eight shoe.... "Ahhh," you say. "So, that is what shoes feel like."

But then people ask, "But, how did you adapt to wearing this size eight shoe? Don't you ever miss the way your size five shoe felt?" Of course not.

Coming home to India has felt like slipping a size eight foot into a size eight shoe: just right. I wake each morning and — just as little children rush into their parents' bed, cuddle under the covers, and lie in Mom's arms before starting their day — I rush down to Ganga, like a very young child. "Good morning, Mom," I say into the wind as it whips off the Himalayas, onto Her ceaselessly flowing waters. I bow to Her and drink a handful of Her divine nectar. I stand, Her waters rushing over my bare feet, an IV of life and divinity into my all-too-human morning sluggishness. I fold my hands in prayer as the sun, rising over the Himalayas, begins to reflect off Her boundless waters:

*Thank you Ma.*
*Thank you for waking me again today,*
*For letting my eyes open*
*In the land of your infinite grace.*
*Thank you for making my legs able*
*To carry me to Your banks, and then to my office.*
*Thank you for bringing me forth to this life of service,*
*This life of light, this life of love,*
*This life of God.*
*Let my work today be in service of You.*

*May You be the hand that guides mine.*
*And most importantly,*
*Please, please, let me be worthy of living on your banks.*

Then I walk back up the steps of the ashram, into the blinding light of the rising sun, and to my office. It is barely 6:30 A.M.

The day is filled with work, work on a computer, sitting in an office: proposals for new projects; reports on the projects that already exist; ideas for how to improve the work we are doing; letters to those who generously fund our schools, hospitals, ambulance, and ecology programs; correspondence for the saint in whose service I live my life; and editing beautiful books on the Gita, the teachings of the Mother, books written by brilliant Indian thinkers but checkered with spelling and grammatical mistakes.

"Don't you ever take a day off?" people ask. I laugh. What would I possibly do with a ""day off"? Sit in bed and paint my toenails? And why would I ever want one? My life is the work. I am more at peace, more joyful, more filled with divine bliss as I work to bring education to the illiterate, training programs to the unemployable, medicine to the sick, sweaters to the cold, and smiles to the teary eyed than I could possibly be anywhere else. This work and this life have been the greatest gift from God I could possibly imagine.

Why am I sharing this with you? Why would people who don't even know me possibly be interested in the joy I have found in life? Because it is not what we are taught. We are taught that joy in life comes from having money, a good education, the latest material possessions, relaxing vacations, and a white picket fence around our home. And, if we have all those things and are not happy, our culture simply says, "Acquire more. Make more money, get another degree, buy this or that, take another sun-soaked trip to Mexico, build a higher white fence." No one ever says, "You have the wrong things!" No one ever tells us that money, education, possessions, and vacations are wonderful, that they bring comfort, but that they are not the key to happiness. No one tells us that to be in service is one of the greatest joys in the world.

There are clichés like "It is better to give than to receive," yet these words are more likely found in a book in the self-help section of a bookstore than on our lips or in our hearts. Today, as I see an advertisement for a skin cream that will "restore your youthful beauty" for only $30, I think of twenty children shivering in the Himalayas who can have sweaters for that same amount of money. Which, I wonder, will truly bring youth to my being, the skin cream or the knowledge that twenty children are no longer shivering?

I have found that all the things I used to believe were essential — as much sleep as my body could take, meals whenever I wanted them, an air-conditioned car — don't begin to bring the health to my being that being in service does.

On a recent trip back to America, I had just arrived into L.A. after forty hours of travel, preceded by days of unusually long hours preparing for the two-week absence. At 9:45 P.M., I received a message that I must write and send a fax to Bombay, to people who wanted to send six truckloads of clothing, utensils, and food to earthquake victims in the Himalayas. They had contacted our ashram requesting specific information immediately in order to dispatch the trucks. Now, I had not slept in over forty-eight hours (other than a few hours caught on the airplane), and I was just about to brush my teeth and head for bed. But the knowledge that these people were going to bring shelter to those who were stranded, clothe those who were without, give food to a region that for weeks had been without water or electricity was enough of a catalyst to send me right to the computer. As I stood over the fax machine, trying to get through to Bombay, my mother came over for the third time, insisting that I go to sleep: "You haven't slept in days. You have to get up in the morning, and it's already 10:15. Enough!" What? Trade six truckloads of disaster supplies for twenty minutes of sleep? In whose world?

But this was a rationale that I used to believe: my needs came first. Only then, once they were met, could I help others. It's like on airplanes when they describe what to do in case the oxygen masks drop: secure your own mask, then help others. But, I have discovered something different in life. I have discovered the incredible health — not only mental and spiritual but also physical — that comes from being selflessly in service. Any friend of mine will vouch for how somatically focused I used to be, always running to take care of this ache, that pain, this "signal" from my body. I would panic at the prospect of getting less than the necessary eight hours of sleep a night, because then I would undoubtedly get sick and the world would come to an end.

Yes, there are times when it is important and healthy to nurture oneself, when one must first take care of one's own needs — be they physical, emotional, or psychological. There are times when this work can actually make one much more able to be selfless later. However, I feel that our culture today is focused backward: we are taught that the majority of our focus should be on ourselves and then, once our needs are met, we should give a token amount of time and energy to charitable endeavors. And we wonder why we don't feel a divine connection, why we don't wake up each day filled with ecstatic joy at the thought of jumping from bed and beginning the day. Could it be that the priorities are backward, that, yes, we must take care of ourselves, but that our own satisfaction does not have to be our primary goal? Could it be that changing the lives of others is exactly what we need to help us change our own lives? Could it be that a beautiful divine connection can also be found in simple surrender to His will, and not only in ardent, arduous, spiritual "practice"?

For me, it has all been about surrender, to truth, to joy, to God's will. What are my plans? Only God knows. I have no plans, per se. If I were "in charge" I would stay in India forever, building schools, orphanages, and hospitals, ceasing work each day only for Aarti on the banks of the Ganga. But, one thing I have learned is that we are not in charge. Who can know what will befall them? A sudden accident, sudden illness, sudden lottery win, sudden ecstatic epiphany....

I have found that, rather than pretend to have any semblance of control over my life, it is better to simply turn it over to Him. "May I live as Your tool," I pray. "May Your will be my will." And the messages come clearly. His voice is loud and unmistakable, if only I am quiet and still enough to hear. Sure, there are times when I will say to Him, "But why this? That's not how I would have done it." Yet, the answer usually comes relatively quickly; a few hours, days, or weeks later I will understand why He pushed me in a certain new direction.

So, my life is in God's hands. If He ever asks I will certainly tell Him that all I want is to be able to stay on the banks of the Ganga forever. But He has not yet asked. By His divine grace, though, He has kept me there, and every day I am more and more grateful.

▼▼▼

**SADHVI BHAGWATI** works in Rishikesh for one of India's most renowned saints, Swamiji Chidananda Saraswati, doing spiritual service for schools, orphanages, ecological programs, and scholarly projects.

## LONE MANZANITA

BY **TYLER ENFIELD**

Following is a series of sixteen Zen-inspired poems, written and painted over the course of several months in 1997.

For every hour I sit listening
To the songs of a creek
All the toil and grief of a lifetime past
Is liberated from my soul
My step becomes light and my heart is lifted
Every time I rest
In the silent shade
Of an old fir tree
I know my place on earth
I know who my elders are
And with each kiss of blue
Upon my skyward eye
I am reminded of loftier regimes
Than any I might subscribe to
In blood or ink
For nature is my Lord
She is the Essential Author
Who whispered it all first
At the feet of her glory
Every poem is but a witness to inspiration
And every poet a scandal—

Her eyes
Were forest-colored
Bent at the seams
With scorching orange bursts
Of high noon
Each time she blinked
The sun set in the woods
And my world
Dissolved —

From atop the waterfall
Our bellies, flush upon cool stone,
Rush leap and wander like
The river droplets
Spilling from our eyes...

She was not
Good and great,
As I'd once disguised her,
But a mere apparition
Of the heart.

Alone on mountain—
Drunk on the moon
And the notion
That none knows
The secrets she
Hides in these smiling fool eyes.

Pale quietude
Of deep forest glade:
One tree stirring
Has the presence of thunder.
One leaf falling
Is a thousand...

Blessed is he who falls
Thru this world
Into his own
To feel the sound
Of silk tearing in his spine,
For when the moon is high
Her touch is higher
And glows like a last candle
In winter –

If only the winds
Were less bold, i might find this
Crooked path kinder...

To shake off this halter and bridle
the yoke of this life
this impossible fiction
Is to make amends
between thy monk
and the lover
To let obscurity reign till days end...

Nobody home tonight—
Just crickets singing this mind.

Can the right hand
Steal from the left?
No loss or gain in
A world rid of others—

All alone
In this Great House of Mirrors—

Each of us...

No God
No Nirvana
No life
No death
Just this.
Finally just this
And yet...
No one left to know it—

Not the bitter cold
Of the place I was, nor the
Hunger or the thieves,
But only the charmed tendrils
Of your tender prayers that brought
Me home—

Lone manzanita
On ridge, tucked deep in the
Crimson mists of dawn.

▼▼▼

**TYLER ENFIELD** is a rock climber, father, and poet who lives in Boulder, Colorado. His contribution includes sixteen poems and drawings culled from a collection of two hundred that capture elements of the spiritual path in evocative ways. Most were written and drawn in a few weeks while living in a monastery.

# AFTERWORD

BY STEPHEN DINAN

**I HOPE YOU'VE FOUND IN YOUR JOURNEY** through these pages a more radical view of your own spiritual adventure. As our contributors demonstrate, spiritual life involves more than moral codes, compassionate behavior, and wise sayings. It involves expanding one's loving embrace to include everything: mischief and misery, bliss and boredom, trauma and transformation. Life's house of mirrors reflects our essence in amusing, whimsical, and sometimes grotesque ways. We can resist the images we don't like or, alternatively, choose to love each as a creative expression of the Divine.

From God's perspective, our various roles and dramas can all be likened to different flavors of ice cream. Each produces a delightful moment of fresh experience, including the flavors most of us want to avoid. Mmm, Falling in Love Fandango. Yum, Village Shaman Swirl, a tantalizing mix of jungle fruit and psychedelic 'shrooms. And ahh, yes, Despotic Dictator Decadence, festooned with dark chocolate chips, a perennial favorite. Each is a flavorful surprise.

As humans, largely shielded from our ultimate nature, we tend to get very attached to the flavor of the month; or perhaps more accurately, the flavor of this incarnation. We identify with a particular personality, religion, culture, or relationship. We confuse our essential nature, which is both none of these things and all of these things, with the experience of the moment. As this month's flavor melts, we recoil in terror from the "death" that awaits us. But there is no real death, just a migration of experience from one form to another, from one level of being to another. We shed identities and roles and take on new garb before beginning the cycle anew.

There is a danger for spiritual seekers. In our thirst for transformation, we may begin to identify with spiritual practices and a "compassionate" lifestyle. We might become attached to speaking kindly in conversation, dedicating ourselves to charity work, or abiding in rarified states of consciousness. When life asks for greater flexibility — time to get off the *zafu,* raise hell, or get a corporate job — we may resist the new roles as "not spiritual." We may resist the "death" the change represents. Our *image* of spiritual life may thus betray the *actual* flow of lived experience. It is essential, then, to remind ourselves that life evolves continuously. Today's insights may bloom like magnificent flowers, but ultimately they rot and must be composted for next year's crop. The more attachments we create, the more likely that our fingers will need to be pried from yesterday's truth in order to deal with the realities of today.

For example, I once scoffed at vegetarians, arguing that we were born omnivores. But after reading *Diet for a New America,* vegetarianism revealed itself to me as essential for environmental, health, and spiritual reasons. I grieved for having purveyed so much illusion and made it a personal crusade to win others to the Cause. After ten years of vegetarianism, though, I grew concerned about feeling morally superior to omnivores. Was this a barrier to radically opening my heart? Perhaps I needed to re-embrace the carnivore inside, the part of me that *likes* the taste of flesh.

Thus it came about that I spent five days in France eating virtually every type of meat: from beef bourguignon to tender duck, from ham-and-cheese crêpes to escargots. Barely a meal passed without another piece of animal flesh heading down my pristine gullet. In the airport on the return trip, I capped the binge with a Double Whopper with Cheese to perform last rites on my identification as a vegetarian. Despite my rumbling moral pride, it tasted delicious.

In releasing vegetarianism as a bedrock identity, I created a more open, compassionate space inside, which is essential to being able to serve as an agent of evolution. When we can savor *all* the flavors of samsara, we are no longer resistant to doing what real love requires. We can adopt a radically new lifestyle while recognizing it is just another face of Spirit. We can rage when situations call for it and whisper tenderly when that best serves. The fullest love is not limited to saccharine sweetness but flows with the moment, which might sometimes demand fangs.

Slowly, this process of loosening our attachment to a single way of being creates fluidity. This fluidity is not the same as indifference. Some spiritual practitioners deny the gamut of emotions from delight to anger in order to break the attachment cycle. They choose the dull coma of indifference over the hot fire of attachment. However, I find that it is those who can truly, utterly, passionately engage life while remaining fluid and free in their roles who have discovered the real key. They relish each turn of the karmic wheel, embracing highs and lows, breakthroughs and failures, while their identity sticks to no single experience. They are capable of feeling great sadness, outrage, and joy but they let each feeling pass through them like a weather system. Fog can be as beautiful as sun and snow as enjoyable as rain. Those who love reality want only More, a heightened and deepened dose of life in all its complex, tantalizing glory.

Each author in this book has delivered this "Moreness" as each stretches beyond the paradigms they've inherited and explores ever wider orbits. With each passing year, the authors show up with More of their fullness, More of their care for others, and More of their adventurous spirit. In this expansion, they answer love's call, which is to embrace literally everything and to amplify it all into radiant fullness. This process continues through each of us as we release our resistances, expand the depth and breadth of our experiences, and relish pain and pleasure alike. As we do so, we begin to not just see through the veils, but *feel* through the veils of reality until the entire drama is revealed as waves of divine grace crashing on the shore of an evolving universe. It is all a perfect gift, just for us, right now, exactly as it is. In that recognition, we glimpse ourselves as God embodied, cocreating this radically delightful, deeply mysterious world. We awaken to our Home.

May this book, a love offering from us to you, help you reach that most blessed destination.

# TRANSFORMATIVE BOOKS

**I OFTEN ASK INTERESTING PEOPLE,** "What books have had the most transformative impact on you?" This is a different question than "What are the best books you've read?" or "What was the most intellectually stimulating?" We've all read books that are superbly crafted, impeccably argued, or exhibit technical expertise but that don't really change us in the reading. Every once in a while, though, we read something that fundamentally opens our eyes, cracks open our heart, and shakes the fabric of our being. Paradigm busters. Growth enhancers. Revolution igniters. They are books that reverberate with the hidden knowledge inside each of us that is still waiting to be unveiled. In that resonance between words and soul, we awaken in some small way. They may not be the best written books. Their plots may ramble. Their ideas may be dense or abstruse. But somehow they reach into our depths and, almost without our consent, wring loose more hope, more passion, more truth, more whimsy, or more intelligence. More Spirit. Each contributing author has listed below the five books (as editor, I indulge myself and list ten) that most fit this description for them. Hopefully some of these books will spark you in your journey.

## SADHVI BHAGWATI

*Diet for a New America* by John Robbins
*Reinventing Eve* by Kim Chernin
*Autobiography of a Yogi* by Paramhansa Yogananda

*The Gospel of Sri Ramakrishna*
*They Lived with God: Stories of the Lives of Devotees of Sri Ramakrishna*

## GEORG BUEHLER

*The Denial of Death* by Ernest Becker
*The Complete Works of Carl Sandburg*
*Magical Child* by Joseph Chilton Pearce
*Till We Have Faces* by C. S. Lewis
*I Am That* by Sri Nisargadatta Maharaj

## JULIA BUTTERFLY HILL

*In the Absence of the Sacred* by Jerry Mander
*The Fifth Sacred Thing* by Starhawk
*Ishmael* by Daniel Quinn
*My Life Is My Sundance* by Leonard Peltier
*The Lorax* by Dr. Seuss

## MARIANA CAPLAN

*Layla and Majnun* by Nizami
*The Alchemy of Transformation* by Lee Lozowick
*Daughter of Fire* by Irina Tweedie
*Guru's Grace: Autobiography of Mother Krishnabai*
*Duino Elegies* by Rainer Maria Rilke

## ERIK DAVIS

*I Ching* Wilhelm/Baynes translation
*The Marriage of Heaven and Hell* by William Blake
*The Principal Teachings of Buddhism* by Tsongkapa
*In Search of the Miraculous* by P. D. Ouspensky
*Valis* by Philip K. Dick

## STUART DAVIS

*Tao Te Ching* by Lao-tzu
*The Cloud of Unknowing*
*Tibetan Book of the Dead*
*The Essential Rumi* translated by Coleman Barks
*Sex, Ecology, and Spirituality* by Ken Wilber

## BOB DEARBORN

*Beyond Therapy, Beyond Science* by Ann Wilson Schaef
*No Boundary* by Ken Wilber
*Focusing* by Eugene Gendlin
*Tropic of Capricorn* by Henry Miller
*In My Own Way* by Alan Watts

## MICHAEL DINAN

*The Holographic Universe* by Michael Talbot
*Fingerprints of the Gods* by Graham Hancock
*Jitterbug Perfume* by Tom Robbins
*Ultimate Journey* by Robert Monroe
*Conscious Dreaming* by Robert Moss

## STEPHEN DINAN

*Grace and Grit* by Ken and Treya Killam Wilber
*Diet for a New America* by John Robbins
*Golf in the Kingdom* by Michael Murphy
*Zen and the Art of Motorcycle Maintenance* by Robert Pirsig
*The Prophet* by Kahlil Gibran
*Natural Capitalism* by Paul Hawken, Amory Lovins,
    and L. Hunter Lovins
*The Adventure of Self-Discovery* by Stanislav Grof
*Even Cowgirls Get the Blues* by Tom Robbins
*Hidden Journey* by Andrew Harvey
*The Magus of Strovolos* by Kyriacos Markides

## TYLER ENFIELD

*Unveiling Reality* by John DeRuiter

## VIPASSANA ESBJÖRN

*Collision with the Infinite* by Suzanne Segal
*Grace and Grit* by Ken Wilber and Treya Killam Wilber
*Freedom Has No History* by Andrew Cohen
*The Sorcerers' Crossing* by Taisha Abelar
*Everyday Zen* by Charlotte Joko Beck

## DENISE FUEHRER

*The Courage to Create* by Rollo May
*The Aquarian Conspiracy* by Marilyn Ferguson
*Reinventing Eve* by Kim Chernin
*Tao Te Ching* by Lao-tzu
*Being Intimate* by John Amodeo and Kris Wentworth

## SOREN GORDHAMER

*Way of the Peaceful Warrior* by Dan Millman
*A Gradual Awakening* by Stephen Levine
*Of Water and the Spirit* by Malidoma Patrice Somé
*How Can I Help?* by Ram Dass and Paul Gorman
*The Little Engine That Could* by Watty Piper and Ruth Sanderson

## RONAN HALLOWELL

*How the Other Half Dies* by Susan George
*The Sane Alternative* by James Robertson
*The Chalice and the Blade* by Riane Eisler
*Where Do We Go from Here? Chaos or Community* by Martin Luther King, Jr.
*The Universe Story* by Brian Swimme and Thomas Berry

## SUSANA HERRERA

*A Course in Miracles*
*Siddhartha* by Hermann Hesse
*I Know Why the Caged Bird Sings* by Maya Angelou
*The Color Purple* by Alice Walker
*Their Eyes Were Watching God* by Zora Neale Hurston
*A Return to Love* by Marianne Williamson

## CLAUDIA HORWITZ

*This Bridge Called My Back* edited by Cherríe Moraga and Gloria
    Anzaldúa
*There Is Nothing Wrong with You* by Cheri Huber
*Way of the Peaceful Warrior* by Dan Millman
*Letters to a Young Poet* by Rainer Maria Rilke
*A Return to Love* by Marianne Williamson

## RABBI DANIEL KOHN

Book of Psalms, Hebrew Bible
*Emotional Intelligence* by Daniel Goleman
*God Was in This Place, and I, I Did Not Know* by Lawrence Kushner
*Stranger in a Strange Land* by Robert Heinlein
*Aikido and the Harmony of Nature* by Mitsugi Saotome

## KIMBERLEE ANN KUWICA

*Living the Eternal Way* by Ellen Grace O'Brien
The Bhagavad Gita, translated by Paramahansa Yogananda
*Prayers of the Cosmos* by Neil Douglas-Klotz

## RACHEL MEDLOCK

*The Razor's Edge* by W. Somerset Maugham
*Tuning into Grace* by Andre Louf
*Memories, Dreams, Reflections* by C. G. Jung
*Thus Spake Zarathustra* by Friedrich Nietzsche
The Dhammapada

## HALEY MITCHELL

*Conversations with God* by Neale Donald Walsch
*The Only Dance There Is* by Ram Dass
*Confessions of St. Augustine* by Augustine
*Way of the Peaceful Warrior* by Dan Millman
*Breaking the Cycle of Birth and Death* by Gourasana

## OCEAN ROBBINS

*Diet for a New America* by John Robbins
*Initiation* by Elizabeth Haich
*The Eyes of Horus* by Joan Grant
*The Ecology of Commerce* by Paul Hawken
*The Kin of Ata Are Waiting for You* by Dorothy Bryant

## ELIZABETH SHAVER

*Women in Praise of the Sacred* edited by Jane Hirshfield
*The Spell of the Sensuous* by David Abram

*Woman and Nature* by Susan Griffin
*Women of the Light* edited by Kenneth Ray Stubbs
*Nacidos de la Tierra* by Ramon V. Albareda and Marina T. Romero

## ABIGAIL SUTKUS

*The Return of the Great Goddess* by Burleigh Múten
*The Politics of Women's Spirituality* by Charlene Spretnak
*Uncursing the Dark: Treasures from the Underworld* by Betty DeShong
    Meador
*The Circle of Simplicity* by Cecile Andrews
*The Chalice and the Blade* by Riane Eisler

## ASHLEY WAIN

*Adventure of Self-Discovery* by Stanislav Grof
*Pearl Beyond Price* by A. H. Almaas
*Reflections on the Art of Living: A Joseph Campbell Companion*
*Plays and Stories* by Anton Chekhov
*The Open Society and Its Enemies* by Karl Popper

## SOLA WILLIAMS

*Appearances: Clearings through the Masks of Our Existence* by Rusty Berkus
*All I See Is a Part of Me* by Chara M. Curtis
*The Power of Silence* by Carlos Castaneda
*The Experiment Is Over* by Paul G. Lowe
*The Alchemist* by Paulo Coelho

## ALBERT WONG

*The Writing Life* by Annie Dillard
*Absolute Living* by Karlfried Graf Durckheim
*Iron John* by Robert Bly
*I and Thou* by Martin Buber
*The Phenomenology of Spirit* by Georg Wilhelm Friedrich Hegel

## COMMUNITY

## CREATING YOUR OWN CIRCLE

***RADICAL SPIRIT* IS MORE THAN A BOOK.** It is also the start of a larger community, a community with circles that are linked in their desire for personal awakening and planetary change. As explorers and adventurers, we often hunger for a tribe to call our own. Teaming together with others to release old wounds, create lasting love, and work for social change can rapidly accelerate our path and ease the ache for friendship on the journey.

We will be offering a series of programs to become guides for local Radical Spirit circles. We will provide templates for spiritual cross-training, relationship-building, and worldly change. Radical Spirit circles are designed to be easy to implement, effective, and income-generating. A typical circle meets three weeknights each month and one full weekend day. One weeknight is dedicated to spiritual cross-training, a second to intimacy, and a third to supporting each other in world-transforming work. On the weekend, circles bring in experts on meditation, leadership, healing, communication, relationships, and the most pressing issues the community faces. Guides will also provide monthly consultation sessions.

If you want to join an existing local circle, find the guide closest to you on our Web site. We hope that our circles, trainings, and Web offerings will help you deepen your own spiritual path, create more community, and foster lasting change in our global family.

Visit http://www.radicalspirit.com for more details!

# RECOMMENDED RESOURCES

**THE FOLLOWING RESOURCE GUIDE** does not attempt to be comprehensive. Rather, it is simply a way for readers to engage in some of the techniques, practices, and perspectives that are found in this book in a deeper way. Virtually everything included below is something that one or more contributors have personally been involved in. Our feeling is that the spiritual path must unfold in unique ways for every individual. One's own heart is the best compass. Nevertheless, if readers are particularly intrigued by something found in this book, we feel confident in recommending the following avenues for exploration and action.

## FEATURED PHILANTHROPY

We're proud to announce the involvement of many of the authors of this volume in a special philanthropic project called the Parmarth Shiksha Mandir project in rural India, a project of the India Heritage Research Foundation, an international nonprofit humanitarian organization for which Sadhvi Bhagwati works in Rishikesh, India. Twenty-five percent of all author royalties will sponsor small schools with local teachers as part of a rural development project to bring education, vocational training, ecological and family planning programs into areas of India that have largely been neglected. A full description can be found on our Web site: www.radicalspirit.com.

Why, the reader might ask, engage in projects on the other side of the world when we have so many problems to attend to close to home? The answer is that one of the main purposes of this book is to go beyond merely local or self-centered ways of being. What we are generally trained to do from a young age is to help those closest to us to a great degree and then extend a watered-down version of that compassion outward. In subtle ways with this approach, our sphere of love remains small. A philanthropic project involving people we will never see or meet on the other side of the world helps us open to a wider family.

Our actions and intentions build a web of interconnection and give us the strength to move in positive directions. When we build those bonds only locally, we are not fully moving into a global consciousness. We need to *feel* globally, *connect* globally, and *act* globally in order to truly become global citizens. It's not enough to just think about the big picture. So that's one reason we decided to sponsor a program in India: it creates a subtle thread of interconnection that weaves us into a more cohesive planetary civilization.

The second reason is that the project produces a lot of bang for the buck. Five hundred dollars of funding provides for a whole school of forty students for a year. The seeds planted in this way will eventually blossom in many other places and ways. A small amount of money by U.S. standards can thus give a lot of people access to the skills to enter modern India with grace, intelligence, and awareness.

If you get inspired by this project, you, too, can sponsor a school, either on your own or in collaboration with friends, colleagues, fellow employees, or students. You can sponsor a school in memory of a loved one, or for a loved one's birthday or anniversary, or in the name of your children.

All donations are completely tax deductible. The foundation, named the India Heritage Research Foundation (an umbrella organization involved in many projects) is a registered nonprofit in India, the United Kingdom, Canada, and the United States. Rather than sending the money directly to India, donors can send it to the U.S. office, and the money will then be transferred to the headquarters of the program in India.

If you have any questions, feel free to E-mail Sadhvi Bhagwati at Bhagwati333@aol.com. If you would like to sponsor a school for a year, please send a check for $500 to the India Heritage Research Foundation, c/o Parmarth Shiksha Mandir, 621 Illini Drive, Monroeville, PA 15146-1917, USA. Smaller donations are also most welcome. Please send an E-mail, as well, to Bhagwati333@aol.com, with the details of when you sent the donation, the amount, and the name in which you'd like to sponsor the school.

## ACTIVISM AND OUTREACH

### CIRCLE OF LIFE FOUNDATION

Julia Butterfly Hill founded the Circle of Life Foundation to help inspire, support, and network with individuals and communities working on environmental and social solutions. The Circle of Life Foundation envisions a sustainable culture that honors biological and cultural diversity. Through education and outreach, it promotes efforts to protect and restore the Earth. Circle of Life is a project of the Earth Island Institute. Ten percent of all author royalties for this book will be contributed to this foundation. Contact: P.O. Box 3764, Oakland, CA 94609, (510) 601-9790, www.circleoflifefoundation.org.

## STONE CIRCLES

stone circles is a nonprofit organization that finds unique ways to integrate faith, spiritual practice, and social justice. It serves nonprofit, social change organizations and activists through organizational development training, workshops on contemplative and spiritual practice, practical publications, community gatherings, and interfaith celebrations. Individuals find (1) concrete tools to join the work of the spirit with the spirit of work; (2) experiences that reconnect them with the strength and wisdom at the core of their being; and (3) a network of like-minded individuals. Contact: Claudia Horwitz, stone circles, 301 W. Main Street, Suite 280, Durham, NC 27701, (919) 682-8323, claudstone@aol.com.

## YOUTH FOR ENVIRONMENTAL SANITY (YES!)

In 1990, sixteen-year-old Ocean Robbins founded Youth for Environmental Sanity (YES!) to educate, inspire, and empower his generation to take positive action for healthy people and a healthy planet. Since then, this nonprofit organization has held sixty-six weeklong training camps for youth from thirty-eight nations, sharing support and skills with thousands of fifteen- to thirty-year-old young people who want to make a difference. For more information on YES!'s environmental leadership trainings and other work, contact: YES!, 420 Bronco Road, Soquel, CA 95073, (877) 2-YES-CAMP, www.yesworld.org, camps@yesworld.org.

## THE LINEAGE PROJECT

Cofounded by Soren Gordhamer, the Lineage Project offers yoga programs and mindfulness-based meditation to at-risk and incarcerated teens in both New York and California. It works with some of the most dangerous and violent youth in society, providing support to this population through both classes at the facilities as well as literature that speaks to the possibility and practice of transformation. Though inspired by Buddhist teachings, the focus of the organization is not to convert youth to any particular religion or ideology. Instead, it offers tools to help them access their own inner wisdom and to use their passion and longing for aliveness in more beneficial ways. Contact: P.O. Box 366, Mt. Vernon, NY 10552, (914) 699-8479, www.lineageproject.org, lineagepro@aol.com.

## THE ALLIANCE FOR SUSTAINABLE JOBS AND THE ENVIRONMENT (ASJE)

ASJE is a network of individuals and organizations dedicated to building a world where nature is protected, the worker is respected, and unrestrained corporate power is rejected through grassroots education, organization, and action. Check out the Alliance Web site: www.asje.org.

## EARTH ISLAND INSTITUTE (EII)

EII develops and supports projects that counteract threats to the biological and cultural diversity that sustains the environment. Through education and activism, these projects promote the conservation, preservation, and restoration of the Earth. The Circle of Life Foundation is proud to be a project of EII. Contact: (415) 788-3666, www.earthisland.org.

## THE ENVIRONMENTAL PROTECTION INFORMATION CENTER (EPIC)

EPIC works to protect the long-term health of the coastal forest ecosystem of Northern California through education, advocacy, and litigation. EPIC is at the forefront of state forestry reform. Contact: (707) 923-2931, www.wildcalifornia.org.

## FULL CIRCLE FUND (FCF)

Full Circle Fund is a growing community of business professionals who partner with social entrepreneurs to create breakthrough solutions for pressing social problems. It commits financial, human, political, and social capital to nonprofit partnerships, and teaches its members to use "all of the tools in the social change tool box." Members are entrepreneurs, venture capitalists, and other business professionals. Contact Haley Mitchell, program coordinator, at (415) 793-4483, or visit www.fullcirclefund.org.

# HIGHER EDUCATION

## CALIFORNIA INSTITUTE OF INTEGRAL STUDIES

The California Institute of Integral Studies is an accredited institution of higher learning and research that strives to embody spirit, intellect and wisdom in service to individuals, communities, and the Earth. Contact: 1453 Mission Street, San Francisco, CA 94103, (415) 575-6100, www.ciis.edu.

## INSTITUTE OF TRANSPERSONAL PSYCHOLOGY (ITP)

ITP is a private, accredited, nonsectarian graduate school offering residential and distance-learning degree programs for professional, educational, and personal growth. Its unique curriculum focuses on six core areas of inquiry: the intellectual, emotional, spiritual, physical, social, and creative. Contact: 744 San Antonio Road, Palo Alto, CA 94303, (650) 493-4430, itpinfo@itp.edu, www.itp.edu.

## NAROPA UNIVERSITY

Naropa is a private, nonprofit, fully accredited liberal arts college offering undergraduate and graduate degrees in transpersonal psychology, contemplative psychology, Buddhist studies, writing, environmental studies, gerontology, somatic psychology, early childhood education, and more. Naropa is nonsectarian and characterized by its unique Buddhist educational heritage. Contact: 2130 Arapahoe Ave., Boulder, CO 80302, (303) 444-0202, info@naropa.edu, www.naropa.edu.

# TRANSFORMATIVE PROGRAMS

## GROF TRANSPERSONAL TRAINING (GTT)

Featured in Ashley Wain's contribution, GTT is a multiple-year training program involving different facets of transpersonal psychology and intensive periods of experiential work, using especially Holotropic Breathwork. Holotropic Breathwork is a powerful approach to self-exploration and healing that integrates insights from modern consciousness research, anthropology, various depth psychologies, transpersonal psychology, Eastern spiritual practices, and mystical traditions of the world. Contact: 20 Sunnyside Ave., A-314, Mill Valley, CA 94941, (415) 383-8779, www.holotropic.com.

## DIAMOND HEART AND TRAINING INSTITUTE (DHAT)

The Diamond Approach is the spiritual teaching, the path, and the method of the Ridhwan Foundation and its educational branch, the Diamond Heart and Training Institute (DHAT). The approach has been developed by A. Hameed Ali (A. H. Almaas ) over the last twenty-five years. The Diamond Approach utilizes the insights of modern psychology about the human ego and personality and extends that understanding into the spiritual dimension. The purpose of this work is to access our essence or spiritual self. Contact: Ridhwan School, P. O. Box 10114, Berkeley, CA 94709, www.ridhwan.org.

## THE ESALEN INSTITUTE

Esalen is a premiere venue for transformative workshops and features several hundred seminars each year with pioneering teachers in most disciplines related to human growth or spirituality. It is located on the coast of Big Sur in California. Catalogs available from the Esalen Institute, Highway 1, Big Sur, CA 93920-9616, (831) 667-3000 x7100, www.esalen.org.

## VIPASSANA

With hundreds of centers around the world, Goenka's style of *vipassana*, which carries on a Burmese lineage and is highlighted in Stephen Dinan's contribution, has spread rapidly. The ten-day introductory courses are a rigorous and powerful way to begin to clarify and purify the depths of the mind and to initiate a more serious meditation practice. Courses at the major centers run nearly continuously. The Web site provides links to regional centers around the world: www.dhamma.org.

## SELF KNOWLEDGE SYMPOSIUM (SKS)

SKS was created ten years ago by philosopher/businessman August Turak to fulfill a growing hunger among college students for an accessible means to address questions of meaning and spirituality. It has since grown into a large network of students and young adults with a bimonthly magazine. It is particularly interested in people who would like to create seed groups at universities where there are currently no chapters. Contact: 5440 Atlantic Springs Rd., Suite 115, Raleigh, NC 27616, (919) 878-3717, www.selfknowledge.org.

## BUSINESSES

### TRANSFORMATIVE COMMUNITY NETWORK, INC. (TCN)

Founded by Stephen Dinan, TCN creates and connects transformative communities in the service of global awakening. It provides resources, networking, and training for those who wish to create local communities that link into a larger system. One pilot project is the Radical Spirit Community, a San Francisco Bay Area group dedicated to awakening together, creating deeply loving relationships, and helping each other in world-transforming work. Contact: www.transformunity.com, www.radicalspirit.com.

### SOLA DESIGNS

When you commission a piece of custom jewelry from Sola Designs, you join in a dance of alchemy. You and I become collaborators in transforming the desires of your heart and the visions of your mind into a stunning, wearable art form that speaks eloquently of your essence. To begin the dance, please call: (510) 482-7492 or go to www.soladesigns.com.

## WEB SITES

**WWW.TWISTEDMYSTIC.COM** features a wide array of mystical texts and mystically oriented art, from visual pieces to songs to poetry and essays. It aims to go beyond mystical dualism and embrace works of a more mischievous, humorous, or shadowy origin as well as those with a more "white-light" flavor.

**WWW.ESALENCTR.ORG** showcases articles, papers, conference summaries, and book reviews from scholars, teachers, and theoreticians doing leading-edge intellectual work, including research on topics like psi, reincarnation, hands-on healing, and transformative practices.

**EARTHSAVE INTERNATIONAL** was co-founded by John Robbins and promotes food choices that are healthy for people and the planet. They educate, inspire, and empower people to shift towards a plant-based diet and to take compassionate action for all life on Earth. Contact: http://www.earthsave.org.

**WWW.AMMACHI.ORG** links to a variety of activities and tour schedules related to Ammachi, a remarkable living saint. Ammachi is often referred to as the embodiment of Divine Love.

**WWW.LEVITY.COM/FIGMENT** is the official site for Erik Davis and his intoxicating brew of Figments and Inklings — more than just journalism, cultural criticism, or flights of fancy. All thought provoking.

**WWW.ATHENAGRAPHICS.COM** is a Web design business, owned and operated by Rachel Medlock.

**WWW.REALSPIRITUALITY.COM** is a Web site for Mariana Caplan's books, articles, counseling services, and writing consultation, as well as a bunch of sometimes stubborn and uncompromising views on the contemporary spiritual movement.

New World Library is dedicated to
publishing books and cassettes that inspire
and challenge us to improve the quality
of our lives and our world.
Our books and cassettes are available
at bookstores everywhere.
For a complete catalog, contact:

New World Library
14 Pamaron Way
Novato, California 94949
Phone: (415) 884-2100
Fax: (415) 884-2199
Or call toll free: (800) 972-6657
Catalog requests: Ext. 50
Ordering: Ext. 52
E-mail: escort@nwlib.com
newworldlibrary.com